AFTER UTOPIA

The Decline of Political Faith

After Utopia

THE DECLINE

OF POLITICAL FAITH

BY JUDITH N. SHKLAR

PRINCETON, NEW JERSEY

PRINCETON UNIVERSITY PRESS

First Princeton Paperback Printing, 1969
Second Hardcover Printing, 1969

Grateful acknowledgment is made for
permission to quote from *Situations III*
by Jean Paul Sartre, published by
Librairie Gallimard, Paris.

Printed in the United States of America
by Princeton University Press, Princeton, New Jersey

219040

To My Parents

Preface

EVERY reader who opens a new book takes a certain chance. For until he has read the book he cannot know whether it is at all worth reading. It is, therefore, no more than fair that an author should tell him right at the beginning what the book is about, and why it was written, even though this is not easy to do.

This book is about political philosophy or, to be entirely exact, about its disappearance in recent years. For the sense of political helplessness induced by years of instability, war, and totalitarianism manifests itself intellectually no less than in popular feeling. To think of politics in broad terms has come to seem futile. Instead we have culture consciousness, a concern for Western culture and history as a whole. No one could ignore the avalanche of works with such titles as "whither modern man?" or "good-by to the West," or "the destiny of European culture." And the absence of original theories about government and political life is equally evident. Historical surveys are plentiful, as are descriptive analyses of political processes and institutions. But the urge to construct grand designs for the political future of mankind is gone. The last vestiges of utopian faith required for such an enterprise have vanished.

It is not only that no reasonable person can today believe in any "law" of progress. In the age of two world wars, totalitarian dictatorship, and mass murder this faith can be regarded only as simple-minded, or even worse, as a contemptible form of complacency. But more has happened than just a decline of optimism. Rather than look to the future at all, we tend to turn backward and ask ourselves how and why European civilization has reached its present deplorable condition. In-

deed, if any unifying characteristic can be said to exist in the
social ideas of a period as complex as ours, it is the tendency
to judge Western civilization, or at least modern history, as a
whole, and to find it wanting. It is with these judgments that
this book deals.

The sense of cultural disaster is not entirely new, though
the extent to which it is now felt is unprecedented. Even during the last century romantic and Christian thinkers felt alienated from the social life about them, and the representatives
of these philosophies are today the most impressive exponents
of the various theories of social decay. For the romantic, then
and now, civilization has become mechanical, crushing the
individual and drowning in mediocrity. To many a Christian
it seems that a Europe without religious faith is doomed to
inner, and eventually outer, decay. To both it is evident that
political action is utterly inadequate to deal with such deeply
set troubles; that, indeed, our political problems are merely an
expression of a far more fundamental spiritual disorder. Politics, in short, have become futile. Now these attitudes are not
just a response to recent events; they are, in fact, part of a considerable tradition of social criticism. What is new is not only
that they have become widely accepted, but that they are not
challenged by any serious rival *political* philosophies. The
spread of romantic and Christian political fatalism has been
accompanied by a virtual absence of the political ideas that
dominated the last century. Above all, there is nothing that
could be called a genuinely radical philosophy today. Liberalism has become unsure of its moral basis, as well as increasingly defensive and conservative. Certainly it has not presented an answer to a social despair that it fundamentally
shares. The case of socialism has been similar. Especially those
socialist theories which depended most upon some form of
historical determinism have seen all their "scientific" expectations shattered, and have not been able to create a new sys-

tem of concepts that might serve both as an explanation of the present and as a program for the future. They too are the victims of a general political fatigue. Intellectually, the prophets of cultural despair have not yet met any serious competition, even now that the extremes of postwar despair have abated and that we are all adjusting to permanent insecurity.

The following pages are devoted mostly to a discussion of romantic and Christian social despair, because they offer the clearest expression of the contemporary mood. Romanticism, especially, has captured the intellectual imagination of sensitive and reflective people, and its spirit is the subject of the greater part of this book. To complete the picture, there is an account of the decline of liberal and socialist thought. While it is clear that these trends are a reaction to historical events, it is not the aim here to relate ideas to social circumstances, valuable as such analyses are. This is, rather, a chapter in the history of ideas, an effort to understand contemporary modes of thought in terms of their spiritual antecedents. It is, in brief, the story of the gradual decline of rational political optimism since the Enlightenment. Regrettably, perhaps, the reader need not expect to find a "new" theory to confront prevailing attitudes. The author shares in the spirit of the age to the extent of being neither able nor willing to build an original theory of politics. The fact is that it is next to impossible to believe strongly that the power of human reason expressing itself in political action is capable of achieving its ends. The various theories of historical determinism prevalent since the last century have long since undermined this hope, and historical disaster has completed the process. Without a glimmer of such optimism, however, political theory becomes impossible. In its place today we have only cultural fatalism. Of these the cultural alienation of the romantic and the despair of Christian fatalism are the most extreme and convincing expressions. It is not, however, the purpose of the following study to lend them support. On the contrary, it is an effort to criticize them, not because they are simply "wrong," but because they fail to explain the world they so dislike. That more adequate explanations may well be impossible at the present time is one of the uncomfortable conclusions that emerge from this analysis. However, even if a certain degree of cultural fatalism is inescapable, there is no reason why the theories advanced in its defense should be uncritically accepted. It is with this end in view that this detailed examination of their history and arguments has been undertaken.

Contents

Contents

AFTER UTOPIA

The Decline of Political Faith

CHAPTER I

Introduction: The Decline of the Enlightenment

"IN THE BEGINNING was the Enlightenment." Any study of contemporary social thought might well begin with these words. Yet nothing is quite so dead today as the spirit of optimism that the very word Enlightenment evokes. Indeed, we are faced not with the mere end of the Enlightenment but with the prevalence of theories that arose in opposition to it. If the Enlightenment still figures in the realm of ideas it is as a foil for attack, not as an inspiration to new ideas. Romanticism, the earliest and most successful antagonist of the Enlightenment, has numerous successors today, especially in existentialism and in the various philosophies of the absurd. The revival of social thought that was almost forced upon Christians by the French Revolution is still active today. But the gradual decay of the radical aspirations of liberalism and the evaporation of socialist thought have left the Enlightenment without intellectual heirs. The Enlightenment is the historical and intellectual starting point of contemporary social theory, but only because a great part of our thinking today is based on ideas, romantic and Christian, that were from the first consciously directed against it.

In retrospect the Enlightenment stands out as the high point of social optimism from which we have gradually, but steadily, descended, at least philosophically. The less reflective public, certainly until 1914, remained cheerfully indifferent to the intellectual currents of despair that had been swelling throughout the 19th century. Moreover, the Enlightenment is not just an historical point of departure. Consciously, or often only half-consciously, the Enlightenment is still the intellectual focus for many who no longer share its beliefs, and who develop their own viewpoint in refuting the attitudes of a past era. For the romantic the rationalism associated with the Enlightenment is still an object of scorn. The orthodox Christian still finds its unreligious, if not actively anti-religious, radicalism abhorrent. It is therefore still worthwhile to ask oneself what is meant by the term Enlightenment. What matters here is not what it really was in all its internal complexity, but only those of its aspects which stand out in retrospect, and which, from the very first, entered into controversy.

The three cardinal traits of the Enlightenment were radical optimism, anarchism, and intellectualism. The optimism rested in the belief that the moral and social condition of mankind was constantly improving. Progress was not only a hope for the future but a law that marked the entire course of history. Though the philosophers of the Enlightenment were extremely critical of the institutions and mores of their own age, they had no sense of alienation from European history as a whole. The darkest ages of the past were but steps to a brighter time. Though the present might seem deplorable, it was infinitely better than the past, for history, like individual man, was rational, and reason was bound to manifest itself to an ever greater extent. This faith in reason made the Enlightenment thinker feel secure in his society and in history as a whole.

"The 18th century is imbued with a belief in the unity and immutability of reason. Reason is the same for all thinking subjects, all nations, all epochs, and all cultures. From the changeability of religious creeds, of moral maxims and convictions, of theoretical opinions and judgments, a firm, lasting element can be extracted which is permanent in itself, and which in this identity and permanence expresses the real essence of reason."[1]

If progress was inevitable it was not, however, a matter of supra-personal forces. It was not as a "law" of economic development or of biological evolution but as the commonsense notion that men learn through experience that the Enlightenment believed in progress. Its hopes were truly radical, which is not true of the pseudo-scientific theories of progress, for the essence of radicalism is the idea that man can do with himself and with his society whatever he wishes. If he is reasonable he will build a rational society; if ignorant he will live in a state of barbarism. To the Enlightenment the political and economic future were open. And since everywhere its proponents saw the growth of useful knowledge, they assumed that knowledge had merely to increase and spread until it was put to social use. Though the philosophers were not prophets of violence they were a great deal more radical in their philosophy than later social revolutionaries, for they did not regard men as the agents of historical destiny, but as the free creators of society.

The intellectualism of the Enlightenment was an integral part of this optimism. Even those who believed that utility, rather than reason, governed human action agreed that a purely intellectual appeal was sufficient to perfect conduct. Condorcet argued that since all political and moral errors were based on philosophical fallacies, science, by dispelling false metaphysical notions and mere prejudices, must lead men to social truth and virtue as well.[2] There was, however, another side to this intellectual optimism. If reason was the supreme guide to progress, the intellectuals, as the most reasonable of

[1] E. Cassirer, *The Philosophy of the Enlightenment*, tr. by F. C. A. Koelln and J. P. Pettegrove (Princeton, 1951), p. 6.
[2] *Esquisse d'un Tableau Historique des Progrès de l'Esprit Humain*, ed. by D. H. Prior (Paris, 1933), pp. 191-192.

men, were entitled to a position of leadership in society. Indeed, many intellectuals felt that they were achieving this
goal. Marmontel declared quite frankly that the philosophers
had already succeeded a negligent clergy in its "noblest function," that "of preaching from the roof-tops the truths that
are too rarely told to sovereigns."[3] And Duclos could not
conceal his pride when he considered the importance of
philosophers: "Of all the empires that of the intellectuals,
though invisible, is the widest spread. Those in power command, but the intellectuals govern, because in the end they
form public opinion, which sooner or later subdues or upsets
all despotisms."[4] This "empire of the intellectuals" was, moreover, inhabited by only one group of the species. The poets,
the artists, like the clergy, were excluded. It was only "rea-
soners,"—scientists and philosophers, the professional moralists
—who were truly enlightened and reasonable, "lumières," as
they called themselves in France.

The notion of the secular moralist as the ideal intellectual
was not an accident. It sprang directly from the Enlightenment's attitude to both religion and art. After all, "enlightenment" meant the illumination of minds hitherto beclouded
by religion. Opposition to the Roman Catholic Church was
the strongest bond uniting the philosophers. Here rationalists
and utilitarians, deists and atheists, were at one. Reason meant
"non-religion," and the rational, harmonious universe was free
from the arbitrary interference of its Creator. Thus, the sane
society would be without an established church, at the very
least; at the extreme, it would be delivered from all priests.
In aesthetics the Enlightenment philosophers accepted, in
the main, the canons of neo-classicism inherited from the 17th
century, with all the restrictions on the poetic imagination that

[3] Quoted in M. Roustan, *The Pioneers of the French Revolution*,
tr. by F. Whyte (Boston, 1926), p. 262.
[4] *Ibid.*, p. 265. M. Roustan adds wisely, "La Bruyère would not
have written that."

this implied. Indeed, at the beginning of the century Fontenelle had declared prose supreme, and had relegated poetry to a very inferior literary position. Even if the Enlightenment as represented by Voltaire and Marmontel, for example, did not go so far, it continued to subordinate art to the demands of philosophy. In a sense they made art superfluous by demanding that it be totally realistic—that is, follow the pattern set by a supposedly harmonious natural universe. The stage was to show nothing but the probable, the typical, the general—in short, only themes of universal significance. Moreover, the purpose of art was to instruct, to moralize. Shakespeare was condemned alike by Voltaire and by the conservative Dr. Johnson for a lack of decorum. Homer was disliked and Vergil praised on the same grounds. Taste, not strength, was the final criterion. Even Diderot and Lessing, who modified Aristotelian theory by the demand that drama should stir the audience emotionally, did not abandon the prerequisites of ethics. The spectators were to be moved only to virtuous feelings, especially to pity. The addition of sentimentality to literature was only an educational device, not a concession to the spirit of poetry.[5] The vocation of the intellectual was, in the eyes of the Enlightenment, to reform and to teach society until all mankind was free from irrational urges, whether of an artistic or a religious sort.

This feeling that they were destined to redeem mankind naturally inspired the philosophers of the Enlightenment to work energetically at drawing up projects for the imminent betterment of society. Philanthropy is the term that best describes this zeal for practical reform. It was a passion that seized a rather simple man like the Abbé de Saint-Pierre no more severely than sensible or profound people like Bentham or Kant. Indeed, it was the good Abbé who gave currency, in

[5] The above remarks are largely based on Professor René Welleck's *A History of Modern Criticism: 1750-1950*, vol. I, "The Later Eighteenth Century" (New Haven, 1955), pp. 12-104.

the earlier years of the century, to the word, "bienfaisance" which was to become so dear to the writers who followed him.[6] Though in France and Germany, especially, there was no scope for political activity on the part of intellectuals, the dream of citizenship, and especially of political leadership, was intensely felt. It was a profoundly political age.

The politics of the intellectuals were, however, of a peculiar nature. They were the politics to end all politics. Force was not only unnecessary in a society composed of reasonable persons; it was the prime instrument of unreason. Anarchism was the logical attitude for those who felt so great a confidence in intelligence in general and in the professional intellectual in particular. All existing political and religious institutions were irrational, obsolete, and so "unnatural," designed to prevent an inherently self-regulating society from achieving universal felicity. Coercive institutions, especially the traditional state, were not only unnecessary; they actually prevented an orderly social life. The function of the state was to be educational and its repressive activities were to be limited to protecting society against unenlightened nations and against those few aberrant persons whose anti-social urges led them to a life of crime. The radical aspiration of the Enlightenment was to substitute the educative leadership of the intellectuals for the state that was based on power and habit. Education and legislation were identical to Helvetius.[7] Once the art or science of educative legislation was mastered, social perfection would be at hand.

The "invisible hand," so easily laughed at now, was not

[6] M. Leroy, *Histoire des Idées Sociales en France* (de Montesquieu à Robespierre) (Paris, 1946), p. 10. C. Becker, *The Heavenly City of the Eighteenth Century of Philosophers* (New Haven, Conn., 1952), p. 70.
[7] Helvetius, *A Treatise on Man*, tr. by W. Hooper (London, 1810), vol. II, pp. 438-443. To these attitudes there were, of course, exceptions, especially during the earlier Enlightenment. Voltaire, for instance, was far from being an anarchist.

really a mysterious mechanism. It merely implied that social harmony was inevitable in a society of perfectly free and reasonable persons. To be sure, there was some inconsistency in believing that educational restraint was necessary in political but not in economic life.[8] But even in the latter realm, monopoly was regarded as so reprehensible that society had a right to prevent it and punish those who practiced it. Freedom, however, was regarded as the necessary condition of human development in all areas, just because it allowed the best, the most reasonable, impulses to assert themselves in every sphere of action. Moreover, the Marxist contention that the Enlightenment was nothing but the bourgeoisie coming into its own finds little support in the writings of that period, and is forced to rely almost exclusively on Voltaire's frequently expressed contempt for the "canaille."[9] Most of the writers of the 18th century, by no means Rousseau alone, felt that great differences in wealth were scandalous, and that one of the chief blessings of the abolition of the existing state was to be a reduction of these discrepancies. Almost all agreed with Helvetius that bad legislation alone created excessive economic inequalities, and that these could be mitigated by law.[10] Among the many charges that Tom Paine brought against all the prevailing forms of government was that "in countries that are called civilized we see age going to the workhouse and youth to the gallows" as well as "a mass of wretchedness that has scarcely any other chance, than to expire in poverty or infamy."[11] It was not that the Enlightenment was indifferent to poverty, but that it blamed it exclusively on obsolete and

---

[8] E. Halévy, *The Growth of Philosophic Radicalism*, tr. by M. Morris (London, 1934), p. 127.

[9] E.g., H. Laski, *The Rise of European Liberalism* (London, 1947), pp. 161-264.

[10] *Treatise on Man*, vol. II, p. 205. The article on "Indigent" in the *Encyclopédie* states unequivocally that poverty is the result solely of maladministration. M. Roustan, *op.cit.*, p. 269.

[11] *The Rights of Man* (Everyman's Library, London, 1915), p. 221.

immoral legislation. With the exception of monopolists, Adam Smith spoke of no one with greater contempt than of politicians.[12] Beneath his accusation lies the common anarchism of the Enlightenment, which essentially amounts to a belief that society is inherently good, but that governments, and they alone, prevent it from flourishing.[13]

While nothing was more sacred to the philosophers of the Enlightenment than individual liberty, they were not individualists. The word does not appear in their writings. For, though they saw a clear conflict between society and the state, between conscience and power, they did not envisage a similar tension between the individual and society. The inevitability of such a struggle, and the entire doctrine of the inviolability of individuality, were unknown to the Enlightenment. That the individual's conscience, his moral will, or at least his sense of utility were the ultimate arbiters of all public as well as of private action was taken for granted. There was, however, no suspicion of a necessary conflict between private and public interests, between individual freedom and social needs. For the utilitarians there was only a conflict between immediate and long-term interests, not between altruistic and self-regarding motives, and this conflict was to be resolved easily by education and by a few laws. The utilitarians regarded freedom as a necessity because it was in the interest of society no less than of the individual. Those who believed in an absolute moral law, on the other hand, saw freedom as the imperative first condition of all ethically valid action. In the last resort both schools thought freedom essential because man was a rational and social being.

Though it has become a cliché, there is nothing wrong with

[12] *The Wealth of Nations*, ed. by E. Cannan (Modern Library, New York, 1937), pp. 435 and 460-461.

[13] Thus Tom Paine, "Society performs for itself everything which is ascribed to Government," *The Rights of Man*, p. 157.

the phrase "the Age of Reason" as a description of the Enlightenment. It was reason that bound men to the past and to the future. It was reason that brought men together. It was reason that provided every standard for action and for judgment. Reason was to rule art as it guided science. As its ultimate aim the Enlightenment visualized the perfectly rational society of men as equal as they were alike in their common rationality. Such a summing up, though just in many respects, leaves out what so many antagonists forget about the Enlightenment—its humanitarianism, its very profound sense of justice. Thus Condorcet specially defined humanitarianism as tender compassion for all those who suffer the evils that afflict mankind, as horror for all that in public institutions and in private life adds new sorrow to those which nature has already inflicted on mankind.[14] Of d'Alembert it was said by his eulogist, Marmontel, that he was "highly gifted with sensibility" and that he "blazed with indignation when he saw the innocent and weak crushed by the injustice of the strong."[15] Ultimately everything—the optimism, the intellectual excesses, the anarchism—were animated by this spirit. Justice is the center of Stoic thought, old and new. To ridicule this preoccupation is easy enough; whether anything superior has ever been considered is, however, quite another matter.

It would be a mistake to assume that the 18th century and the Enlightenment coincide exactly. Such symmetry is not to be expected in history. Even before the French Revolution, the Enlightenment was vehemently rejected by at least one group of intellectuals, the romantics. Moreover, even in the midst of the Enlightenment there were deviations. Sentimentalism in literature, a considerable concern about "genius," began to be felt. Romanticism did not fall fully developed from the skies. The aesthetic revolt against neo-classicism did

[14] *Esquisse*, pp. 164-165.
[15] Roustan, *op.cit.*, p. 251.

not find full expression until Herder, who was the first outstanding man of letters to throw overboard the entire system of aesthetics that had flourished during the Enlightenment. He was the first to discard those rationally imposed rules upon art, and to champion the supremacy of primeval poetic feeling. For in its origins romanticism was the revolt of aesthetic sensibility against the philosophic spirit. Eventually, moreover, this aesthetic difference implied a break with the Enlightenment as a whole, and the birth of a new attitude toward nature and society as well.

Romanticism, therefore, needs to be defined clearly. There are two extreme approaches to this question. One school of thought regards the classicist and the romantic as two eternal human types. The former seeks harmony in the contradictory elements of all existence; the latter glories in the individual and in the differences in all that he sees and feels.[16] These opposed characters are expressed in religion, in art, and in philosophy throughout history. Christianity can thus be regarded as a romantic religion; the Gothic style, all music, and Platonic philosophy in their turn are somehow romantic. At the other pole are those who would call only one generation, that of the brothers Schlegel, romantic. For them, at best the romantic movement is over by that momentous year 1848. Indeed, among those who favor a narrow definition there is one scholar who advises us to speak only of "romanticisms," in the plural.[17] Individual and national variations seem to him so great that no single definition can cover all the authors who have been called romantic. This idea has its merits, for the most significant differences were bound to arise among

[16] E.g., F. Strich, *Deutsche Klassik und Romantik* (Bern, 1949).

[17] A. O. Lovejoy, "On the Discrimination of Romanticisms," *Essays in the History of Ideas* (Baltimore, 1948), pp. 228-253. In reply to this, there is an impressive argument showing the unity of romanticism, in R. Welleck, "The Concept of 'Romanticism' in Literary History," *Comparative Literature*, 1949, vol. I, pp. 1-23 and 147-172.

writers who stressed individuality as their highest aim. Moreover, not all romantics remained romantic. Herder himself
returned partially to the Enlightenment. Others became
Christians. Also, there were endless quarrels among authors
who at a distance seem to have so much in common. Thus
Goethe was in turn the idol and the chief antagonist of the
younger German romantics. Lastly, the task of defining romanticism has not been made easier by the polemical and
colloquial use of the term. To some French authors, particularly, romanticism is just mysticism, irrationalism, and emo-
tionalism of a German sort. It is a hideous, un-French infec-
tion, which undermines the true Latin, Catholic, and classical
heritage of France.[18] In popular usage, of course, a romantic
is simply an impractical person.

The political and abusive exploitation of the word romanticism need not concern us here, but what of the two scholarly
attitudes? A compromise between the two may well prove
helpful. For, if romanticism is an eternal human urge, it becomes very difficult to understand what was so peculiarly new
in the aesthetic opposition to the Enlightenment. If, however,
romanticism is to be applied to only a handful of poets who
chose that name, the great affinity that so many later writers
have to that original group becomes inexplicable. It seems
expedient, therefore, to look for both the unique and the
enduring aspects of the romantic movement. For if it began
as a specific theory of art, opposed to the standards of neo-
classicism, it was also the expression of a general temper, of a
state of mind, and this condition is still prevalent today, even
though the aesthetic form it originally took has long since
been discarded.

[18] The best known of these politically inspired studies of roman-
ticism are probably the innumerable works of Baron Ernest Seillière.
A brief, but complete, statement of this viewpoint can be found in his
Romanticism, tr. by C. Sprietsma (New York, 1929).

In art the romantics, beginning with Herder, declared a total war against the neo-classicism of the Enlightenment. Instead of reason and form, the intuitive imagination of the poet was hailed as the sole creative force. Not the universal, the typical, and the probable, but the unique, the original and the fantastic were to be the aim of literature. Literature was to stir the reader, not to instruct him. To follow nature now meant not to seek harmony, but to imitate nature's dramatic intensity. Not civilization, but primeval energy was the greatest virtue. The odes of Horace were rejected in favor of Homer, and Shakespeare was idolized for just those qualities which Voltaire and Dr. Johnson had disliked as barbarisms. Not philosophical fables, but the novel of private experience became popular. Above all, the place that the Enlightenment had reserved for the philosophers was now claimed for the poets. They were now regarded as the founders of religions and of nations, and as the guardians of the highest truth. In fact, after neo-classicism the romantics went on to reject the entire Enlightenment, and the entire attitude that it represented. Instead of cold analysis they wanted the experience of life itself. Not man, the rational animal, but Prometheus, the defiant creator, was the new ideal. Historical optimism was rejected in the consciousness of the tragic in both life and art. Beauty cannot improve, and Hellas has passed. To all complacency the "genius" sneered: "Philistine." The present was no better than the past, and "things as they are," every convention, all set institutions, were only chains on the creative faculties of the artist. Individuality, not social reason, was to become the highest moral aim. All politics were suspect as unartistic. From the "quantitative individualism" of the Enlightenment, the romantics moved to "qualitative individualism"; from rational autonomy, to limitless self-expression and self-differentiation. To concentrate merely on reason was to remain a "rational oyster." An artistic personality must have a limitless number of qualities; it must be Protean, colorful, and, above all, different.[19] This is by no means like the humanistic ideal of the full man. For the whole man is made up of a limited number of qualities in a preconceived state of balance. The humanistic ideal is based on a universal pattern, not on the romantic aspiration of each person to be completely different from every other. No wonder that all were permanently at odds with their environment!

The aesthetic revolt of romanticism was, then, only part of a more general dissatisfaction with the entire age. If we look deeper, beyond even the conscious expressions of romantic thought, we discover a specific consciousness. What appeared in the republic of letters at that time was very early, and with unrivalled subtlety, described by Hegel as the "unhappy consciousness." This is the "alienated soul" that has lost all faith in the beliefs of the past, having been disillusioned by skepticism, but is unable to find a new home for its spiritual longings in the present or future. Hopelessly tossed back and forth between memory and yearning, it can neither accept the present nor face the new world.[20] This is essentially a religious phenomenon, what Miguel de Unamuno was later to call the "tragic sense of life," a longing for immortality which is constantly harrowed by doubts of its possibility.[21] However, this consciousness did not express itself in religious terms in the early years of romanticism. It was not only that "God is dead," but that culture had perished. The "unending yearn-

[19] *The Sociology of Georg Simmel,* tr. and ed. by K. H. Wolf (Glencoe, Ill., 1950), pp. 58-84.

[20] *The Phenomenology of the Mind,* tr. by J. B. Baillie (London, 1931), pp. 250-267 and 752-756. This, like most translations of Hegel's works, is inadequate, but since there are few direct quotations, the usual English versions will be referred to. Their general meaning has been checked in the German original.

[21] *The Tragic Sense of Life,* tr. by J. E. C. Flitch (New York, 1954), pp. 1-57.

ing" was felt primarily as culture longing.[22] It was a yearning for Greece, first, then for the world of Ossian and for the colorful Middle Ages, and later for the Renaissance as well—indeed for any time more blessed than the present.

This sense of lostness in the "real" world that marks the unhappy consciousness, and that lies at the root of the romantic revival, is also what gives the movement its continuity. It is this which allows us to speak of romanticism as prevalent throughout the last century and today, in spite of the inner dissensions, the changes in modes of expression and in literary subject matter. The refusal to accept a world of nature in which all must die, or a social universe in which "the whole" counts more than each person, marks the entire course of romantic thought. The Enlightenment was able to rationalize and live at peace with these conditions; the romantic rebelled against them. The senselessness of death and the crushing force of society are the constant themes of all the poets who have been conventionally called the romantic school; so is the rejection of all existing cultural life. This attitude appears in Kierkegaard's hatred of optimistic philosophy and in his call to "the one," and again in Nietzsche's dream of the super-artist who would subdue nature and society. Burckhardt's longing for the artistic periods of the past is essentially the same as Herder's dream of primitive societies dominated by poets. Many romantics, of course, eventually made their peace with God, with the established social order, with history, with politics, even with reason, but they ceased to be romantics when they did so.

As an aesthetic theory romanticism still has its votaries.

[22] It is my firm conviction that the longing for Hellas was not only the first manifestation of romanticism but also the essence of its cultural attitude. Mediaevalism was nowhere as important, or as universal. See, e.g., E. M. Butler, *The Tyranny of Greece over Germany* (Cambridge, 1935); G. Highet, *The Classical Tradition* (New York, 1949), pp. 355-465.

The supremacy of art and of the artist is still a vital concern to André Malraux, to Albert Camus, and to Stephen Spender, for instance. In literary criticism, Sartre and his followers still belabor authors who adhere to the classical tradition and deal in stereotypes, thus denying man's freedom to behave unpredictably. American literature, especially the "tough" kind, is, one suspects, admired for what, to Europeans, seems to be its exotic character. The German philosopher Martin Heidegger still seeks the highest wisdom in poetry. And among existentialist thinkers, Karl Jaspers joins Goethe in the battle against Newton and the age of prose that he represents. However, when we speak of romanticism here, we mean primarily the manifestations of the unhappy consciousness, for today it is no longer the implicit basis of a new literature, it is a conscious attitude. Existentialism and the less systematic philosophies of the absurd regard themselves openly as the awareness that "God is dead." While the early romantics showed considerable combative vigor, and really believed that the spirit of poetry might yet conquer the world of prose, the contemporary romantic cherishes no such hope—indeed, no hope of any sort. Instead of dramatic energy there is now only a feeling of futility. Romanticism now expresses itself in a denial of the very possibility of our knowing—much less controlling—history, nature, or society. It asserts our freedom from God and social determination, but this implies only an absence of permanent attachments. Man has become a foreigner wandering aimlessly around unknown territory; the world, both historical and natural, has become meaningless. The relevance of all social thought and action becomes doubtful in the face of a human situation in which nothing is certain but the individual's reactions to the external world and his need to give expression to his inner condition. As seen with the inner eye, the world appears as a strange and hostile prison which one cannot either understand or alter; at best it can be evaded. The great tragedy of the present age is that history, society, and politics, for all their insignificance to our real self, press upon us unavoidably. The outer world is crushing the unique individual. Society is depriving us of our selfhood. The entire social universe today is totalitarian, not just some political movements and some states. Technology and the masses are the conditions of life everywhere today, and these, forming the very essence of totalitarianism, are the epitome of all the forces in society that have always threatened the individual personality. This is the romanticism of defeat, the ultimate stage of alienation. It is also the very farthest point from the spirit of the Enlightenment. Romanticism began by denying the facile optimism of the men of reason, but under the stress of the social enormities of the present age it has come to reject the entire modern world, and implicitly, the very possibility of social knowledge and amelioration.

Romanticism was not the sole hostile reaction to the Enlightenment. Christian believers could hardly be expected to rejoice in its doctrines, and the 18th century was by no means wholly irreligious. Pietist and Evangelical movements flourished. In Saint-Martin the century even had its mystic. But all this religiosity did not amount to a theological refutation of the Enlightenment, least of all in the realm of social theory. Not until the French Revolution shook the very foundations of ecclesiastical institutions was such a reply forthcoming. With the politically inspired literature of the Theocrats, chief among them Joseph de Maistre, a point by point attack on the Enlightenment from a Catholic position appeared. It is worth noting that even Maistre had in his youth flirted with Enlightened ideas, spoken favorably of liberty, and referred to God as the "Supreme Being."[23] The Catholic reaction to the Enlightenment, emerging as it did in the course of the Revolu-

[23] C.-A. Saint-Beuve, *Portraits Litteraires* (Paris, n.d.), vol. II, pp. 394-399.

tion, was from the first primarily political in character, and its contemporary descendants, in their rejection of the whole post-Revolutionary world, retain this orientation. In this respect, therefore, the religious opposition to the Enlightenment has been rather less intricate, in a sense less profound, than that of romanticism. It is, however, superficial to regard the opposition as merely a matter of extreme political conservatism. In the case of a thinker of Maistre's caliber political "reaction" was only a part of a wider realization that Europe had ceased to be Christian and that the whole modern age was in every respect a failure. It is this awareness, not his authoritarian bias in matters of government, that has given Maistre's answer to the Enlightenment such a lasting influence.

That the faith in progress is repellent to most Christian thought is obvious, for it rests on the denial of original sin. Maistre, however, went even further than to deny its validity. Indeed, hardly anyone since Luther was more impressed by human corruption than Maistre. Though he professed to admire St. Thomas, he did not seem to accept his doctrine that the faculties of natural reason had remained largely unimpaired. Actually his pessimism was not merely social; it was cosmic in scope. His contribution to the controversy about the significance of the Lisbon earthquake of 1755 was a return to the belief that Providence was just but mankind so wicked that these disasters occurred because men deserved them. That the apparently good should perish together with the guilty was no injustice, since none of us is really innocent.[24] The picture of violence on earth that he painted was far grimmer than Hobbes'. Hobbes' natural man at least kills for understandable purposes, but Maistre saw violence as a law of all life, even that of vegetables. Men cannot help killing each other. They kill

[24] Soirées de Saint-Petersbourg (Classiques Garnier, Paris, 1922), vol. I, pp. 170-177 and 201-211.

for justifiable reasons, and they kill merely to amuse themselves. In either case they are merely fulfilling their destiny.
The world is an endless scene of carnage.[25] It is violence that
forms the essence of all human activity, of even its positive
forms. Society ultimately depends for its survival on the public executioner.[26]

Like the Enlightenment, Maistre placed great emphasis on
the power of thought, but he regarded it as an almost wholly
evil force. Religion and the "national dogma," a mixture of
religious and traditional moral and political precepts, were to
be propagated by the clergy and the nobility, and to dominate
the world of ideas.[27] As for the savants, they were not to speak
on moral matters. They could have the natural sciences to
amuse them, but nothing else, and he was even suspicious of
these. The natural sciences were the creatures of pride and
brutalized men. Also, by emphasizing the laws of nature, they
made prayer seem superfluous.[28] Human reason and will were
the enemies of faith and, as such, suspect. Men of learning
were to give up all political ambitions. History, according to
Maistre, shows that men of learning have no talent for practical affairs, while priests, on the other hand, have always made
excellent statesmen.[29] This conclusion follows logically from
his belief that in politics reason and practice stand unalterably
opposed to each other. The rationality of political theories
only demonstrates that they are useless or pernicious,[30] for
they always forgot the profound irrationality of mankind in
general, and of social units especially.

For the world about him Maistre felt a deep dislike. The
Revolution he sometimes regarded as the direct work of Satan
or as the punishment justly visited upon an irreligious genera-

[25] *Ibid.*, vol. II, pp. 21-25 and p. 121.
[26] *Ibid.*, vol. I, pp. 29-33.   [27] *Ibid.*, vol. II, pp. 102-104.
[28] *Ibid.*, vol. I, pp. 192-197.   [29] *Ibid.*, vol. II, pp. 174-176.
[30] *Ibid.*, vol. II, pp. 108-109.

tion. Only occasionally did he hope that it was a salutary purging of a corrupt nation.[31] As to its historical origins there could be no doubt—it was the offspring of Protestantism, the child of heresy. Conversely only through a revival of religion, indeed only under the domination of the Catholic Church, could Europe hope to survive. It is this interpretation of history which gives Maistre a contemporary significance. Many Christian thinkers, both Catholic and Protestant, today subscribe to the idea that civilizations live and die with their traditional religious faiths, and that ultimately all social events are the expression of some religious attitude. As for the Enlightenment, the English Catholic historian, Christopher Dawson, who is perhaps the most perfect representative of the school of Christian fatalists today, can still speak of it as "the last of the great European heresies."[32] Moreover, it is the historical fatalism implicit in a theory that makes cultural life dependent upon one factor—religious faith—that unites so many Christian social theorists today. War, totalitarianism, in short, the decline of European civilization—all are inevitable results of the absence of a religious faith in the modern age. Since a real renewal of Christianity is unlikely, the end of Western culture is more than likely. In this, Protestant theologians like the Swiss Emil Brunner and the English Nicholas Micklem, Anglo-Catholics like V. A. Demant and T. S. Eliot, and such Roman Catholic thinkers as Hilaire Belloc, Christopher Dawson, Romano Guardini, and Erich Voegelin quite agree. Here the democratic Jacques Maritain is at one with the authoritarian monarchist Henri Massis.

The relation of this type of religious thought to romanticism is not obvious. To be sure, both dislike much in common. But even if they shared a common distaste for the Enlightenment,

[31] *Considérations sur la France* (Paris, 1936), pp. 17-32.
[32] *Progress and Religion* (London and New York, 1933), pp. 192-193.

it was for different reasons. It is one thing to reject neo-stoicism as a rationalist disregard for revelation; it is quite another thing to despise it as lifeless and unpoetic. Again today the Christian in revolt against the present age. is no less in a state of cultural alienation than the romantic. The external aspects that arouse his indignation—rootless city life, technology, the prevalence of modes of thought that derive from the natural sciences, the popularity of totalitarian parties and ideologies—also offend the romantic. However, for the romantic, cultural alienation involves an absolute estrangement, whereas the believer can still rest securely in his faith. To long for such a haven without being able to find it is the essential condition of the unhappy consciousness. For the Christian thinker it is only the lack of faith among those about him that is terrifying, not the emptiness within himself. This distinction, though crucial, is not without difficulties. Particularly among the early romantics, "infinite yearning" ended in an acceptance of Catholicism. Friedrich Schlegel in fact became a great admirer of Maistre's works.[33] Again, the emotional, internalized religion of feeling which flourished at the same time as early romanticism resembles the latter in many respects. Hegel, indeed, regarded it as a manifestation of the unhappy consciousness.[34] However, the insistence upon individuality as the sole guide to God which is characteristic of both the optimistic religion of Schleiermacher and the tragic faith of Kierkegaard bears but little resemblance to any of the established forms of Christianity. This too is evident

[33] *The Philosophy of History*, tr. by J. B. Robertson (London, 1846), pp. 464-470.

[34] Jean Wahl in his study of this subject feels that Hegel regarded all Christianity as "unhappy consciousness," but I think that this is false, since Hegel discusses the unhappy consciousness as a specifically pre- and post-Christian phenomenon, and describes it as a response to a climate of skepticism. See J. A. Wahl, *Le Malheur de la Conscience dans la Philosophie de Hegel* (Paris, 1929).

in the ideas of the contemporary Christian existentialist and playwright Gabriel Marcel. Similarly, the aestheticized reverence of a Chateaubriand is foreign to the ancient faith. Moreover, the worship of the creative imagination and the excessive disdain for reason as well as the insistence on individuality in all matters are distasteful to the orthodox forms of Christianity, both Catholic and Protestant. To Thomists in particular they are anything but appealing. There is thus no real affinity between romanticism and Christianity. The romantic and the Christian fatalist are alike only in a negative sense: in their common alienation from the age of the Enlightenment first; then from the entire world of science, industry, commerce; and now from a culture apparently doomed to war and totalitarianism.

Romantic and Christian despair in the realm of social thought are different, then, and would be more so if the end of European culture did not for the Christian have an even deeper religious meaning. However, the end of the West may very well mean the disappearance of Christianity in the world, and this possibility has aroused many Christians to a new and dramatic awareness of the old prophecy of the end of the world. The eschatological consciousness, already present in Maistre and in Lammenais, before his apostasy, is today the Christian equivalent of the unhappy consciousness. For the sense of doom is extended from the merely cultural level to the supernatural, and all mankind is faced with its final hour —a finality that for the romantic is already accomplished in the end of civilization. Thus recently Josef Pieper, a German Catholic thinker, in a brief but complete statement of the doctrine of the last things, foresees the apocalypse in the events of recent years.[35] In specific political events, especially in totalitarianism, he discerns a foretaste of the rule of Anti-

[35] J. Pieper, *The End of Time*, tr. by M. Bullock (London, 1954).

Christ. Totalitarian ideologies represent the devil's counter-religions. The martyrdom of Christians in totalitarian states is a prelude to that heightening of tensions between the forces of Christ and Anti-Christ that precedes the end of time. Implicitly or explicitly the apocalypse has haunted all those Christian thinkers who since the French Revolution could see nothing but decadence and decline in the life of the modern age. It is difficult to imagine anything farther removed from the spirit of the Enlightenment than this.

These apprehensions are far from ridiculous. After all, the society that the romantic and Christian alike revile has rejected them. Both are excluded from the general current of popular thought. Political developments are hardly such as to encourage either. However, the Enlightenment has not triumphed—far from it. Even those who once opposed romantic and Christian despondency, the obvious successors of the Enlightenment, the liberals and socialists, have ceased to offer genuine intellectual alternatives to the doctrines of despair. Since the last century liberalism has itself become increasingly conservative and fearful of democracy. Today a conservative liberalism flourishes that also sees Europe doomed as a result of economic planning, egalitarianism and "false" rationalism. Socialism, on the other hand, has suffered as a theory because of its too intimate connection with the "movement." Today, rejected by the left and assimilated by the right, socialism appears incapable of providing a philosophy that is anything but a defence of its immediate parliamentary position, and even here it falters. Such radicalism as still survives is usually only a belief in the infinite extension of individual liberty for its own sake, without any of the Enlightenment's faith in the harmony and progress of society as a whole that would accompany freedom. As for the two major forms of totalitarian ideology, Nazism and communism, they are not philosophical interpretations of the modern world so much as a verbal form of warfare. As such they are rather the subject of theoretical analysis, not replies to it. In any case, though both regard themselves as the "wave of the future," they too take a catastrophic view of modern history. Only after the violent overthrow of existing social institutions do they foresee a more perfect era, the nature of which remains vague. Certainly Nazism was in its racial monomania a fatalistic denial of all that the Enlightenment stood for, while the élitism and violence lying at the very root of communism make its use of the word "progressive" a crime against its Enlightenment meaning.

The end of the Enlightenment has, in fact, meant not only a decline of social optimism and radicalism but also the passing of political philosophy. This has not been the work of recent years only. The ascendancy of ideas opposed to the entire Enlightenment has been a rather slow and very intricate development. It is to the analysis of this process that the following pages are devoted.

CHAPTER II

The Romantic Mind

The Background: Rousseau, Godwin, and Kant

ROMANTICISM found its first clear expression in the aesthetic revolt against the Enlightenment. But even before the appearance of a romantic literary school there were stirrings of dissatisfaction with the ruling ideas of the 18th century. The unhappy consciousness, at odds with society, with every established faith, uncomfortable with skepticism and longing for some imaginary retreat, was awakened even before romanticism appeared in the literary world. Romanticism itself was nourished by two streams of feeling: a longing for a more purely aesthetic culture and a profound disgust for the rationalist excesses of the Enlightenment. On one hand it was the revolt of poetry against philosophy; on the other a simple reassertion of the emotional and natural in human experience against the eternal reasonableness of the moralist.

This distinction between romantic feeling and romanticism proper is particularly important in tracing the origins of the movement. The intention, as is usual, preceded the act. Rousseau is the first great example of romantic feeling, but his philosophy is not at all romantic, and this discrepancy between impulse and fulfillment is the key to an understanding of Rousseau. The romantics were entirely right in loving him as their older brother, but none of them accepted the conclusions that he drew from their common source of experience. He shared their conviction that European civilization was a failure, but he did not propose to reconstruct it in their way, for Rousseau had no theory of aesthetics. It was thus quite consistent for Schiller to address admiring verses to him and then to refute all his ideas on art and society.

The only serious thought that Rousseau ever gave to art as such was in his *Lettre sur la Musique Française*. There, indeed, he did call for more freedom of style, for more emotion, melody, and drama.[1] But when one hears his own compositions this outburst seems a little empty. Certainly his harmless rococo operettas lack even the suspicion of sound and fury. Here, as everywhere, the protest is romantic, the execution in the convention of the 18th century. Art, in general, however, was uncongenial to this semi-Calvinist. To him it remained a sinful occupation, a sign of social decadence. It only interferes with our civic duties.[2] If he detested the calculating philosophers, he was very far from admiring the artists. His real hero was Cato, who had tried to drive the Greek artists and scholars out of Rome.[3] His social universe contained only three types: natural man, historical man, and the citizen, that is, ideal man. The creative man, the genius, was unknown to this world.

To be sure, Rousseau detested the philosophers as unfeeling and irresponsible. The world of salons was infinitely too artificial for him and his personal life was a model for all later bohemians. No conceivable real state or church could ever have suited him. He was doomed to loneliness because he was impelled to alienate everyone about him. While he could well be discussed as a psychiatric case, he was also the proto-

[1] It has even been noted that the *Lettre* was the basis of later French romantic musical theory, especially Berlioz's. Such was the fate of many of Rousseau's purely polemical works. J. Barzun, *Berlioz and the Romantic Century* (Boston, 1950), vol. I, p. 371.

[2] That is the entire burden of the first *Discourse*, and the *Lettre à D'Alembert*; also of his "Letter to Voltaire," September 10, 1755, *Citizen of Geneva*, tr. and ed. by C. W. Handel (New York, 1937), p. 135.

[3] *Discourse on Political Economy*, p. 502; *Discourse on the Arts and Sciences*, pp. 155-157.

type of the generation of intellectuals who followed him, for in him the restless longings of the unhappy consciousness were already fully at work. However, it was only a mood, and it did not lead him to a new philosophy. What about Rousseau's dislike of the artificial, his love of solitude, of simple, natural, spontaneous existence? There is in these Arcadian reveries a real indictment of a society that has destroyed man's original inner unity. This is a feeling all romantics shared. But Rousseau did not suggest that the work of civilization be undone, but that it be completed. Society gives man the idea of morality, without offering him an opportunity to realize it. Society must restore man to completion by making him wholly social, wholly moral.[4] Its failure lies in destroying instinct without replacing it completely with reason. Man is left in a social twilight where he is neither totally unconscious of morality nor a fully moral being. The *Social Contract* is the picture of a society in which men are restored to inner and outer unity through the triumph of the social and moral will. Again, it is only in our semi-social state that solitude becomes a moral necessity. It is not that Emile is not educated for citizenship, but that there is no society in which citizenship can be effectively exercised. That is why he must live in isolation—not because society rejects genius or creative originality, not even because solitude is good in itself. True freedom is to be found only in submission to law and to the voice of conscience. When the two coincide the problem of the one and the many is solved.

Rousseau not only made the individual submit to society on moral grounds; he also offered a very similar answer to the other great problem of romanticism—the conflict between reason and feeling. The great foe of all that was irrational in

---

[4] "Le Bonheur Publique," *The Political Writings of Rousseau*, ed. by C. E. Vaughan (Cambridge, 1915), vol. I, p. 326.

romanticism, Kant, would hardly have admired Rousseau as much as he did, had Rousseau chosen feeling. Yet even those who see Rousseau as a precursor of Kant insist that Saint-Preux is the model for Werther.[5] Now it is true that in drawing his self-portrait Rousseau created a new literary figure, the desolate man of feeling. Even the notion of such a recreation of personal experience is romantic.[6] But just as in the *Social Contract* Rousseau has pictured a society in which people like himself could never appear, so in the *Nouvelle Heloïse*, Julie, the heroine, is made to appear a being entirely superior to Saint-Preux and she demonstrates her virtue by finding a rational and moral solution to a romantic dilemma.[7] The shocked moralists who later tried to rewrite Werther with a more edifying end should have remembered that Rousseau had already written a *Werther* with a suitable last act.[8] He had meant the novel to be didactic, and that is just what it is.[9] In making it a story of love thwarted by convention he set the pattern for an endless number of romantic tales. But if his had been a typical *Sturm und Drang* novel, the heroine would have defied her parents, run off with her lover, given birth to an illegitimate child, killed the child out of shame,

[5] E. Cassirer, *The Question of Jean-Jacques Rousseau*, tr. by P. Gay (New York, 1954), p. 88.

[6] According to Dilthey, Rousseau is the first romantic, because he created a work of art out of inner experience alone, without any concern for the behavior and circumstances of other men. *Das Erlebnis und die Dichtung* (Leipzig, 1929), pp. 217-221.

[7] The following interpretation of the novel is greatly indebted to a detailed study by M. B. Ellis, *Julie ou La Nouvelle Heloïse* (Toronto, 1949).

[8] R. Pascal, *The German Sturm und Drang* (Manchester, 1953), pp. 150-151.

[9] His second preface to the novel emphasizes just that point, for Rousseau had realized that the public was ignoring his message. *Oeuvres* (Paris, 1826), vol. VIII, pp. 27-55. He also noted that his novel was far less romantic than Richardson's tales, since it did not depend on improbable events and flights of imagination. *Confessions* (Modern Library Edition, New York, n.d.), pp. 565-566.

and then died alone and in misery. The hero would, after similar disasters, have killed himself or gone mad. All this would have been shown, again and again, to be the fault of a heartless, conventional society.[10] Julie does none of these things. After joining her lover in his revolt against forced marriages, sexual inhibitions, class distinctions, and all artificial conventions, she finds that her affair with him was a mistake. She submits to the wishes of the parents, whom she really loves, marries a perfect 18th century gentleman, and finds her happiness in running a model estate with him. She dies contentedly, having achieved her two greatest desires: to convert her husband to natural religion and to restore her lover to a useful life of tutoring her sons. This story is not an inconsistent wavering between sentiment and reason.[11] It is a clear illustration of Rousseau's awareness of the romantic situation and his eminently rational and conventional solution to its problems. The ethics of duty, not of feeling, conscience, not desire, are the true guides of man.[12]

The "unhappy consciousness" does not, in itself, constitute romanticism. Rousseau was able to wring a rationalist morality from such a mentality. Unless the romantic spirit is certain of the futility of *all philosophy*, it does not assert itself to

[10] L. Kahn, *Social Ideas in German Literature, 1770-1830* (New York, 1938), pp. 12-16.

[11] This contention is the main argument of Baron E. Seillière's critical study, *Jean-Jacques Rousseau* (Paris, 1921), pp. 105-112 and 330-379. Baron Seillière's dislike of everything romantic does not, however, blind him to the peculiarity of Rousseau's position in the movement. In this respect he is far more discriminating than I. Babbitt, in whose *Rousseau and Romanticism* (Boston, 1919) can be found a rehash of all Seillière's early ideas, without his caution or wit.

[12] This aspect of Rousseau's philosophy, of course, makes him the great precursor of Kant. Hegel, for one, saw Rousseau's ideas as a stepping-stone to Kant's ethics of pure duty, and his view is today finding an increasing number of supporters. G. W. F. Hegel, *Lectures on the History of Philosophy*, tr. by E. S. Haldane and F. H. Simson (London, 1896), vol. III, pp. 400-402. Cassirer, *op.cit.*, pp. 96, 99-100.

create a congenial world view for itself. Nor does every demonstration of the bankruptcy of philosophy imply, in itself,
that a romantic mind is at work. There never was a less romantic soul than William Godwin, yet step by step he was
forced to destroy the basis of his own thought and flee to romantic ideas, not because of any inner urges, but as a matter
of intellectual necessity. He did not, like Goethe, feel instinctively repelled by the mechanistic philosophy of Holbach,
nor did he find the ethics of pure duty cold. He even accepted
the idea of natural harmony, on both utilitarian and rational
grounds. Yet, by drawing excessively logical conclusions from
these principles, and by trying to apply them to actual life, he
revealed their emptiness.

In England Godwin is the immediate predecessor of romanticism even chronologically. This fact has troubled many
people. How could so "pedantic," "colourless," and even
"clammy" a man appeal to virtually every English romantic
poet?[13] The attractions of Godwinism, one suspects, were in
its excesses. There is a degree of reasonableness that borders
on the irrational. Shelley found it easy to integrate Godwin
into the most perfect expression of romanticism in English.
His contemporaries did not regard Godwin as the antithesis
of romanticism. Hazlitt speaks of him with affection, while
he heaps scorn upon Bentham for being what in truth he was,
the epitome of unromanticism.[14] Moreover, Godwin's integrity, his determination "to see things as they are," and his
refusal to disregard the incongruity between life and thought

[13] C. Brinton, *The Political Ideas of the English Romantics* (Oxford, 1926), p. 70; C. E. Vaughan, *The Romantic Revolt* (Edinburgh
and London, 1923), pp. 142-143. For a more sympathetic understanding of Godwin's relations to the poets, especially to Shelley, one
ought to read H. N. Brailsford, *Godwin, Shelley and their Circle* (London, 1951), especially pp. 38-41, 113-114, 121-133.

[14] W. Hazlitt, *The Spirit of the Age* (Everyman's Library, London,
1910), pp. 171-194.

destroyed philosophy, his own included, and forced him and his admirers to seek new solutions.[15] Godwinism was a self-liquidating state of mind, even for its originator, who preserved his unromantic, cautious personality to the end.

The means by which Godwin came to ruin philosophy began with his attempt to combine all strands of 18th-century thought. In the ensuing confusion all were discredited. Godwin had no system; he was merely an honest philosophizer. For instance, he never gave up his belief in necessitarianism. Free will was a "fantasy," he knew, but though determinism had its humanitarian advantages in proving that criminals "could not help it," it was also an idea "at war with the indestructible feelings of the human mind." We cannot judge, we cannot even act nobly, without believing in free will. When applied to life, Godwin candidly admitted, necessitarianism is nonsense, even though the philosopher knows it to be true.[16] Few thinkers have been as ready to face so fully the distance between truth and living.

Actually Godwin had dispensed with necessitarianism even before he made this confession. For the ethics of hedonism he had only contempt. Self-interest clearly does not in practice lead to beneficent action, except by accident.[17] Only "disinterested benevolence" implies virtue; to Godwin a useful action was one that aimed at the greatest good of the greatest number. At times he more or less agreed with Kant that a good will acting on universally valid norms alone ensures morality. Truth for him was, moreover, an eternal standard

[15] For the importance of this favorite phrase of Godwin's, and for many new insights, I am indebted to D. H. Monro, *Godwin's Moral Philosophy* (Oxford, 1953).

[16] W. Godwin, *Thoughts on Man* (London, 1831), pp. 226-242.

[17] *Political Justice*, ed. by F. E. L. Priestley (Toronto, 1946), vol. I, pp. 433-438. (Unless otherwise indicated, this is the edition referred to below. It is a copy of the third and last edition.) *Thoughts on Man*, pp. 205-225.

which we are absolutely obliged to follow.[18] This in fact was his first axiom of morality. All of this clearly means that we are free to choose good or evil, truth or error. Indeed, this belief can lead only to the ethics of reason and pure duty, and so it does—fatally, for Godwin knew no compromise. In case of a fire, whom must I save, Fénelon or his chambermaid, who also happens to be my mother? Clearly Fénelon, the benefactor of mankind; not my mother, who may be a fool. "What magic," asks the eternal philosopher, "is there in the pronoun 'my' to overturn the decisions of everlasting truth?"[19] Love, gratitude, and feeling cannot influence "disinterested benevolence." Such reasoning makes philosophy absurd. The distinction between feeling and duty was carried farther only by Kant, and with the same effect. After all, it was he who noted that the really good man does not even live because he feels like it, but only because it is his duty.[20] The second instance of both Godwin's and Kant's ascetic intellectualism concerns the absolute obligation to sincerity. Is it right to tell a lie to save my neighbor's life? No, says Godwin, the interest of all mankind in truth is prior to the existence of any one person.[21] Kant had been asked this very question, and he had replied exactly as Godwin did.[22] But he was an old man when he did so. Godwin could not really accept such a suicidal philosophy forever. He modified his stand, both in the case of "mother or Fénelon" and of sincerity, but he could never show that his first conclusions were not the logical ones. Nor did the romantic critics of Kant really care whether logically

[18] *Political Justice*, vol. I, pp. 307-315.
[19] *Political Justice* (1st ed., London, 1793), vol. I, pp. 81-83. Later Godwin changed "mother" to a "valet and brother."
[20] "Critique of Practical Reason" in *Critique of Practical Reason and Other Writings in Moral Philosophy*, tr. and ed. by L. W. Beck (Chicago, 1949), p. 194.
[21] *Political Justice* (1st ed.), vol. I, p. 282.
[22] "On the Supposed Right to Lie from Altruistic Motives," tr. by L. W. Beck, loc.cit., pp. 346-350.

any other system of ethics was possible. Their only complaint was that its principles fell short of the demands of real life.

There was actually in *Political Justice* itself a principle sharply opposed to such rationalism. Necessitarianism had its value, after all. For if we are the creatures of external circumstances, none of us can turn out to be alike. It is therefore impossible to make general rules about human behavior. The "true dignity of reason" consists in making decisions without the help of general rules.[23] Rules are only abstractions we invent to evade our responsibilities to each other. We must treat each person and each event as unique. When Godwin took a second look at his ideas on sincerity, he decided that, after all, a man's life was worth more than any principle, and that in morals no "absolute judge" can exist.[24] We must simply make up our minds anew on each occasion. It seems, then, that no system of ethics is possible; indeed, that philosophy, the art of generalizing, is both immoral and futile. Certainly law and justice become totally incompatible. If no two persons and no two actions are alike, no legal rule can be invented to cover both, nor can the same law be applied twice in fairness. Law is never just.[25] "The fable of Procrustes presents us with a faint shadow of the perpetual effort of the law," he noted.[26]

Systematic philosophy, like systematic legal society, is then clearly a complete failure. Only a perfect moral, social, and intellectual anarchism will do. This, indeed, was Godwin's aim, but how was it to be achieved? What was to provide that minimum of social cohesion that even an anarchical society needs? Certainly there was nothing in the present state of society and of human intelligence to warrant hopefulness.

[23] *Political Justice* (Priestley ed.), vol. I, pp. 344-347.
[24] *Ibid.*, vol. I, pp. 351-356.
[25] *Ibid.*, vol. II, pp. 347-352 and 397-419.
[26] *Ibid.*, vol. II, p. 403.

No one had criticized every existing institution more vehemently than Godwin. The deleterious effect of the established order upon individual lives was, in fact, the constant theme of his gloomy novels.[27] Yet Godwin continued to believe that reason would pull men out of their present irrationality and maintain them in harmonious anarchy forever after—and this after he had so clearly demonstrated that reason can only disintegrate, and never provide the basis for reconstruction! His continued optimism was a tribute to his own classical disposition, not to his philosophy. But the latter was the necessary condition for the flourishing of the "unhappy consciousness." Past and present had been rendered hateful, yet no means of rehabilitation seemed at hand. Philosophy was in disgrace. In Germany, indeed, Kant had earlier had much the same influence. The greatest and most influential of modern philosophers managed to dismay the poets as much as he aroused the admiration of his fellow philosophers. In the realm of literary ideas he produced a reaction that was in every way hostile to his real aims and to the many philosophers who continued to appreciate him. It is difficult today to imagine how shattering an effect the first reading of the Critique of Pure Reason could have. But we need only read Kleist's heartbroken letter, telling how it destroyed all his certainties, to remember.[28] To Nietzsche, Kleist's experience still seemed close.[29] That, too, was why Heine claimed that Kant had been more destructive than Robespierre, and why he sneered

[27] A. Wilson, "The Novels of William Godwin," World Review, June 1951, pp. 37-40.

[28] J. C. Blankenagel, The Dramas of Heinrich von Kleist (Chapel Hill, N.C., 1931), pp. 14-15; P. Kluckhohn, Das Ideengut der Deutschen Romantik (Halle, 1942), pp. 6-9; W. Silz, Early German Romanticism (Cambridge, Mass., 1929), pp. 6-8; O. Walzel, German Romanticism, tr. by A. E. Lussky (New York, 1932), pp. 250-254.

[29] "Schopenhauer as Educator," Thoughts out of Season (II), tr. by A. Collins, Works, ed. by O. Levy, vol. v, pp. 123-124.

at him as "unpoetic" and "Philistine."[30] In first revealing the
limits of reason, and then setting up a system of morals in
which reason lived at the expense of every natural impulse,
Kant helped to inspire among poetic spirits a general mood of
despair, and then of aversion to all philosophy.

The new world of reason more than compensated philosophers and scientists for the loss of a secure religious universe,
but to people of a more ardent imagination it was intolerable.
For them the recognition that "God is dead" was a tragedy.
Their one hope was to find a poetic vision of reality which
could fill the emotional emptiness of the world of prose, of
political maxims, and of scientific logic. Here the young rebels
of the *Sturm und Drang,* even the mature Schiller and Goethe,
all the poets of the romantic revival in England, France, and
Germany, and such later imaginative thinkers as Kierkegaard
and Nietzsche were quite at one. This quest of the unhappy
consciousness, not just its sense of alienation in the modern
world, formed the core of 19th-century romanticism.

Romanticism did not grow out of any philosophy, but philosophy did set the intellectual stage for the new spirit, and
for a war between poetry and philosophy. Philosophy itself
provided the occasions for the eruption of the "unhappy consciousness," and a great part of 19th-century intellectual history consists in a war between philosophy and poetry. Poetry
tried to "heal the wounds reason has inflicted on us," and
philosophy sought to defend itself against the growing prevalence of anti-rational forms of thought. In the course of this
dialogue both sides were modified, until today we have excessively intellectual poetry and philosophers who constantly
call for more life. In the beginning, however, it was the aesthetic view of life which tried to save human existence from
the excesses of the analytical spirit.

[30] "Zur Geschichte der Religion und Philosophie in Deutschland,"
Werke, ed. by E. Elster, vol. IV, pp. 249-261.

The War between Poetry and Philosophy

The man who saves Fénelon suffers from a malady that Coleridge called "the alienation and self-sufficiency of reason."[31] It was against this analytical fragmentation of man, rather than against reason itself, that romanticism protested. From the first outbursts of the *Sturm und Drang*, romanticism was dedicated to the ideal of human totality, the integrity of the entire personality. Its excesses of "feeling" were assertions of vitality, of unphilosophic living strength. If the hero of the *Sturm und Drang* was a mere *Kraftgenie*, and if its cult of energy and spontaneity was exaggerated, this must be seen as an effort to redress the balance that the excesses of analytical reason had upset. Life was not just identified with energy; the inner unity of man's powers was sought, instead of their departmentalization into "feeling" and "reason."

Manfred spoke for all when he claimed that "the Tree of Knowledge is not that of Life," but the real question remained; "what is life itself?"[32] Especially for the later, more reflective romantics, emotion alone was not enough.[33] For them life was never really here, in the present, but always a distant goal, an aspiration, something unreachable, an object of longing rather than something experienced. For most romantics life was a desire, not a reality.[34] Their constant call for more life and less thought was really a demand for a new way of looking at life—the artist's way, to be exact, creatively. It was the intense wish to put together again all that philosophy had torn asunder, reason and experience, duty and inclination. Not analysis, but the restorative powers of the crea-

[31] "The Statesman's Manual" in *The Political Tracts of Wordsworth, Coleridge and Shelley*, ed. by R. J. White (Cambridge, 1953), p. 37.

[32] *Manfred*, Act I, Scene I.

[33] The degree of reflective activity is what basically differentiates the *Sturm und Drang* from romanticism. Walzel, *op.cit.*, pp. 7-9.

[34] Kluckhohn, *op.cit.*, p. 12.

tive imagination, were to recreate man and make him more alive.

The first objection to philosophy was, then, that it is un-creative. "Mind . . . cannot create, it can only perceive."[35] What is more serious is that "mind" can destroy. It can rob us of our simple consciousness of existence, our place in crea-tion, as Herder noted. "A sad occupation," he called philos-ophy.[36] This was the first authentic voice of romanticism. Herder was the first to apply the poetic point of view to every intellectual and social problem.[37] In literature, which was Her-der's field, there is no "man in general" such as philosophy likes to contemplate. There are only concrete individuals— the artist himself and his characters. An author is great if he is original, that is, not like "man in general." His work is beautiful if his characters are living beings, not abstractions representing isolated characteristics. According to Herder, that is why Homer was a Prometheus creating living gods and men, while the didactic poetry of Horace and his imi-tators dealt only with empty symbols.[38] The power of both the poet and his "gods and men" depends on the unity of their inner being. The poem must be an expression of the entire personality of the poet, and his "gods and men" must be believable, many-sided individuals. From this point of view, of course, all talk of man as divided into rational and emo-tional seems fruitless. Again, the idea of a common human nature, a generalized man, seems unreal. Men differ more from each other than do the various species of animals, Her-

[35] Shelley, "On Life," *Essays and Letters* ed. by E. Rhys (London, 1887), p. 76.

[36] *Vom Erkennen und Empfinden der Menschlichen Seele,"* *Werke,* ed. by Suphan, vol. VII, p. 311.

[37] T. Litt in his study *Kant und Herder* (Heidelberg, 1949) il-lustrates very skillfully how Herder applied aesthetic standards to all philosophic problems, and how this orientation was at the root of all his differences with Kant.

[38] *Kritische Wälder, Werke,* vol. III, pp. 94-104.

der insisted.[39] Everywhere in nature he saw the process of individuation at work. Instead of becoming abstract, philosophic "men in general" we should become more distinct, more "whole": "The conviction of our selfhood, the principle of our individuation, lies deeper than our understanding, our reason, or our fancy can reach. . . . As feeling and idea it lies in the word 'self' itself. Self-consciousness, self-activity make up our actuality, our existence." Instead of struggling against it we should follow the great law of individuation, "awaken our true self and strengthen the principle of individuality in us."[40] For him this was not subjectivist ethics, as it was for later romantics, but an affirmation of the value of each being as a whole, as a simple, given unit. He had that sense of selfhood, of simple existence (Daseyn), that Coleridge saw as the salvation of disintegrated man:

> "When he by sacred sympathy might make
> The whole one self! self, that no alien knows!
> Self, far diffused as fancy's wing can travel!
> Self, spreading still! oblivious of its own
> Yet all of all possessing! This is faith!"[41]

Herder had a sense of the unity not only of the inner man but of all existence. To him the idea that experience and knowledge might not be one seemed absurd. Descartes' proof of his existence, or Kant's "hypercritical" examination of the proofs of God's existence, were just examples of intellectual obscurantism. We know that we exist, and that God is, not because we think, but because our whole being tells us that it is so. We are directly and inevitably conscious of existence, just as we cannot even imagine nothingness. There can be no

[39] *Vom Erkennen*, etc., pp. 314-315.
[40] *God: Some Conversations*, tr. and ed. by F. H. Burckhardt (New York, 1949), pp. 211 and 213.
[41] *Religious Musings*.

separation of thought and experience, because our awareness
of existence, of God, is more than either. It is the basis of all
our knowledge and all our happiness, for it is the expression
of our whole being as part of a universal Existence.[42] Over and
over again Herder remarks how our sense of the beautiful
helps us see this.

At the bottom of all this lies Herder's conviction that intuition is our real guide to truth; that it is the highest form of
consciousness—which may be true in art, but is certainly dubious philosophy. While Herder engaged in what he mistook
for philosophic debates, Goethe was quite frank in his dislike
of all speculation and metaphysics.[43] He preferred to depart

[42] *God*, pp. 122-124, 149-155, 165-174 and 211-212.
[43] K. Viëtor, *Goethe the Poet*, tr. by Moses Hadas (Cambridge,
Mass., 1949), p. 14, and *Goethe the Thinker*, tr. by B. Q. Morgan
(Cambridge, Mass., 1950), p. 70. In spite of the vast Goethe literature, and the great variety of possible interpretations, I have relied
almost exclusively on Viëtor. Though other works were consulted,
none proved as suited to the purposes of this study. Viëtor presents
both a detailed analysis of the poetic works and an interpretation of
Goethe's philosophic and scientific writings, but he keeps the two
apart. While this leads to repetition, it is convenient for the non-
specialist. Moreover, Viëtor tends to take a moderate position on most
of the great controversies.
Among the entirely non-biographical presentations of Goethe's
ideas, the philosopher H. Siebeck in his *Goethe als Denker* (Stuttgart,
1922) has much the same general orientation as Viëtor, but does not
deal individually with the poetic works. B. Fairley, *A Study of Goethe*
(Oxford, 1947), is quite thorough, but he puts the poet into an
intellectual vacuum, and discusses his thought only as an emanation
of his personality. Of the other biographical studies, F. Gundolf's
Goethe (Berlin, 1922) is the most impressive. Certainly it is infinitely
above the usual catalogue of Goethe's love affairs, but it is more an
effort to create an image of Goethe as a creative superman than a
study of his ideas.
Of more specialized studies, those dealing with Goethe's relations
to the romantic movement are the only really vital ones for this study.
F. Strich's *Goethe and World Literature*, tr. by C. A. M. Sym (London, 1949), discusses at length the influence of Herder's literary ideas
on Goethe, as well as the latter's impact on the romantic movement in
Europe as a whole. The author, however, tends to separate the early

from the Kantian realm, with its unresolved conflicts, and "escape into poetry."[44] Just as Herder developed his ideas on existence in the process of misinterpreting Spinoza, so Spinoza was Goethe's favorite among the philosophers. To him Spinoza meant that we need not dissect the universe to understand it, but that our own genius builds itself a picture of the universe from its own inner thoughts and feelings.[45] Unlike Herder, he did not feel the need to link his appreciation of life to a teleological, divinely planned system of nature. "Eternity is in the moment," and the energy we display in our life, the creativity we summon up from within, is the real justification of our existence.[46] Again, personality as a whole, not the textbook virtues, makes us both happy and good.[47] Each one of us is gifted with an inner "daemon" which he can develop but never change. Though this implies a degree of fatalism, it does not end in pessimism, but in the recognition that self-expression is the highest aim of man.[48]

However, this serene indifference of poetic intuition to the problems of metaphysics was not typical. Most romantics

---

from the late Goethe too sharply. Perhaps nothing can illustrate the degree of Goethe's romanticism better than his attitude to Kant. E. Cassirer in a short essay tries to prove that though they followed entirely different paths, the poet and the philosopher arrived at much the same conclusions, *Rousseau, Kant, Goethe*, tr. by J. Gutmann, P. O. Kristeller, and J. H. Randall, Jr. (Princeton, 1945), pp. 61-98. On the other hand, G. Simmel in his *Kant und Goethe* (Leipzig, 1916) far more convincingly shows the two to represent two entirely opposite forms of human thought. The present study treats Goethe as a romantic author, but it does not wish to imply that he ought to be regarded as nothing but a member of this or of any other literary "school."

[44] E. Heller, *The Disinherited Mind* (Cambridge, 1952), pp. 24-25; Viëtor, *Goethe the Thinker*, p. 154.

[45] Pascal, *op.cit.*, pp. 170-216; Viëtor, *Goethe the Thinker*, pp. 65-68.

[46] *Goethe the Thinker*, pp. 103-116 and 135-160.

[47] *Ibid.*, pp. 145-146.

[48] *Ibid.*, p. 95, and *Goethe the Poet*, pp. 38-48.

tended to adopt Herder's method of reforming philosophy by imposing a new conception of life on it. The creative imagination, poetry, were to supply the needs of a "metaphysical longing." Imagination was not a quality that classicism had greatly valued. Thus Hobbes, one of the pillars of English neo-classic criticism, had held that fiction ought never "to exceed the possibilities of nature."[49] For the romantic, however, imagination was not only "fancy"; it was the nucleus of all man's powers, rational and emotional, from which creative action grew. It was by definition that force in man which could make him whole again, and even recreate him in a higher form. Imagination, its creations, its originality—these were the divine element in man, the primary quality of Prometheus. One could not miss the religious origin of these ideas. The pious were quite properly shocked by these pretensions.[50] It was the human aspiration to be God. "(Imagination)," wrote Coleridge, "I hold to be the living Power and prime Agent of all human Perception, and as a repetition in the finite mind of the eternal act of creation in the infinite I AM."[51]

Schleiermacher, who like Coleridge thought himself a thoroughly religious man, spoke of "the divine power of imagination which alone can free the spirit and place it far beyond coercion and limitation of any kind."[52] This, however, is only rhetoric. The real question was how? Only two romantic authors, Schiller and Shelley, were able to work out a really cogent answer—the same answer indeed, so that one is really tempted to ask whether "Shelley is not the English for Schil-

[49] L. P. Smith, *Words and Idioms* (Boston and New York, 1925), p. 77.
[50] *Ibid.*, pp. 101-105.
[51] *Biographia Literaria*, in *Selected Poetry and Prose of Coleridge*, ed. by D. A. Stauffer (Modern Library, New York, 1951), p. 263; *Philosophical Lectures*, ed. by K. Coburn (New York, 1949), p. 452, n. 25.
[52] *Schleiermacher's Soliloquies*, tr. and ed. by H. L. Friess (Chicago, 1926), p. 81.

ler."[53] Unlike some romantics, neither abused philosophy as such. Schiller wanted only to make Kant's ethics more viable. He accepted Kant's picture of moral perfection, but he doubted that reason could realize the end it had set itself. What was needed was some faculty that "might pave the way . . . from the realm of mere force to the rule of law."[54] In the "play impulse" he found such a means to morality. But Schiller did not stop here. Even if he claimed to accept Kant's notion of "the primitive and radical opposition between nature and reason," he could not resign himself to it.[55] The aesthetic life in which man is again made one insensibly replaced the Kantian ideal.

The "play impulse" is for Schiller just what the creative imagination was for most romantics—the urge to create beauty. It unites both "the sense and the form impulses," our need for "variation and identity," and thus brings into harmony "our perfection and our happiness."[56] Its end, beauty, becomes "our second creator," for it has as its aim the cultivation of the whole of our sensuous and intellectual powers in the fullest possible harmony.[57] That is why "man is only wholly man when he is playing."[58] We must take the "leap into aesthetic play" to end the "war between intuitive and speculative reason" that has left "man himself . . . only a fragment."[59] Only thus can we reach humanity. And humanity was Schiller's real ideal, a state of perfection that only the Greeks had achieved, "combining fulness of form with fulness of content, at once philosophic and creative, at the same time tender and energetic . . . uniting the youthfulness of fantasy with the manliness of reason in a splendid humanity."[60]

[53] F. A. Lea, *Shelley and the Romantic Revolution* (London, 1945), pp. 221-227 and 253-254.
[54] *On the Aesthetic Education of Man*, tr. and ed. by R. Snell (London, 1954), p. 30.
[55] *Ibid.*, p. 67. [56] *Ibid.*, pp. 74-75. [57] *Ibid.*, pp. 101-102 and 99.
[58] *Ibid.*, p. 80. [59] *Ibid.*, pp. 39-40. [60] *Ibid.*, p. 37.

Now this is very far from Kant, and not only from the letter, as Schiller thought, but also from the spirit of his philosophy. The absolute separation of duty from every emotional motive is the very basis of Kant's ethics. Kant would never have allowed the mediation of beauty in moral education. He insisted that duty could be taught only by example, which, he felt, would awaken a rational response even in the most depraved villain.[61] "The majesty of duty has nothing to do with the enjoyment of life."[62] Schiller simply postponed the rule of duty indefinitely, and Hegel was quite correct in noting that he had freed philosophy from the ethics of duty.[63] And though he admired Schiller, neither Hegel—nor any philosopher— could accept the idea that aesthetic culture is the true and final end of man, and that the artist is the only educator of mankind.

Shelley did to Godwin exactly what Schiller did to Kant. Accepting disinterested morality as the true end of man, he proceeded to show that reason cannot itself achieve this end, but that it requires the aid of the creative imagination, of poetry. But he finally found in poetry ends that transcended morality itself:

"Ethical science arranges the element which poetry has created, and propounds schemes and proposes examples of civil and domestic life: nor is it for want of admirable doctrines that men hate, and despise, and censure, and deceive, and subjugate one another. But poetry acts in another and diviner manner. . . . Poetry lifts the veil from the hidden beauty of the world. . . . The great secret of morals is love; or a going out of our nature, and an identification of ourselves

[61] *Foundations of the Metaphysics of Morals*, tr. by L. Beck, *loc.cit.*, pp. 108-109; *Critique of Practical Reason*, pp. 180-195.
[62] *Ibid.*, p. 195.
[63] *The Introduction to Hegel's Philosophy of Fine Art*, tr. and ed. by B. Bosanquet (London, 1905), pp. 152-155.

with the beautiful which exists in thought, action, or person, not our own. A man, to be greatly good, must imagine intensely and comprehensively; he must put himself in the place of another and of many others. . . . The great instrument of moral good is the imagination; and poetry administers to the effect by acting upon the cause. Poetry enlarges the circumference of the imagination."[64]

Like Schiller, Shelley felt that it was not by preaching, but by the very consciousness of beauty, that art made men good. "Didactic poetry is my abhorrence," he wrote.[65] Though *Prometheus Unbound* celebrates the Godwinian revolution of man against social injustice and prejudice, its hero is conceived primarily as "a poetic character," the perfect image of titanic nobility. Shelley too saw artists as the great reformers of society, standing within yet above their time. The poet also "participates in the eternal and infinite and the one" and poetry "redeems from decay the visitation of the divinity in man."[66] That is, beauty is not just the instrument of reform, it is the reflection of universal harmony in individual form. Like Schiller, he felt that reason had brought discord to man and society: "We have more moral, political, and historical wisdom than we know how to reduce into practice. We want the creative faculty to imagine that which we know . . . we want the poetry of life; our calculations have outrun conception, we have eaten more than we can digest."[67] It is from this that poetry can save us, for it "compels us to feel that which we . . . perceive."[68] Poetry was more than a restorative, a pleasure, or a guide to action. It was "the very image of life expressed in its eternal truth."[69] This aesthetic idealism has been both the most profound and lasting contribution of ro-

[64] "A Defence of Poetry," *Essays and Letters*, p. 12.
[65] "Preface" to *Prometheus Unbound.*
[66] "A Defence of Poetry," pp. 6 and 36.
[67] *Ibid.*, pp. 32-33.   [68] *Ibid.*, p. 37.   [69] *Ibid.*, p. 9.

manticism. Thus today Sir Herbert Read returns to Schiller's idea of education through art as our only hope, and Albert Camus finds comfort in a desolate world in Shelley's celebrated words, "Poets are the unacknowledged legislators of the world."[70]

Not all romantics were capable of rising to this level of controversy. Most of them simply vented their spleen upon philosophy, and made unsystematic claims for poetry. There is no substance in Friedrich Schlegel's and Novalis' aphorisms. "Poetry begins where philosophy ends," the former noted.[71] And "the more poetic the more true," the latter concluded.[72] The old complaint that philosophy was divorced from life was repeated over and over. It was because of this that Schleiermacher objected to Fichte as "a virtuoso, but never a man."[73] The young Schelling observed that no one "can through pure reason become virtuous or a great man"—or even propagate the species.[74] Philosophy was to be poeticized—but to what end? Here a mystical note entered the discussion. What Novalis really disliked about Fichte's philosophy was that it did not lead to ecstasy.[75] Thomas Carlyle, the belated echo of all that was most dubious in German romanticism, exclaimed, "To know; to get into the truth of anything, is ever a mystic act—of which the best Logics can but babble on the surface."[76] This is neither poetry nor philosophy; it is an unresolved de-

[70] H. Read, *Education through Art* (London, 1943), pp. 1, 263, and 278; A. Camus, *The Rebel*, tr. by A. Bower (London, 1953), p. 237. This is the closing phrase of *A Defence of Poetry*, p. 41.

[71] Friedrich Schlegel, "Ideen," *Athenaeum* (Berlin, 1800), vol. III, p. 13 (my translation).

[72] Novalis, *Fragmente, Werke*, ed. by H. Friedmann, vol. III, p. 211 (my translation).

[73] Kluckhohn, *op.cit.*, p. 11.

[74] *Of Human Freedom*, tr. and ed. by J. Gutmann (Chicago, 1936), p. 95.

[75] *Fragmente, Werke*, vol. III, p. 54.

[76] *On Heroes and Heroworship* (T. Y. Crowell & Co., New York, n.d.), p. 78.

sire for two very different things—immediate, raw life, and
mystic exaltation. This sort of romanticism is nothing but "an
encounter between materialism and mysticism."[77]

Not unnaturally, the philosophers rose in ire against these
jibes. There is a real conflict between philosophy and all
aestheticism, not only the spurious kind. The philosopher remains the "priest of truth," in Fichte's words, and as such
the true guide of his fellow men—at least in his own eyes.[78]
In this Fichte, for instance, did not differ from his 18th-cen-
tury predecessors. For him the end of man remained "to subject all irrational nature to himself and to rule over it unre-
servedly and according to his own laws."[79] Even if we can
never reach this goal, to become ever more reasonable is our
highest task. As for the fine arts, Fichte expected the perfect
state to promote them as a good outlet for that surplus of
national energy which remained after man had conquered
nature.[80] Philosophy and religion, however, can never be the
subject of state regulation, for they are superior to society.
They alone link man to the absolute, and so represent his
highest aspirations.[81] Fichte was here opening the philosophers' campaign against the poets, but it was Hegel who really
pursued the war with heat, not by restating the Kantian position but by appropriating for reason all that romanticism had
claimed for art.

Hegel's *Phenomenology* marks his abdication from romanticism; it is also, paradoxically, the most romantic philosophical
attack on romanticism.[82] Not beauty, but truth, is "the baccha-

[77] H. U. von Balthasar, *Prometheus* (Heidelberg, 1947), p. 637.
[78] *The Vocation of the Scholar, Popular Works*, tr. by W. Smith
(London, 1889), vol. I, p. 193.
[79] *Ibid.*, p. 156. X. Léon, *Fichte et son Temps* (Paris, 1924), vol.
II, pp. 180-226.
[80] Fichte, *The Present Age, Popular Works*, vol. II, pp. 183-190.
[81] *Ibid.*, pp. 62-63.
[82] A brief but illuminating account of Hegel's complex relations to
the romantics is to be found in R. Kroner's "Introduction" to Hegel's

nalian revel where not a member is sober."[83] Reason, not art, is to put together the inner and outer life of man. For the work of the poet-philosophers he had the most profound hatred—"fictitious creations that are neither fish nor flesh, neither poetry nor philosophy."[84] The task of philosophy is not, as these dabblers suppose, "to restore the *feeling* of existence, "or to serve enthusiasm and ecstatic longings.[85] "Beauty," he noted bitterly, "hates the understanding" because it is too weak to endure the "death" that is inherent in the analytical process. Reason, however, bears this suffering, rises from it, and eventually reaches absolute knowledge in which all contradictions are resolved.[86] As for the Faust-consciousness of the *Sturm und Drang* that denies all objective limits to the rights of personality, it ends in despair. Because it seeks only enjoyment, it finds itself chained by material necessity and fate on every side. "Instead of having escaped from dead theory and plunged into actual life, (it) has . . . only precipitated itself into consciousness of its own lifelessness, and enjoys itself merely as naked and alien necessity, *lifeless* actuality."[87] It does not even create great art, Hegel felt, for uncontrolled genius is incapable of such heights.[88]

It was not, however, in his disdain for the poetic personality, but in his conception of the relation of art to philosophy that Hegel's debt and his antagonism to romanticism become clear. Having escaped its temptations and accepted the world, he tried to prove that he had aligned himself with the inevitable, the rational, and the only truly living reality. Like the romantics he longed for the union of the objective and subjective

---

Early Theological Writing, ed. by T. M. Knox (Chicago, 1948), pp. 1-66. Also R. Haym, *Hegel und seine Zeit* (Berlin, 1857), pp. 31-37, 135-158, 209-220.

[83] *Phenomenology,* p. 105. [84] *Ibid.,* p. 126.
[85] *Ibid.,* p. 72 (Hegel's italics). [86] *Ibid.,* p. 93.
[87] *Ibid.,* p. 387 (Hegel's italics).
[88] *Philosophy of Fine Art,* pp. 87-88.

in the human spirit. He claimed that Spirit had finally succeeded in its effort to become conscious of this union. Art
and religion were, indeed, expressions of this development,
but "philosophy is the highest, freest and wisest phase."[89]
Thought, not intuition and feeling, leads to truth. Art,
moreover, is great to the extent that it expresses the Idea. It
thus is reduced, from the world-historical viewpoint, to an
inferior form of philosophy.[90] It was a logical, if not a very
happy thought on his part, therefore, to criticize modern love
literature for dealing with feelings that interest only the individuals involved but that have no universal importance at
all.[91] Again, poetry was to him the highest form of art because it is "the universal art of the mind which has become
free in its own nature. . . . (Here) art transcends itself, inas-
much as it abandons the medium of a harmonious embodiment of mind in sensuous form, and passes from the poetry of
imagination into the prose of thought."[92]

The fate of art is, then, to die in becoming philosophy.
Those higher expressions of the Spirit, philosophy and the
state, are not encouraged to suppress art; nothing could have
appalled Hegel more. But the Spirit has passed beyond art.
Art is dead and gone beyond all recovery. Hegel always envisaged art as a form of religious worship. At first, in the
Phenomenology, art had meant Greek art; like his friend
Hoelderlin, he felt that art had died with the passing of the
old gods.[93] In his later work on aesthetics, Christian art received its due, but then, Christianity is as dead as is Hellas.

---

[89] G. W. F. Hegel, *The Philosophy of History*, tr. by J. Sibree (New
York, 1900), p. 49.
[90] *Philosophy of Fine Art*, pp. 177-180; B. Croce, *What Is Living
and What Is Dead in the Philosophy of Hegel*, tr. by D. Ainslie
(London, 1915), pp. 120-133.
[91] *Hegel's Philosophy of Right*, tr. and ed. by T. M. Knox (Oxford,
1942), p. 112, s. 162.
[92] *Philosophy of Fine Art*, pp. 208-209.
[93] *Phenomenology*, pp. 753-755.

We may admire the art of the past, but we cannot relive the experiences that created it; we can no longer worship in art, and we will never become artists again.[94] The age of poetry has passed into the age of prose, and Hegel resigned himself to it—one wonders how happily.

Hegel's claims for philosophy were as immoderate as those of the poets for art. An even more extreme form of the "unhappy consciousness" followed him and found its expression in opposing him as its predecessors had once fought Kant and Fichte. From the romantic point of view a philosophic system that tries to absorb all life is as objectionable as one that simply seems to ignore life altogether. Kierkegaard had, like Hegel, passed through an aesthetic period, but when he emerged from it he did not abandon its inspiration, only its object. The primacy of living over reflecting remained his central thought.[95] To him, as to all romantics, philosophy was "not in the game"; life passed it by.[96] Indeed, it is a form of escapism, a systematic delusion, a retreat from the tragic nature of life. Philosophers know all about abstractions, about death, for example, but nothing about dying.[97] Hegel was just a "pedant." "What it was to live," he never knew.[98] To accept the objective world, to reconcile it to the subjective realm with comforting ideas about mediation, is just cowardice. The "general man" of philosophy is made "to lose himself in objectivity."[99] He is allowed to deny his personal situation and his highest interests. This is treason to life—and it is inherent in all philosophy. For all philosophers, not just Descartes, begin with doubt,

[94] *Philosophy of Fine Art*, pp. 52-56.

[95] J. Wahl, *Etudes Kierkegaardiennes* (Paris, 1949), pp. 58-171.

[96] S. Kierkegaard, *Either/Or*, tr. by W. Lowrie (Princeton, 1949), vol. II, pp. 144-149.

[97] *Concluding Unscientific Postscript*, tr. by D. F. Swenson and W. Lowrie (Princeton, 1944), pp. 147-152.

[98] *The Journals of Soren Kierkegaard*, tr. and ed. by A. Dru (London, 1938), s. 610.

[99] *Concluding Unscientific Postscript*, p. 55.

and look only for some satisfying answer. The really living person begins, not with doubt, but with despair, and he seeks God.[100] This obviously is not the old controversy between religion and philosophy. Traditional Christianity appealed less to Kierkegaard than it did to Hegel. What did matter was the intensity with which man lived and experienced his most vital moments, his relation to God. His outbursts against all "dons" as "eunuchs," as something less than human, were inspired by his resentment against their intellectual indifference to real men.[101] Like Hegel they reduce the person to "an animal gifted with reason," an item in a system.[102] It was not for him, as it had been for the *Sturm und Drang*, a matter of living oneself out; it was not the aesthetic life, either; it was a distinctly religious life, but conceived in terms of the romantic consciousness as something unreflecting, directly experienced, and absorbing the entire personality of the individual. When the chips are down, as in the case of Abraham's sacrifice, ethical judgment is as futile as aesthetic appreciation.[103] In his most crucial experience, in face of God, the individual is beyond either. The ethical man, for all his superiority to the aesthetic man, is also "an affront to God."[104]

To Kierkegaard the choice facing the modern world was clear, aesthetics or religion.[105] He chose romantic religion. Nietzsche, however, decided in favor of art, tragic and dramatic art. If he stood with Kierkegaard in rejecting the optimistic delusions of all past philosophy, he was not, however, ready to discard all philosophy. In him the early romantic

---

[100] *Either/Or*, vol. II, pp. 177-179.
[101] E.g., *ibid.*, ss. 1239, 1264, 1268, 1269, 1323, and 1324.
[102] *The Journals*, s. 1050.
[103] S. Kierkegaard, *Fear and Trembling* (Anchor Books, New York, 1954), pp. 91-129.
[104] *Concluding Unscientific Postscript*, pp. 78-79 and 225-266; *Either/Or*, vol. II, pp. 283-294; *Sickness unto Death* (Anchor Books, New York, 1954), pp. 184-194.
[105] *Journal*, s. 991.

hope of making philosophy aesthetic and creative revived
again. That is why he regarded himself as the "first tragic
philosopher," the only one to say yes to life and no to abstraction.[106] At times, indeed, he longed to escape from truth altogether; for "truth is ugly," and "knowledge kills illusion"
which the active life demands.[107] "Art alone makes life possible," he would say, and call for "an anti-metaphysical view
of the world—yes but an artistic one."[108] But to reject metaphysics is not to deny philosophy itself. It was, rather, a demand for "artist-philosophers."[109] It meant only that philosophic systems do not reach truth and cannot create culture.
He wanted to escape from the asceticism of all past philosophy,
which had merely given Christian values a new coat of paint,
and from the "objectivity, reflection and suspension of the
will," the inartistic conditions from which all suffered.[110]

If he always drew a sharp distinction between the Socratic
hope to fathom life by means of logic, and the tragic needs of
art, Nietzsche did not disdain all Greek thought. In pre-
Socratic philosophy he recognized ideas consonant with the
demands of life, not in modern philosophy, which languishes
"in the throes of unfulfilled desire for life," but a philosophy
that returns to the earliest Greek question, "what is the real

[106] *Ecce Homo*, tr. by C. P. Fadiman in *The Philosophy of Nietzsche*
(Modern Library, New York, n.d.), pp. 868-869. Professor C. J.
Friedrich has suggested that Nietzsche's ideas changed very radically
at least twice during his life. While changes certainly did occur and
Nietzsche was not, in any case, a consistent thinker, there is a basic
unity in his thought that permits its being treated as a single, undifferentiated whole. Romanticism provides the unifying element.

[107] *The Will to Power* (ii), tr. by A. M. Ludovici, *Works*, vol. xv,
p. 822; *The Birth of Tragedy*, tr. by C. P. Fadiman (Modern Library),
pp. 984-985; "The Use and Abuse of History," *Thoughts out of
Season* (ii), *Works*, vol. v, pp. 60-61.

[108] *The Will to Power* (ii), nrs. 853 and 1048.

[109] *Ibid.*, (ii), p. 239.

[110] *Genealogy of Morals*, tr. by H. B. Samuel in *The Philosophy of
Nietzsche*, pp. 717-793; *Will to Power*, vol. ii, p. 257.

of bohemians after another has demonstrated its superiority by despising conventions in dress and manners. Good manners, Fichte observed, spring from the recognition that fundamentally all men are equal.[86] The rejection of manners and convention in Bohemia is infinitely less a desire for freedom than a demonstration of contempt for lesser men. The worship of individuality is inseparable from egoism, and from genius-consciousness. "Individuality," Schlegel noted, "is the primary and eternal aspect of man. . . . To make the creation and development of this individuality one's highest aim would be divine egoism."[87] A few pages later we are told that a really original artist must have his own religion and his own opinion on every subject. Years later Nietzsche repeated this injunction almost verbatim.[88] Whether divine or not, the ethics of genius are egoistic; "the nightingale is proud," it doesn't care. Like ordinary egoism it increases the gulf between what Shelley termed "social and individual man."[89] Indeed, society of every kind is regarded as something of a danger. Artistic creation is possible only in solitude, and the moulding of a truly original individuality requires the same condition. Wordsworth's "self-sufficing power of solitude" became the highest good for all romantics, and gregariousness the worst, the most plebeian sin. With Nietzsche it became an obsessive hatred. What then, if anything, is to tie men together? Only love is to be permitted, since it rises from within, but even here you must be careful, Schleiermacher warns us, lest you lose yourself in your friends![90] One can sympathize with Hegel when in the face of these "excrescences" of subjectivism, he cried out that "the glory of philosophy is departed" where no common ground of understanding is left. His contempt for this despicable "artist

---

[86] *The Present Age*, pp. 249-251.   [87] *Ideen*, p. 15.
[88] *Ibid.*, p. 6; Nietzsche, *Human-all-too-Human* (1) nr. 286.
[89] "Speculations on Morals," *Essays*, pp. 134-135.
[90] *Soliloquies*, pp. 56-57.

existence," these pretensions of "god-like geniality," was one that every social philosopher must, and did, share, especially the unfortunate Fichte whom Hegel accused of having started this whole mess.[91]

The negative side of self-glorification, however artistic, is only too obvious. What, after all, do the ethics of genius offer society? Nothing. The genius himself is not part of society. He asks only the question, "What does society owe me?" and "Why has it always failed to give it to me?" The social attitudes of genius are, in fact, nothing but an elaboration of one situation, that of the artist facing his public. On one side stood the young heroes of the battle of *Hernani*, "drunk with art," certain that there was no decent occupation in life other than writing verse or painting. On the other side stood the forces of "wealth, power, and society" that let them starve or made them earn their livelihood in some pedestrian fashion, robbing them of hours that might have been spent in creation.[92] Society makes genius, the gift of the gods, a curse. The genius is bound to be unhappy as a necessary consequence of "his inner nature and environment. Society is a republic. When an individual strives to rise, the collective mass press him back. . . . (Against) him, who by the invincible power of genius towers above the vulgar mass, society launches its ostracism, and persecutes him."[93] The word "republic" is revealing when one recalls the hopes that an earlier generation had attached to it. Now it is not any particular form of government but society as such that is hated, for every society is "the public." The poet is maltreated alike under monarchical and under representative governments, Vigny's Docteur Noir, who instructs young Stello in the miseries of the poet's life,

[91] *The History of Philosophy*, vol. III, pp. 507-510; *The Philosophy of Fine Arts*, pp. 158-168.

[92] T. Gautier, *Histoire du Romantisme*, pp. 153, 259 and 268.

[93] H. Heine, "Introduction to Don Quixote" in *The Romantic School*, p. 250.

explains.[94] The inevitable destruction of the poet by society was, indeed, Vigny's major theme. With him the glorification of genius is always coupled with despair over the artist's fate. The typical romantic cycle from extravagant aspiration to utter defeat was repeated in the realm of social life. The genius who begins as a miracle ends as the "poète maudit." Vigny firmly believed that the poet was the highest form of humanity. Yet in a vulgar society, the morose Docteur Noir explains, the poet can only assume a position of "armed neutrality," of aloofness, for it is his best defense against its attacks.[95] There is an inevitable conflict between a flourishing inner life and a repelling outer world, he felt, which always ends in the victory of the latter.[96] The fate of young Thomas Chatterton haunted him, and he told his story twice, once in *Stello* and again in a play in which "he tried to show a spiritual man stifled by a materialistic society, in which calculation exploits talent and work."[97] His own solution to the poet's tragedy was to renounce all hope as a danger and his only longing was "to flee, flee to a few elect."[98]

Stoic despair is, however, not possible for all. Baudelaire, who felt as isolated in the crowd as did Vigny, was far more vituperative in venting his spleen. The dandy is "a Hercules out of work" in a corrupt society. Gifted with great natural ability, he is concerned only with his personal appearance, while his only social function is to scorn the crowd.[99] This was Baudelaire's vision of a spiritual aristocracy in "miserable times" but actually he thought *all* times bad for heroes. Nations do not willingly produce great men, and so must be con-

[94] A. de Vigny, *Stello* (Paris, 1852), pp. 91-92.
[95] *Ibid.*, pp. 247-251.
[96] *Ibid.*, p. 20.
[97] "Dernière Nuit de Travail," *Chatterton, Théatre Complèt* (Paris, 1864), p. 13 (my translation).
[98] *Journal*, p. 23.
[99] *L'Art Romantique*, pp. 91-96; *Intimate Journal*, p. 74.

quered by them.[100] It is worth remembering that today Baudelaire is accepted as a prophetic voice, a man who already knew the situation of the contemporary artist. Again Nietzsche, who so violently scorned the decadents, was quite at one with them in assigning only one function to society: to serve as "a scaffolding" for higher men. In return, every exceptional man is bound to hate society.[101] Society as a whole, for him and for all romantics, is nothing but the Philistines making sport of Samson, and as such an object of boundless contempt.

It has often been suggested that the decline of the old patronage system, the disappearance of courts, salons, and private patrons greatly worsened the artist's social position. One need, however, only recall the difficulties of Erasmus, Mozart, and Dr. Johnson with their respective Maecenases to doubt this. There never was an adequate patronage system, and the "general public" and its chief representative, "C. Snobius Maecenas—the really paying patron of art in our society," are no worse than their predecessors.[102] In any case, it is unsound to look for an explanation for romantic social attitudes in the general social circumstances of the time. The resentment of the public preceded the French Revolution. The idea of an inevitable conflict between the artist and society was accepted by those who, like the author of *Tasso*, never knew patronage trouble. Certainly patronage was not the origin of Lord Byron's social difficulties. The romantic notion of genius, and the conditions which genius demanded, are in themselves the basis for a resentment of *all* society as an inhibiting obstacle to self-expression. Philistia is merely the symbol of this hostility.

Although social changes were not the original source of their antagonism to society, the romantics were by no means unconscious of their new patrons. Some, like Victor Hugo,

[100] *Ibid.*, pp. 39 and 98.
[101] E.g., *Beyond Good and Evil*, pp. 576 and 410-411.
[102] J. Barzun, *Berlioz*, vol. I, pp. 536-538.

even rejoiced at having so huge an audience,[103] but most romantics did not enjoy serving their social inferiors. Moreover,
because the "general public" is itself an abstract entity, it easily
became the basis of general social theory. "To the public, the
Honorable Nobody," wrote Hamann, in dedicating one of his
books.[104] The public was an unknown, amorphous group of
ticket-holders and readers; it was everybody and nobody. The
new patron, the "general public," like "society as a whole,"
was always "everybody except me and my friends." That is
why it became easy to theorize about both in abstract terms
and classifications. The ethics of genius, combined with the
artist's natural dislike for his patron, could thus become the
basis for general social theories.

To the artist the public was not "vox populi" but his real
or imaginary audience. When Vigny spoke of the multitude
he at once visualized it as a typical theater crowd, hoping only
that the play would be a dead failure.[105] To the genius it
seemed that to be hissed off the stage was a typical social experience, even if he himself had never suffered such an indig-
nity, and only felt his individuality being crushed by conventionality. The striking fact for him was that society was divided into two hostile camps, the culture creators and its
countless, mediocre, uncomprehending consumers. It was clear
to him that by right the world ought to belong to the former,
and that a society controlled by sterile, parasitic audiences was
corrupt. That was essentially the idea behind Saint-Simon's
élite of producers, a theory that was very popular among the
French poets. Even Vigny was drawn to Saint-Simon for a
while, and wrote a workers' song that begins with the line, "Le
monde est un vaste atelier."[106] Among romantics of radical so-

---

[103] Preface to *Hernani* (Editions Nelson, Paris, 1943), pp. 9-14.
[104] R. Unger, *Hamann*, vol. I, p. 452.
[105] *Stello*, pp. 228-229.
[106] *Journal*, p. 152; D. O. Evans, *op.cit.*, pp. 9-30 and 45-50; R.
Picard, *op.cit.*, pp. 289-305 and 309-325.

cial inclinations the creators were thought to include all manual laborers. Those who had élitist instincts felt that only artists, with the possible aid of warriors and priests—a trinity of those who create, who destroy, and who know—should dominate society.[107] This is really a very novel élite. It is not Plato's élite of knowers, nor the traditional nobility of conservatism, nor the radical élite of reformers. It is the élite of those who by their own efforts bring forth something new, the élite of creators. Leagued against them stand the dominant powers of the exploiting consumers of creative labor. If at first Philistinism was a creature of the artistic imagination, it soon became a general social category. Soon the war against the Philistines was carried on by people who were quite incapable of artistic creativity and who had never done any physical labor. Moreover, Philistia and the Third Estate were merged into one group. Karl Marx, for one, no longer bothered to keep the two terms apart.

This merging of artistic experience and social theory was a gradual process. Originally the word Philistine was not taken directly from the Bible but from German students' slang, where it was applied to all who had not attended a university. Its meaning was, however, considerably broadened by the young romantics. Thus Clemens Brentano wrote that a student, in the widest sense, is a person "who is engaged in seeking the eternal, knowledge or God, whose soul mirrors every beam of life, who worships the idea, as such, and the Philistines are his opposite." They are the enemies of "all enthusiasm, genius, of all free, godly creation."[108] Schopenhauer defined the Philistine as a man "whose intellect is of the narrow and normal amount"; that is, he is concerned only with his stomach, not with ideas.[109] In France, indeed, the word "bourgeois" was

[107] Baudelaire, *Intimate Journal*, p. 75.
[108] *Der Philister vor, in und nach der Geschichte*, *Werke*, ed. by H. Preitz, pp. 269-318 (my translation).
[109] *Essays*, vol. I, pp. 41-42.

used from the first, but as Gautier noted, it meant the same thing as Philistine and, as he candidly admitted, the "bourgeois" were just about everybody, all those who lived prosaically.[110] The poet Theodore de Banville has given us the most perfect account of the credo of the *race de 1830*. To them, he wrote, art was an intolerant religion that permitted no heretics. The bourgeois, therefore, had to be destroyed. They felt "an inveterate and irreconcilable hatred for those whom they called the 'bourgeois,' a word not used in its political and historic sense as applying to the Third Estate. In romantic language the word 'bourgeois' meant a man who had no faith except in a hundred cent piece, and no other ideal than to save his skin."[111]

What began as an aesthetic notion soon became definitely a social matter. In Baudelaire the identification of the bourgeois, the "Belgian spirit," and the commercial world is quite clear. To Burckhardt the Philistines, the uncultured, were clearly a social phenomenon. In Matthew Arnold and Nietzsche this becomes entirely obvious. It is a little odd to put the insipid Arnold in the same sentence as Nietzsche. One can well imagine what Nietzsche would have thought of a man who defined culture, especially Greek culture, as "sweetness and light"! Arnold was not a tragic but a simpering spirit, but his views were derived from at least one of Nietzsche's sources —Heine, and his separation of the Hellenes and Nazarenes. Both gave this notion a directly social meaning. To Arnold, England seemed divided into three classes, the barbarians, the Philistines, and the populace, corresponding to the aristocracy, the middle-classes, and the workers. Here a class concept has clearly emerged from the artist's relation to the "public." From each class a few escape who then become "aliens," belonging

110 T. Gautier, *op.cit.*, p. 154.
111 "Commentaire," *Odes Funambulesques, Poésies Complètes*, vol. III (Paris, 1883), pp. 179-180 (my translation).

to none of the great groups that compose the public. The barbarians are animals with social graces; the workers, "raw and half-developed"; but the Philistine is the descendant of the Puritans, a "stiff-necked and perverse" enemy of "sweetness and light." Culture is left entirely to the poor aliens, while the rest of the nation assumes that it has a right to do as it likes, that is, remain mediocre and blind to culture, especially in America which contains nothing but Philistines.[112] To Nietzsche, Europe too had become entirely the preserve of the Philistine. The conventional "worship of the ordinary" that destroys poets was rampant.[113] Nietzsche even identified a second degree of Philistinism, that of the "culture Philistines" who do not shrug off culture but nibble it to death. These uncreative parasites simply dissolve the culture they feed on. The genius is their first victim. These creatures are institutionalized. They are the system, a "firmly established barbarity."[114] Wherever Nietzsche looked he saw their power. Modern society was only collective mediocrity. At times he even felt that raging leveling process was desirable, since it would hasten the collapse of the rotten structure. At other times he cried that it must be halted.[115] Socialism was objectionable, not because Nietzsche knew or cared anything about economics, but because it meant the rule of "the cattle," the enemies of the great.[116] The higher man must declare war upon the masses.[117] Contempt for the mediocre and for the masses are merged here. Today the fear of the mass-man that animates all romantics is still nothing but the old hatred for the Philistine, transferred from the bourgeoisie, which has ceased to be im-

[112] M. Arnold, *Culture and Anarchy* (Cambridge, 1946).
[113] "Schopenhauer as Educator," pp. 120-121.
[114] E.g., *David Strauss, the Confessor and Writer*, pp. 10-22 and 41-42.
[115] *The Will to Power*, vol. II, nrs. 898, 954-965 and 1054.
[116] *Ibid.*, vol. II, p. 206; *Human-all-too-Human* (I), nr. 235.
[117] *Ibid.*, nr. 753.

portant enough to really hate. Before the last war there were still some who could focus on the bourgeoisie. Surrealism was always more of a social protest than a theory of art; it represents the final disappearance of the aesthetic mind in social preoccupations. But surrealism was the last great effort "to shock the bourgeoisie."[118] Its adherents have by now either sunk into the Communist Party or disappeared altogether from the intellectual scene. Generally romantic social feeling is now directed against the Philistine mass-man rather than against the bourgeois. Few poets today can be bothered to write verses like D. H. Lawrence's "How beastly the bourgeois is" and exclaim, "what a pity they can't all be kicked over/like sickening toadstools. . . ." Today it is the mass-man who sickens the aesthetic mind.

The "masses" or the "crowd" have, of course, always been around. They were the "canaille," the people, the uncouth many. All romantics feared and hated crowds, but they did not use the word "masses" to mean anything specific, like the Philistine. Only Kierkegaard used the idea of the crowd to put the conflict between the unique and the many on a new basis. In his earlier works he too had sung the praises of the exceptional man, and despised the Philistines, the half-educated and the mediocre. He too feared leveling as the greatest danger to Europe, and scorned the public for its lack of ideas.[119] In his religious writings he discarded the "superior man" in favor of the "individual," which is something every man can become. Indeed, he claimed that the practices of his earlier days had only been a device to stir people to self-conscious-

[118] Thus André Breton clearly insists that surrealism is the artistic equivalent of the proletarian revolution, "Limits not Frontiers of Surrealism" in *Surrealism*, ed. by H. Read (London, 1936), pp. 95-116.

[119] E.g., *Journal*, ss. 81, 88 and 1408; *The Point of View*, tr. by W. Lowrie (London, 1939), pp. 53-63; *The Present Age*, pp. 23-33; *Sickness unto Death*, pp. 174-175.

ness.[120] He never lost the sense of being an exception, but it was changed from the loneliness of the extraordinary to that of the victim, the one before God. Kierkegaard was also a thoroughly conservative person, a defender of the king and of the established order. It was indeed in the defence of the latter that he got himself involved in a tremendous row with the popular press.[121] He could never forget how much the attacks of the vulgar had hurt him, but the last pamphlet he wrote was an appeal to the "Plain Man" to become an individual and to shun the pastors of the established church like Satan, for they were royal functionaries and, as such, in no way related to Christ.[122] With that his renunciation of "superior" people was complete.

However, even in his aesthetic days, Kierkegaard's religious *alter ego* was with him enough to make his attack on the public something quite different from the genius' diatribes against Philistia. The trouble with the public, Kierkegaard felt, was that it did not exist; it was a mere phantom of the reflective mind, a gruesome abstraction. Who is the public? Certainly it is not any concrete group of people whom we know, for these retain their individual identity. It is not any nation, not a community, not a class—it is nothing. It is not real and it does not exist in a real situation but only provides a "negative unity" for those who by reflection have destroyed their personal, immediate existence. However, the power of nothingness is enormous. The kindest persons can by dint of thinking themselves "the public" become cruel monsters—what we today know as fanatics.[123] There is a remarkable scene in Bernard Shaw's *Saint Joan* which perfectly illustrates this power of nothingness. The English chaplain, the perfect average man,

---

[120] *The Point of View*, p. 126.
[121] W. Lowrie, *Sören Kierkegaard* (Princeton, 1951), pp. 176-187.
[122] *Ibid.*, pp. 251-254.
[123] *The Present Age*, pp. 37-43 and 28; *The Point of View*, pp. 53-60.

has been louder than anyone in screaming for Joan's death. When, however, he has seen the fire he cries piteously: "I meant no harm. I did not know what it would be like . . . it is so easy to talk when you don't know. You madden yourself with words. . . . But when it is brought home to you: when you see the thing you have done, when it is blinding your eyes, stifling your nostrils, tearing your heart, then, then—."[124] Significantly, Shaw notes in the preface that his play is a real tragedy, in which "normally innocent persons," not villains, commit murder. That is exactly what Kierkegaard had in mind when he spoke of the inhumanity of abstractions, especially when raised to a power in the form of "public opinion." That too is the danger he saw in acting "on principle."[125] This is not Burke's counsel of political expediency, which is only another abstraction, but a demand for complete personal responsibility on the part of the individual. For it is only the individual who can face God and make a decision—hence the viciousness of crowds. It was not their mediocrity, nor their inferiority, that he disliked. Moreover, he admitted that the power of numbers may have its value in politics, and temporal life in general.[126] But where truth is at stake, numbers cannot decide anything, and we escape our first responsibility as individuals if we allow numbers to decide for us.[127] Truth, especially religious truth, can be achieved only by the solitary individual taking a "leap" out of the crowd, out of the power of numbers. But this leap, away from the leveling life of crowds, does not make one "an outstanding man or a hero," but "a man and nothing else, in the complete equalitarian sense. That is the idea of religion."[128] Individuality here is a religious not an artistic category. To be a man is not to be distinguished, but to face God, and this is possible to anyone who really wants to be an individual.[129]

[124] Scene VI.   [125] Present Age, pp. 54-58.
[126] The Point of View, p. 112, footnote, and p. 113.
[127] Ibid., pp. 102-122.   [128] The Present Age, p. 34.
[129] The Point of View, pp. 123-140.

Kierkegaard divorced the ethics of individuality entirely from the immanent realm of genius, and made it an object of self-transcendence, something the "Plain Man" is as capable of achieving as the superior person—not that Kierkegaard shared Schleiermacher's optimistic hope that introspection alone brings us to God. Individuality is only the first step for him, but so necessary a step that he disregarded all forms of community, the church included. Only a person can make a decision, and only an individual can become an Apostle, but that individual is Everyman.

It is unfortunate that modern romantics have ignored Kierkegaard's ideas on crowds and on the public. Gabriel Marcel alone has tried to adapt them, but he reduces them to conventional conservatism. Instead, everyone hails Le Bon as a great discoverer, when in fact his book on the crowd is nothing but a jumble of pseudo-scientific racist generalizations, in the service of the most ordinary élitism. But the élitist tendency, rather than Kierkegaard's egalitarian idea of individuality, has predominated in romantic thought, and this has lent Le Bon his totally undeserved appeal. Moreover, Kierkegaard's individual is not a political entity but a complete, living person. Kierkegaard, as a genuine romantic, was an entirely unpolitical writer—even when he dealt with politics.

The Politics of the Unpolitical

The politics of romanticism are negative in the extreme. The one concern of romantics was to defend non-political man against the encroachments of public life. Whether they rejected all political activity or tried to transform it into aesthetics, the romantics were anti-political. When the poets allowed themselves to participate directly in political affairs, they ceased to be romantics—just as they did when they joined the church.[130] Politics implied the same sort of loss of self. The

[130] To that extent it is perfectly sound to say that romantic politics

ethics of genius demands that individuality must be preserved against society, and the fruit of individuality, culture, must be guarded against the state. Culture is the highest aim of man, and the state is its natural enemy. No external agency, least of all the state, can assist man in the labors of self-development and of artistic creation. It can only hinder it. The anarchism of the Enlightenment consisted in rejecting the coercive state because it interfered with a society that should be self-regulating, in accordance with the laws of reason or of self-interest. The anarchism of romanticism was based on the conviction that all external restraint was a threat to culture.

Freedom, for the romantics, meant freedom from all social control, from law as much as from arbitrary regulation. The cult of individuality finds law as much of an alien imposition as a tyrant's fiat. With the rejection of reason as man's best guide in social matters, reason's public voice, the law, lost its appeal as well. "I am an utterly unjuristic person," Novalis wrote naively, "I feel no need for law, at all."[131] Culture is not created by law, or by any kind of social rule, however reasonable it might seem on other grounds. It was this trend which so appalled Kant. In tones of unusual vehemence he begged the men of genius "to consider what you do, and where you will end with your attacks on reason."[132] If reason is not the supreme value, and if arbitrariness rules intellectual life, what is to prevent rulers from arbitrarily interfering with freedom of thought? What purpose does freedom serve, if it is not the necessary condition for the sovereignty of reason? When

---

are a self-contradiction, though this need not imply a criticism of romanticism, as it usually does; B. Croce, *The History of Europe in the Nineteenth Century*, pp. 49 and 51; C. Schmitt, *Die Politische Romantik* (Muenchen and Leipzig, 1925), pp. 50-76 and 153-228.

[131] *Fragmente, Werke*, vol. III, p. 158.

[132] *What Is Orientation in Thinking?* tr. by L. W. Beck, *loc.cit.*, pp. 303-305; E. Cassirer, *Kant*, pp. 392-393.

reason is abused, freedom loses its justification and oppressors will hasten to exploit this fact. The argument reveals how intensely Kant was concerned with liberal politics, for there was no indication at that time that the romantics took any interest at all in politics. As Kant admitted, they were as fond of freedom as he was. Nevertheless, Kant's criticism of its irrational tendencies has remained until today the most popular of all attacks on romanticism, but it is not an entirely valid one, for it points only to the possible consequences of romanticism, not to its actual aspirations. Inherently romanticism is a longing for the most complete personal freedom.

In the war between culture and power, romanticism took several positions. First of all there was the complete rejection of the state, or at least the desire to limit its activities greatly. Participation in politics was regarded as an inexcusable disregard for man's most vital concerns. Thus Friedrich Schlegel advised, "Do not waste your faith and love on the political world. Give your inner self only to the divine realms of knowledge and art."[133] Many romantics were not, however, always ready to dispense with all politics; they wanted to transform them. The state was to become an object of aesthetic admiration and something that grew naturally out of the soul of a people, like poetry. Political action and opinion were to be matters of self-expression. Schleiermacher wrote to his father, for instance, "I *love* the French Revolution very much."[134] And Byron said of Italian liberation that, "it is a grand object— the very *poetry* of politics."[135] This kind of politics was an exercise of individuality, and as such always meant opposition to the trend of the times. Wherever public opinion was, the

[133] *Ideen*, p. 23 (my translation).
[134] Quoted in G. P. Gooch, *Germany and the French Revolution* (London, 1920), p. 244 (my italics).
[135] C. Brinton, *The Political Ideas of the English Romanticists*, p. 153 (his italics).

poet, explicitly, was not.[136] Lastly there was the hope that politics might be made the servant of culture, its mere expression. The culture creators were not to exercise political power but to direct the spirit of a people and so rule indirectly. That was the aim of Coleridge's "clerisy," for instance, a corporate body of the nation's cultural leaders that moulds the nation's spirit and thus indirectly dominates its life, including its political life.[137] Shelley's belief that poets are the heralds of political reform, the conscience of society, and the prophets of an ideal state of anarchy was a radical's version of the same notion.[138] It is therefore possible to speak, in a limited sense, of romantic political theory, but it must be understood as the infusion of entirely unpolitical motives in political life and thought. Nevertheless, Schiller's belief in the mission of art, or Nietzsche's dream of the aesthetic powers of the super-man who would forge men into a new humanity—these are essentially political ideals. Their origin and ends, however, spring directly from aspirations which have nothing to do with any definable power structure or any concrete institution. It is a matter of exploiting political power for aesthetic ends, but it remains politics for all that. Romantic political theory, though meaningful enough, is inevitably a paradoxical term. It applies to the political conceptions of people who are alienated from every existing society, from every possible historical form of political life, and from all the undramatic world about them.

The extreme distaste for politics was most common among German romantics, though it was by no means limited to them. This is not surprising. Germany in the 18th century presented a "spectacle of political decrepitude and intellectual

[136] R. Huch, *Ausbreitung und Verfall der Romantik* (Leipzig, 1902), pp. 306-332.

[137] Coleridge, *On the Constitution of Church and State*, Works, ed. by W. G. T. Shedd, vol. VI, pp. 51-55.

[138] Shelley, "A Philosophical View of Reform" in *Political Tracts*, pp. 211-227 and 248-262.

rejuvenescence."[139] There was nothing in Germany's political life that could attract an ardent spirit, while the republic of letters, in glaring contrast, seemed to offer everything. Goethe lived in that conviction to the end of his days, long after Napoleon had succeeded in making most Germans intensely conscious of politics—not the least of the Emperor's many sins. In 1794, Goethe, Schiller, and Wilhelm von Humboldt formed a closed circle, of which Goethe said, "We seek together to maintain ourselves in the aesthetic life as far as possible and to forget everything outside ourselves."[140] More than thirty-five years later he still felt that politics were not a fit object for a poet—either as a subject for verse or as a field of activity. Art is inherently above politics, and as soon as a poet enters the political arena he must choose a party, and so lose his free spirit and broad outlook. Hatred, moreover, is the death of poetry. In any case, how could he have hated the French, who were the most cultured people of Europe? For nationalists he had the most profound contempt. As a man and a citizen he was ready to love his fatherland—the fatherland of the poetic life, that is, of all that is good, noble, and beautiful.[141] These had, indeed, been the beliefs of all German romantics before the Napoleonic invasion. Even those two later super-patriots, Clemens Brentano and Achim von Arnim, begged each other to take no part in the war, when it began.[142] Wackenroder wrote to Tieck that he was too preoccupied with "ideal beauty" to care whether Germany or France won.[143] "Not Hermann and Wotan, but art and science are the national gods of the Germans," Friedrich Schlegel noted.[144] In France, Vigny represented the same point of view. All governments loathe poetry and conspire to destroy it. To be free

---

[139] Gooch, *op.cit.*, p. 1.   [140] Viëtor, *Goethe the Poet*, p. 99.
[141] Eckermann, *Gespraeche mit Goethe*, March 14, 1830, and (early) March, 1832.
[142] Huch, *Ausbreitung und Verfall*, etc., pp. 306-307.
[143] Silz, *op.cit.*, pp. 91-92.   [144] *Ideen*, p. 28.

means to keep far away from the state. Only in the republic of letters does liberty prevail.[145]

The most detailed defense of this kind of anarchism is, ironically, to be found in the youthful work of a future Prussian minister of education, Wilhelm von Humboldt. It is a curious book, a non-political investigation into the limits and purposes of the state. Not forms of governments or their historical origins, but only the effect of the state in general on culture is discussed. There is no evidence of political emotion. If less radical than Kant, Humboldt was no conservative, either. Freedom was his passion, and freedom meant self-development, originality. His main target, therefore, was the "schoolmaster-state" of 18th-century theory. Like Godwin he felt that the state could educate men only to uniformity, but unlike the latter he was not ready to subject men to the regiment of reason, which would only have had the same result. Morality was individuality in beauty and inner harmony. The state is clearly not able to promote such ethics; it can only destroy them. Humboldt, moreover, like Herder regarded energy as a high virtue. War was therefore not a bad thing, if the state kept out of it, for its disciplined armies give no scope to individual energy. The state must provide a certain minimum of security for culture, but beyond that it can have no end.[146]

What, however, would a society dominated by aesthetic culture and its standards be like? The ethics of genius provide the answer. There is a strong aristocratic bias inherent in all these "unpolitics" which springs both from the individual genius' sense of personal distinction, and from the obvious fact that equality is a meaningless value in aesthetic

[145] *Journal*, pp. 31 and 36; *Stello*, p. 299.
[146] W. von Humboldt, *The Sphere and Duties of Government*, tr. by J. Coulthard (London, 1854); G. P. Gooch, *op.cit.*, pp. 103-118; F. Meinecke, *Weltbuergertum und Nationalstaat* (Muenchen, 1919), pp. 39-61 and 192-205.

judgment. The demands of aesthetic culture are bound to be hostile to egalitarianism. A society dominated by artists and artistic standards would be aristocratic through and through. This becomes clear in the ideas of the less unpolitical romantics, but it is clear even among the anarchists, for all democratic and radical ideals of citizenship involve a high degree of politicization. The anarchism of the Enlightenment was not unpolitical, but, on the contrary, aimed at extending civic consciousness. But the anarchism of the unpolitical is concerned not only with eliminating power; it wants to escape from social consciousness altogether. That is why Heine observed that democracy is bad for poetry. Not only does democracy cause poets to write tendentiously—that is, unpoetically—but it wants to raze all heights, including Parnassus. "In highly political times, pure works of art are rare," he noted, and democracy is ultra-political.[147] Though after 1848 there were few really unpolitical people left, the most outstanding, Burckhardt and Nietzsche, shared Heine's views fully. Indeed, their chief objection to their own time was that his predictions had already been fulfilled. This may seem strange, since there was nothing remarkably democratic about 19th-century Germany. But politicization and democracy seemed to them to be marching hand in hand against culture, especially German culture and its standards. Nowhere is the attempt to impose an alien hierarchy of values on the social world more evident than in Burckhardt's and Nietzsche's critique of politics in general and of their own times in particular.

Burckhardt renounced all politics, especially all forms of radicalism. "Freedom and the State haven't lost anything in me," he wrote as a young man. "With people, such as I, you cannot build States. . . . For society as a whole I have no use,

---

[147] *Gedanken und Einfaelle, Werke,* vol. VII, pp. 418-419 (my translation).

I look upon it with involuntary irony. . . . And even if I can, when it becomes necessary, understand higher politics, I won't ever participate in them."[148] Unlike Carlyle, he thought it impossible that there should be great men in political life, for no "greatness of soul" can exist where power is the highest stake.[149] Nothing disgusted him more than Bismarck's Empire —in which the state was busily conquering culture, and thus destroying it.[150] Government is, by definition, concerned with utility, and so is the enemy of genius.[151] Unlike many other romantics, Burckhardt did not believe that culture could or should rule the state. The two are hostile empires; the state is a monument to power, the antithesis of culture, something that is itself the offspring of unhappiness and can only make others miserable.[152] At best politics are futile; at worst they interfere with culture. In this, at least, Nietzsche quite agreed with Burckhardt. "I am the last anti-political German," he announced.[153] Every political organization, even the Greek *polis*, is inherently opposed to culture.[154] Dionysius is the anti-political god. Culture is a matter of style, of the aesthetic unity of a people, not of politics.[155] The "highly civilized state" is a cultural menace. With its politically dominated herds it brings neither happiness nor comfort to anyone.[156] Indeed, no problem of existence can ever be solved by a political act, and no political innovation can make us a "contented race."

[148] Letter to H. Schauenburg, February 28, 1846, *loc.cit.*, pp. 147-148.
[149] *Force and Freedom*, pp. 184 and 331.
[150] Letter to F. von Preen, April 26, 1872, *loc.cit.*, pp. 348-349; to the same, June 16, 1888, pp. 476-478, and March 25, 1890, pp. 488-490.
[151] *Force and Freedom*, p. 344.
[152] *Ibid.*, pp. 110-115, 117-119, 180-184, and 209.
[153] *Ecce Homo*, p. 821.
[154] *Human-all-too-Human* (I), nr. 474.
[155] "David Strauss, the Confessor and Writer," p. 8.
[156] *Human-all-too-Human* (II), nr. 277; "Schopenhauer as Educator," p. 161.

The new state worship, he warned the Germans, was "not a relapse into paganism, but into stupidity."[157]

Yet Nietzsche was not content to leave politics alone. He wanted the rule of an aesthetic élite—a direct exercise of power by the culture creators, in their own interest and that of culture. He resented the "mediocrity" of democracy and liberalism, and admired hierarchies of power. Political power, conquest as an expression of creativity and love, like that which "impels an artist to his material," was a sign of greatness, and he longed for a new aristocracy "based on self-discipline" which would work "as artists upon man himself" and transform him.[158] The will to power over other men—that is politics, whether Nietzsche knew it or not. His is a form of politics—even if an aestheticized form, in which artistic norms determine the action. It is culture politics, an idea of power as an aesthetic activity. It had, in fact, already occurred to Schiller, who saw in art, in supra-political creation, the only means of reforming the decrepit state of his time.[159]

The mission of the artist did not have to be postponed, as Nietzsche thought, to the coming of the super-man. Schiller called for immediate action, but it was a demand for indirect action. Both he and Shelley saw in art such a recuperative power that the artist rules *qua* artist. He makes art a substitute for politics, but art itself does not change. Some romantics, however, wanted to make politics a form of aesthetic enjoyment. They wanted to make politics artistic, into a new art form, a new field of self-expression, and they wanted to do it at once. They wanted to be "engaged," to use a modern catchword. The great example of such politics is surely Lamartine. As a poet he regarded himself as above all parties. In the Cham-

[157] *Ibid.*, pp. 134-135.
[158] *The Will to Power* (I), nr. 125 (II), nrs. 764, 854-864, 873, 960 and 962.
[159] *On Aesthetic Education*, pp. 24-30, 50-51, and 139-140.

ber of Deputies he therefore chose to be an independent, but not, like Benjamin Constant, in the interest of reason. Politics were to him a form of religion, or poetry. "A great statesman," he said, "is a poet in the act of transforming Words into Deeds." As a poet he felt himself endowed with special powers to divine the true state of the national soul. He had, he claimed, "the instinct for the masses." His hand was on the nation's pulse.[160] This is, of course, nothing but the romantic image of the poet-prophet transplanted to the political scene— and Lamartine's fate shows how misplaced it was there.

Lamartine's was not the only way of playing aesthetic politics. If politics could be made into a poetic activity, why should not the state be made into a romantic work of art? The state must be beautiful, Novalis demanded; it must have individuality. The traditional state, and the state of laws even, were mechanical. To Novalis, Frederick the Great's Prussia was just a big factory. The true relation between ruler and subject ought to be one of love. In the young Frederick William, and especially his pretty queen, Novalis found objects of aesthetic pleasure. His hope was that the new king would be artistic and make his state into something poetic.[161] This sounds like sheer gibberish, and it may very well have been nothing else. It is, however, indicative of an important trend in romantic "unpolitics." The objection to the existing state as a mechanical external imposition was already familiar to Herder. His antipathy to all states was such that his lengthy philosophy of history contains barely half a dozen pages dealing with the subject, for Herder was discussing man's cultural growth, in which the state played either no part at all or was only a detriment. But in Herder's "biological-vegetative" con-

---

[160] A. de Lamartine, *History of the French Revolution of 1848* (Bohn's Library, 1905), p. 44; H. R. Whitehouse, *The Life of Lamartine* (Boston, 1918), vol. I, pp. 6, 399-464; vol. II, pp. 52-72.

[161] *Fragmente, Werke*, vol. II, pp. 159, 163, 173-175; Kluckhohn, *Persoenlichkeit und Gemeinschaft*, pp. 47-81.

ception of historical development, the national community, as opposed to the state, is of paramount importance. Herder did not just see great men creating culture. Culture, and indeed its creators, were the offsprings of a collective "daemon," the national soul. Though Herder was too truly romantic to draw any very concise political conclusions from the fact, he undoubtedly believed that the national state would at least be a culture-dominated state, not a political one. This was still an unpolitical nationalism, as was that of Herder's truest disciple, Burckhardt. If the culture-creating, true *Volksgeist*, was to flourish again, he wrote, political nationalism would have to be destroyed first.[162]

"Group romanticism," the consciousness of communal individuality, however, did not stop there. The urge for totality asserted itself here, as in every other realm of romantic thought. Individuality was, after all, not enough. Community, too, was needed. At first this meant that associations of like-minded friends were to replace existing states and societies. Or, as in Novalis' case, the actual state was to be transformed into such a community. Even the young Hegel had felt that the state was something alien that had to be superseded by a more personal form of communal life. It was fondly believed, moreover, that such a personalized community would involve no sacrifice of individuality. Even Adam Mueller, the most illiberal of the romantics, agreed to that. But the meaning of individuality subtly changed in the new context of "group romanticism." It was the group that had a personality, that had an individuality of its own, and the individual man derived his individuality only through the group. The national soul, or the communal spirit, lends individuality to the person now, rather than being the object of genius' defiance.[163] "We

[162] Letter to F. von Preen, December 31, 1872; *loc.cit.*, p. 356.
[163] E. N. Anderson, "German Romanticism as an Ideology of Cultural Crisis," *Journal of the History of Ideas*, vol. ii, 1941, pp. 301-317;

need roots to grow," Coleridge asserted, after congratulating himself on being an Englishman.[164] Today, after the original nexus of ideas about the cultural fecundity of the national soul has been all but forgotten, the "need for roots" remains a major theme of romantic political thought. Man, like a vegetable, it seems, requires a root—though, why, no one really knows. It is the unhappy consciousness itself longing for rest that wants roots, but refuses to abandon its aloofness, its supra-social freedom. It accepts roots as a general need, "for the others," but for itself it retains a position of dissatisfied, yet self-admiring freedom.

That group romanticism was eventually put to the service of ordinary politics was the last of the many self-inflicted defeats of romanticism. "Blood and soil" and political nationalism are not properly part of romantic thought; they represent its degeneracy. To submit to politics was an act of resigning to actuality and, as such, an abandonment of romanticism. However, though the first great period of romanticism ended ignominiously, romanticism has survived. The unhappy consciousness thrives today, finding expression in existentialism, the philosophies of self-transcendence, historical despair, aesthetic anarchism, the old cult of individuality, and hatred for the masses. Indeed, it is not too much to say that the second great age of romanticism has begun. The unhappy consciousness again finds itself in the conditions Hegel described—the sense of a lost past, of an actual world that is too revolting to accept, and of a hopeless or non-existent future.

G. Briefs, "The Economic Philosophy of Romanticism," *ibid.*, pp. 279-300; H. Kohn, "Romanticism and the Rise of German Nationalism," *Review of Politics*, vol. 12, 1950, pp. 443-472.

[164] A *Lay Sermon*, *loc.cit.*, pp. 61-62.

CHAPTER IV

The Romanticism of Defeat

The Unhappy Consciousness Today

IT IS quite possible that pure romanticism no longer exists. The unhappy consciousness, however, flourishes as never before. Hegel's account of the alienated soul fits many of our contemporaries better than it ever did his own romantic friends. To be sure, romanticism does not express itself today in spontaneous outbursts of feeling. Indeed, it has become quite reflective. But this change in tone has not brought it an inch closer to traditional philosophy. What has happened is that the unhappy consciousness has become acutely aware of itself as such. It knows itself as the realization that God is dead, and it analyzes its condition with a detachment unknown to the earlier romantics. The effect of this new self-consciousness, however, has been only an intensification of the romantic predicament. The distance between the unique self and the surrounding world has increased, and the unhappy consciousness today openly admits its sense of meaninglessness. It is now ready to deny that we can understand ourselves, each other, society, history, or nature—much less control or improve them. The creative imagination has failed in its battle against an obtuse world. Aesthetic idealism survives only in its negative form, as a basis for social criticism. Again, the dramatic view of life as struggle remains, but it is now a story of defeat. We are left with a romanticism deprived of all its positive aspirations, wallowing in its own futility.

The unhappy consciousness knows today that spirit is alienated from itself and from the world because God is absent, for the death of God means far more than a mere decline of religious faith. It implies the end of all the highest values, and the disintegration of the world as a coherent whole.[1] With that arise all sorts of fearful possibilities. Is man dead too?[2] Is it possible to maintain any cultural or artistic life under such conditions? Can we still think of a future at all? How can one face one's complete isolation in the cosmos? All this is quite beyond answering. Mind has reached the end of its tether.[3]

To some thinkers these miseries appear as man's permanent fate; to others it is a matter of our present historical situation. For instance, the French school of existentialism and the various poets of "the absurd" regard all consciousness as unhappy consciousness.[4] Heidegger regards our "homelessness" as a matter of both social and metaphysical alienation, the latter being the disaster of the entire post-mediaeval age. We have excluded ourselves from "being" and have made the world a "picture," "an object" to be observed by "subjects."[5] Jaspers speaks even more explicitly of a dual tragedy. There is a uni-

[1] M. Heidegger "Nietzsche's Wort 'Gott ist Tot'" *Holzwege*, (Frankfurt am Main, 1952), pp. 193-247.

[2] André Malraux has especially asked this shattering question, and Gabriel Marcel, who does not believe that God is dead, sees in the death of *man* the same disasters. A. Malraux "Man and Artistic Culture," tr. by S. Gilbert, in *Reflections on Our Age* ed. by D. Hardman (New York, 1949), p. 84. G. Marcel, *Men against Humanity*, tr. by G. S. Fraser (London, 1952), pp. 9-10.

[3] That this was the final conclusion of H. G. Wells, the most ardent optimist since Condorcet, is an interesting reflection on the attractions of the unhappy consciousness in our time. In poor Wells's mind the end of meaning was somehow bound up with the physical annihilation of the world as well. *Mind at the End of Its Tether* (London, 1945).

[4] J. P. Sartre, *L'Etre et le Néant* (Paris, 1949), pp. 133-134; H. Marcuse, "Remarks on Jean-Paul Sartre's *L'Etre et le Néant*," *Philosophy and Phenomenological Research*, vol. VIII, 1947-1948, pp. 309-336; M. Nathanson, "Jean-Paul Sartre's Philosophy of Freedom," *Social Research*, vol. XIV, 1952, pp. 364-380.

[5] M. Heidegger, *Ueber den Humanismus* (Frankfurt am Main, 1949), pp. 27-29; "Die Zeit des Weltbildes," *Holzwege*, pp. 69-104.

versal tragedy in the fact that reality is split up and that truth must ever remain beyond our grasp, but there is also an immediate historical tragedy that has aggravated the human situation. Technology has disrupted history and mass life has deprived us of individuality. Intellectually "we are losing substance and gaining knowledge."[6] This, too, is Gabriel Marcel's view. To the tragic nature of existence we have added a social life that leaves us no choice between the "termite colony and the Mystical Body." We have cut ourselves off from the past and left ourselves no future save that of the most vulgar epicureanism.[7] Lastly, there are those for whom alienation is solely a social matter. They suffer mostly from "the death of Marx," which is, however, part of the end of all certainties. "This is an age of discouraged revolutionaries" Alex Comfort, the anarchist poet, writes.[8] His French counterpart, Albert Camus, has built an entire theory around the "rebel's" new sense of hostility to "revolution" and to all grandiose utopias. But all these different conceptions of alienation are only aspects of the "unhappy consciousness" as a whole. One of Jaspers' disciples speaks for this entire mentality when she announces: "Today we consider both history and nature to be alien to the essence of man. Neither any longer offers us that comprehensive whole in which we feel spiritually at home." Though we must now build our own nature and history without the aid of any eternal verities, our failures and successes are nothing to an indifferent nature and to a dead God. Whether we

[6] E.g. K. Jaspers, *Tragedy Is Not Enough*, tr. by H. A. T. Reiche, H. T. Moore and N. W. Deütsch (Boston, 1952), pp. 94-96. Although this volume is only an excerpt from a larger German work, *Von der Wahrheit*, to which I shall refer later, I have used it so as to avoid untranslated work wherever possible. *Origin and Goal of History*, tr. by M. Bullock (London, 1953), pp. 99-100, 152. *Existentialism and Humanism*, tr. by E. B. Ashton (New York, 1952), pp. 65-66.

[7] G. Marcel, *Men against Humanity*, pp. 138 and 140.

[8] A. Comfort, *Authority and Delinquency in the Modern State* (London, 1950), p. 80.

achieve or fail, we act "in the bitter realization that nothing has been promised us, no Messianic Age, no classless society, no paradise after death."[9]

The great difference between the romanticism of the last century and that of the present is that for the former the defeat of Zeus meant the triumph of Prometheus, while for the latter the death of God means the defeat of man as well. It is now accepted that man's great curse is his *inability* to become divine.[10] Prometheanism has now reversed itself. Man is no longer celebrated as the master of all his creations; he is mourned as the victim of all that he has not created. Whatever hopefulness remains is still, in true romantic style, vested in the value of creative activity, especially art. But it is very far from the artistic self-assurance of a Schiller or a Shelley. Not even those poets who feel closest to the romantics can still believe that poetry is capable of saving civilization.[11] Most would agree with Auden that the artist is not a heroic figure, nor would they worship an "Art-God." The "age of anxiety" evokes other responses. Even those who do not, like Auden, flee from it into tradition and orthodoxy, know as well as he does that: "We are less likely to be tempted by solitude into Promethean pride: we are far more likely to become cowards in the face of the tyrant who would compel us to lie in the service of the False City. It is not madness we need fear, but prostitution."[12]

Self-betrayal, helplessness and frustration in the face of an overpowering external world—such are the conditions of all existence, or at least of life today. If in a world without God

[9] H. Arendt, *The Origins of Totalitarianism* (New York, 1951), pp. 435 and 436.
[10] S. de Beauvoir, *The Ethics of Ambiguity*, tr. by B. Frechtman (New York, 1948), pp. 12-13; J. P. Sartre, *L'Etre et le Néant*, p. 664; K. Jaspers, *Tragedy Is Not Enough*, pp. 55-56.
[11] S. Spender, *The Creative Element* (London, 1954), pp. 38-39.
[12] W. H. Auden, *The Enchafèd Flood* (New York, 1950), p. 153.

we are "doomed" to self-creation, our task no longer gives us the slightest joy. In fact, man is always the victim of some external situation. History and nature leave us few choices. For, though all romanticism tends to be a form of cultural despair, it has now tried to give itself a universal significance. Victimhood has today become a metaphysical category. Everywhere death is seen hovering around us, ready to render all our efforts meaningless. No one today believes in the possibility of really conquering death; at best we may resign ourselves to it heroically. But, as in the novels of André Malraux, heroism, however admirable, is always rewarded with defeat and frustration. Without God or eternity, death becomes formidable, the most difficult of all our "situations." To this must be added all the concrete public and private "situations" that the world imposes upon us. All of them are far too foreign to the self ever to be mastered intellectually. The unhappy consciousness does not really try to explain them; it only hopes to express its awareness of their power. The reflective romantic's occasional efforts to formulate a general ethical or social theory, therefore, always fail. They never become more than limited forms of self-expression, illuminations of particular "situations."

This is a weakness inherent in romanticism, which is not lessened by some of the other traits that the unhappy consciousness has kept from the last century. The old hostility to "abstraction" in thought and society remains. All systems, philosophical or social, are still regarded as mere fetters upon the self. Abstraction today is what it was to Kierkegaard, a means of hiding from one's situation. Thought is valid only as an expression of the thinker's personality, as something "lived." In society the division of labor, functionalism, all that is mechanical, is hated more than ever. The tension between the one and the many has, if anything, become even greater. Political life remains abhorrent. Horror at technology and hatred of the masses are only part of the romantic's estrangement in a "totalitarian world." To him the entire external world is totalitarian today. The 19th-century fear that politics would swallow up all human culture and individuality is revived. If, therefore, romanticism regards totalitarianism as a political phenomenon at all, it is only within its own idea of politics as "anti-culture" that it does so. Consequently, there is no romantic analysis of totalitarianism; there are only attempts to reveal the entire "world," the whole "situation of man," in a totalitarian universe. Romanticism cannot, and does not wish to, explain history. It wants to "live" it, or, since that has become too painful, to escape it altogether in a devotion to a transcendent "existence" apart from the world. But even that is only a hope bound to fail.[13]

There are some signs that this extreme form of the unhappy consciousness is in abeyance. Everyone is beginning to settle down more comfortably to permanent insecurity. In any case, romanticism has a tendency to peter out. The best existentialist works were written between the wars. Jaspers is now trying to find his way back to older forms of philosophy. Heidegger has produced only brief essays lately. The great vogue of French existentialism during the Occupation and right after the war is now diminishing. Its chief exponents, moreover, have deserted their former positions and are making common cause with the communists. This sort of retreat has been characteristic of romanticism from the first. Even more significant is the revival of an aesthetic idealism in the works of Malraux and Camus, for instance. The unhappy consciousness may very well be on its way back to older forms of romanticism. This would not be surprising, for the state of mind expressed

---

[13] The word "existence" when put in quotation marks is used in the same sense as the German "Existenz" in existentialist philosophy.

in "reflective romanticism" is clearly a reflection of the decades of war and totalitarianism in Western Europe.

Between Philosophy and Religion

Philosophy has never recovered from the blows dealt it in the last century. Hegel was the last great thinker really to believe in the mission of philosophical reason to command absolute truth. Disregarded by the natural sciences and scorned by poetry, philosophy gradually lost self-confidence. Today existentialism represents the final collapse of all its claims. It is the "revolt of philosophy against itself."[14] One might well argue that the word "philosophy" ought not to be applied to existentialism at all. Jaspers refers to his thought as "philosophizing" directed at the "illumination" of "existence." Heidegger, in his rejection of all post-Platonic thought, speaks of his reflections as "Andenken an das Sein."[15] No existentialist philosopher wants to be a "priest of truth," or even just a contemplative observer. The very language of existentialists, which is dramatic and emotional, separates them from traditional philosophers. It is romantic thinking, from the point of view of the actor, or, rather, it is a matter of self-expression. All existentialist writers want to emulate Nietzsche's portrait of Schopenhauer and to present philosophies that have been "lived." Thus both Jaspers and Gabriel Marcel give accounts of their "ways in philosophy" in autobiographical essays.[16]

This romantic intrusion into philosophy also explains why

[14] H. Arendt, "What is Existenz Philosophy," Partisan Review, vol. XII, 1946, pp. 34-36. To an unfriendly critic it appears less like a revolt than "a destruction of philosophy," N. Bobbio, The Philosophy of Decadentism, tr. by D. Moore (Oxford, 1948), p. 6; P. Tillich, "Existential Philosophy," Journal of the History of Ideas, vol. V, 1944, pp. 44-70.

[15] M. Heidegger, Uber den Humanismus, p. 42.

[16] Jaspers, Rechenschaft und Ausblick (Muenchen, 1951), pp. 323-365; G. Marcel, The Philosophy of Existence, tr. by M. Harari (London, 1948), pp. 77-96.

existentialist ideas may be as well, if not better, expressed in novels and dramas.[17] As Simone de Beauvoir has well noted, an Aristotelian or Spinozist novel is impossible, but not an existentialist one. Metaphysics is no longer regarded as system building, but as an experience, a realization of "metaphysical experiences" within oneself. This experience, especially the striving toward transcendence, is best expounded indirectly, with the aid of fiction or poetry.[18] Moreover, the demand for the "sum" of Descartes' "cogito" has acquired a purely personal meaning. Philosophy is reduced to elucidating the writer's own situation.[19] According to existentialism, this is what makes philosophy concrete. Indeed to Marcel "the spirit of abstraction" has become the main object of attack, which would be strange in a conventional philosopher. However, for him philosophy is an essentially tragic mode of thought, whose path, like that of romantic poetry, leads inward.[20] Again, Jaspers speaks of philosophy as "self-illumination" and as a state of mind.[21] No wonder that his logic bears no resemblance to anything usually understood by that word. Logic is not a method of thought at all now, but ways of reaching inner consciousness of truth.[22] The end of philosophy is to reach selfhood, not to reveal anything about man and the world.[23] Thus this philosophy of self-expression is particularly open to Hegel's

[17] That is why writers such as Kafka and Rilke are regarded as predecessors of, and contributors to, existentialist philosophy.

[18] L'Existentialisme et la Sagesse des Nations (Paris, 1948), pp. 103-124.

[19] O. F. Bollnow, Existenzphilosophie (Stuttgart, 1949), pp. 53-54.

[20] Marcel, The Philosophy of Existence, pp. 14-15; Men against Humanity, pp. 1-3; F. H. Heineman, Existentialism and the Modern Predicament (London, 1953), p. 138.

[21] Philosophie (Berlin, 1932), vol. II, pp. 325-328.

[22] Von der Wahrheit (Muenchen, 1947), pp. 1-28.

[23] E.g., Man in the Modern Age, tr. by E. and C. Paul (London, 1951), p. 161. "Philosophy," he writes, "is the thought with which, or as which, I am active as my own self," ibid., p. 179; Philosophie, vol. II, pp. 411-414.

criticisms of romanticism. On so subjective a plane philosophic communication becomes impossible. No amount of paper and ink can express the ineffable. In fact, existentialist philosophers admit that the ultimate goal of their efforts, "existence," is beyond verbal definition.

"Existence," writes Jaspers, "cannot be explained in terms of objective reason."[24] "Being," Marcel insists, cannot even be discussed, only "non-Being." "Being" is a mystery, not a problem, and so beyond rational analysis.[25] Heidegger, the most genuine romantic of all, simply dispenses with metaphysics and logic as ways of expressing Being. Poetry alone can reveal Being. It is the poet who mediates between God and the people, who creates language and who penetrates to the holy.[26] Even his rejection of the abstract, however, differs from romanticism as well as from older forms of "life philosophy." The representatives of the latter also spoke of "filthy logic" and of the eternal opposition of reason to spontaneous vitality.[27] But unlike them, existentialists do not really long

[24] *Philosophie*, vol. II, pp. 4-6.

[25] *Men against Humanity*, pp. 129-130; *Philosophy of Existence*, pp. 5-31.

[26] *Ueber den Humanismus*, pp. 5-8. For Heidegger, Hoelderlin has become *the* poet, the "namer" of the gods, and he proposes to base his philosophy on Hoelderlin's verse. "Remembrance of the Poet" and "Hoelderlin and the Essence of Poetry," tr. by D. Scott in *Existence and Being*, ed. by W. Brock (London, 1949), pp. 253-315, and "What is Metaphysics," tr. by R. F. C. Hull and A. Crick, *ibid.*, pp. 355-392. Jaspers, however, regards such an attempt as futile, *The Perennial Scope of Philosophy*, tr. by R. Manheim (New York, 1949), p. 163, and W. Kaufmann "Philosophie, Dichtung und Humanitaet," *Offener Horizont, Festschrift fuer Karl Jaspers* (Muenchen, 1953), pp. 368-380.

[27] Bollnow, *op.cit.*, offers a detailed account of the differences as well as similarities of "life philosophy" and existentialism. At his suggestion Unamuno and Ortega y Gasset have been taken as representative of the former, pp. 28-29. M. de Unamuno, *Essays and Soliloquies*, tr. by J. E. Crawford Flitch (New York, 1925), p. 83; Ortega y Gasset, *Concord and Liberty*, tr. by H. Weyl (New York, 1946), pp. 8-82; and *The Modern Theme*, tr. by J. Cleugh (New York, 1933), pp. 55-57.

worth of life?"[111] Moreover, a genuine philosophy like poetry expresses the personal nature of the philosopher. It is something that has been lived.[112] To create culture, philosophy must discard the empty "esse," Descartes' uncreative "cogito," in favor of "the full green vivere," "vivo ergo sum."[113] Nietzsche did not call simply for life, but for creation, for men to complete nature's highest aim, the building of culture. Nature needs "artists, philosophers and saints."[114] It is the call for Prometheus. Philosophy is absorbed by art, and art by the creation of culture, and a higher form of humanity.

Prometheus

The revolt against the intellectual world of the 18th century was only the first act of the romantic tragedy. The dramatic sense of life is not satisfied by the merely negative act of attacking abstraction. Its real object is to reveal and experience the struggling forces in man's environment, in nature, in the entire universe. At first an energetic generation expected to grasp these, to harness them, and, even, to improve them. Prometheus defied the gods; he even wanted "to be a greater artist than God."[115] Nature was to impart all her secrets to him, so that he might imitate her fecundity and even complete her highest aims, the surpassing of man in the creation of culture. The ambitions of Prometheus did not last, and soon only the defiance remained. In the end the stoic Titan was overcome by self-pity, so that one of today's most genuine romantics can define romanticism as the "sense of victimhood" in a hostile universe.[116] Nature was discovered to be

[111] "Schopenhauer as Educator," pp. 131-133.
[112] *Ibid.*, p. 126.
[113] "The Use and Abuse of History," p. 94.
[114] "Schopenhauer as Educator," pp. 152-155.
[115] Quoted in L. P. Smith, *op.cit.*, p. 128.
[116] Alex Comfort, *Art and Social Responsibility* (London, 1946), p. 14.

nothing but a death-mill, and man the creator was found to be incapable of living up to his own vision. The gap between the actual and the possible grew ever wider; longing expressed itself in irony, and eventually in despair, and in flight from the romantic world to that of the state and orthodox religion. "The true sorrow of humanity consists in this—not that the mind of man fails, but that the course and demands of action and life so rarely correspond with the dignity and intensity of human desires."[117] Thus spoke Wordsworth in his disappointed maturity, and it was this realization that marked the end of romantic aspirations. But before this sad end Prometheus had fought and created brilliantly; for one last time, in Nietzsche, the old image arose again in its full vigor.

In the beginning was the act, the act of creation, and Prometheus, not God, is man's true model of the creator. Indeed, the idea of God as an artist had already dominated the philosophy of both Plotinus and Giordano Bruno. Even Kierkegaard in an "aesthetic" moment thought of God as a poet, who creates a world out of himself but is not, thereafter, identified with it.[118] For most romantics the poet was the greatest of human creators. "The poet is, on a small scale, but the imitator of the Creator, and also resembles God in creating his characters after his own image," Heine said in speaking of Goethe and Schiller.[119] All romantics regarded the poet as a prophet, as semi-divine, god-like. "A just Prometheus under Jove," Shaftesbury called the poet.[120] For he is like God, but not yet God. Because he lives in an imperfect world, because the gods and nature have not yet been mastered, he must ac-

[117] W. Wordsworth, *The Convention of Cintra*, in *Political Tracts*, p. 192.
[118] *Journal*, s. 1377.
[119] *The Romantic School*, tr. by S. L. Fleischman (New York, 1882), p. 57.
[120] O. Walzel, *Das Prometheussymbol von Shaftsbury zu Goethe* (Munich, 1932), pp. 12-15.

cept the position of Prometheus, of the defiant, the struggling creator, not that of an omnipotent deity. In its hopes the "unhappy consciousness" is Prometheus the creator. In its unfulfilled longing it is Prometheus the defiant Titan. And so Aeschylus' hero haunted the romantic imagination. For Goethe he was always the defier of gods and the kindly benefactor of man. Shelley's Prometheus is as much in revolt, but even more explicitly a moral hero who rises above hatred. Nietzsche saw him as the culture creator, "the barbarian who comes down from the height" to mould men.[121] To rise above mere humanity, to surpass man as he is, that is the real task of the romantic Prometheus. "We must become more than man," Novalis wrote. And "man must be a god," "a self-creation."[122] Prometheus' first step is self-transcendence. Nietzsche merely echoes Novalis when he demands that men must not just live, which is but to be a beast, but strive toward an image of man that is above us.[123] But only Prometheus, who is a poet, philosopher, and saint, can achieve this, the end of nature, which nature is incapable of achieving herself.[124]

To give nature a helping hand was the greatest ambition of romanticism. It has been said that the romantics idealized nature. Nothing could be farther from the truth. They admired the endless creativity of nature, its dramatic qualities, and these they wanted to imitate. "Nature has artistic instincts," Novalis observed.[125] But to emulate nature meant only to be as energetic in production. The end of human creation was a new man, and a new culture, which were aims higher than those that nature could herself reach. Not that the early romantics dreaded nature. She was their true ally. And indeed only to the poet does nature really reveal herself. The

[121] *The Will to Power*, ii, nr. 900.
[122] *Fragmente, Werke*, vol. iii, p. 131, and vol. iv, p. 74.
[123] "Schopenhauer as Educator," pp. 149-50.
[124] *Ibid.*, pp. 152-155.
[125] *Fragmente, Werke*, vol. iii, p. 195.

scientist was consequently the deadly foe of all romantic poets. "Poets," wrote Novalis, "know nature better than scientists."[126] "We cannot understand nature by pure reason," Coleridge amplified, "the true naturalist is a dramatic poet."[127] They all dabbled in the sciences, not in search of empirical data, but as a form of black magic. Thus neither Schiller nor Goethe thought much of Alexander von Humboldt as a scientist, since he spent his time in exact, empirical investigations which seemed to lead to nothing momentous.[128] There are few more pitiful incidents in intellectual history than Goethe's futile war against Newton. He even deluded himself into thinking that this was his greatest achievement, that with it he had "made an epoch in the world."[129] The end of his efforts, however, was not to discover scientific truth, but to save nature for the creative imagination, for the inner life of man, to defend it against the dissecting, mechanizing, alienating work of science. Though man is an integral part of nature, she can be understood only by those who are ready for her message, the creative few—hence his opposition to such mechanical instruments as the microscope and the telescope.[130] Schelling, whose ideas he admired, spoke in the same spirit when he exclaimed that "only to the inspired investigator is (nature) the world's holy, eternally creating primal energy, which engenders and actively brings forth all things out of itself." To copy her then means "to emulate this creating energy," and this the scientists who "have done away with nature" cannot grasp, for they have reduced her to dead matter. The artist must not subordinate himself to nature, in any case. He must rise above her products, "apprehend her spiritually," and create something

[126] *Ibid.*, p. 217.
[127] *The Statesman's Manual*, *loc.cit.*, pp. 39-40.
[128] Silz, *op.cit.*, pp. 135-136.
[129] J. P. Eckermann, *Gespraeche mit Goethe* (May 2, 1824).
[130] Viëtor, *Goethe the Thinker*, pp. 12-52; Heller, *op.cit.*, pp. 3-49.

true that is more than merely natural.[131] This, too, was Nietzsche's feeling. Science must be seen "through the eyes of the artist, and art through the eyes of life."[132] His loathing for the scientist as the creative artist's worst enemy, as a "levelled down being," knew no bounds. It was Prometheus, and he alone, who knew nature—and also how to surpass her. This enmity toward science and the scientist as a specialized plebeian has remained part of all romanticism. Only Byron accepted the Newtonian universe, and this was ominous; for it only meant that he recognized the poet's exclusion from nature, that Prometheus had been rejected by a hostile universe.

Even for the nature worshippers among the romantics, nature had never been a tame affair. The dramatic sense of life is fascinated by its violence and destructiveness. "In the ecstasy of destruction the seed of divine creation reveals itself," Friedrich Schlegel wrote to his brother.[133] Nietzsche, years later, could still marvel at the exploitation and destruction inherent in all organic and creative life.[134] "All the life of creatures depends upon the destruction of other species, . . . man lives on animals, animals on one another. . . . I see murder and death in creation."[135] Those are not the words of the gloomy Maistre or the wicked Marquis de Sade, but of the gentle Herder. Creation is tragic; it rises only out of destruction. Every romantic from Herder to Nietzsche knew that. But only with the later romantics, with Baudelaire especially, has creation ceased to justify such cruelty. And then, indeed, nature becomes the unspeakable horror that Sade had felt it

[131] F. W. J. von Schelling, "Concerning the Relation of the Plastic Arts to Nature," tr. by M. Bullock, in H. Read, *The True Voice of Feeling* (London, 1953), pp. 325 and 332.
[132] *Ecce Homo*, p. 937.
[133] Quoted in Silz, *op.cit.*, p. 164.
[134] *Beyond Good and Evil*, tr. by H. Zimmern (Modern Library), p. 577; *The Will to Power* (I), *Works*, vol. XIV, nr. 416; (II), nrs. 768 and 769.
[135] Herder, *God*, p. 185.

to be.[136] And then Prometheus can no longer face his final
enemy, death. For death is the great obstacle in his path to
omnipotence. Death haunts the Promethean consciousness,
and death is its final defeat.

> "Death is here and death is there,
> Death is busy everywhere,
> All around us and, beneath,
> Above is death—and we are death.

> "Death has set its mark and seal
> On all we are and all we feel
> On all we know and all we fear."[137]

"Oh how can anyone be happy here—where everything ends
in death?" Novalis asked, and his question was repeated over
and over again.[138] But romanticism did not despair at first.
Life was to subdue death. Herder, who could not love life,
as Goethe did, even if nature was purposeless and unfeeling,
found comfort in the idea of palingenesis. Death does not
really exist in creation. It is only an appearance; the root of
our being lives on in some changed form. Death is not lifelessness, but only a metamorphosis.[139] Though Goethe had no
use for teleological concepts of nature, death did not frighten
him either. Death, Prometheus tells Pandora, is the most intensely felt moment of our life, in which we lose ourselves,

[136] C. Baudelaire, *L'Art Romantique, Oeuvres* (Paris, 1868), pp.
99-104; M. Praz, *The Romantie Agony*, tr. by A. Davidson (London,
1933), pp. 95-186.
[137] Shelley, *Death*. Death was Shelley's central concern even in his
youthful and most Godwinian days. In later years it became a virtual
obsession—as well as the theme of his best poetry. Indeed it is more
than likely that the passionate sailor who couldn't swim did more than
just long passively for death; B. Kurz, *The Pursuit of Death* (New
York, 1933).
[138] Quoted in Silz, *op.cit.*, p. 175.
[139] *God*, pp. 187-188; Viëtor, *Goethe the Thinker*, pp. 35-38;
Pascal, *op.cit.*, pp. 203-216.

only to live again. Demogorgon in the end grants Shelley's Prometheus that victory over "chance, death and mutability" that he had not been able to achieve himself. But this was not enough for Shelley. Death must be abolished altogether, and transformed into a higher form of life, not its antithesis. And so *Adonais* does not really die. "He is made one with Nature." And " 'Tis death is dead not he." "The One remains, the many change and pass." Finally death becomes a desired end; die, "If thou wouldst be with that which thou dost seek." Fear of death has been transformed into a longing for death. Novalis went through exactly the same process. He even convinced himself that the human spirit's power over life and death was such that one could die by longing intensely to join one's dead friends.[140] "May it be my highest goal to be able to wish to die," Schleiermacher repeated after him.[141] Kleist, who all his life was tortured by the thought of the millions already dead, succumbed to a death longing that ended in suicide. Death had become the final step to self-transcendence.[142] Prometheus conquers oblivion and becomes more than himself. That was the ultimate meaning of the poet's share in eternity.

Death, however, is not conquered quite so easily. Hegel warned that death would defeat Prometheus. The Faustian man, who tries to "take" and "possess" life, finds that he has only taken "hard hold on death." Hegel was not surprised that these "vehement aspirations" led to helplessness and mysticism.[143] He had given up Prometheus with the rest of romanticism. A sensible philosopher can always avoid despair

· [140] *God*, pp. 187-188; Viëtor, *Goethe the Thinker*, pp. 35-38; Pascal, *op.cit.*, pp. 203-216.
[141] Dilthey, *op.cit.*, pp. 283-288.
[142] R. Unger, *Herder, Novalis und Kleist* (Frankfurt a.M., 1922), pp. 94-114 and 143.
[143] *Phenomenology*, p. 388, and *History of Philosophy*, vol. III, pp. 505-508.

although, like Hegel, he may know that even absolute knowledge is always behind life, that it only looks back upon life to "paint its grey on grey" in the dusk, when life itself has departed.[144] But Prometheus is not capable of resigning himself like that. In defeat he is *Manfred* calling for pure oblivion, for a death that puts an end to a life of disappointment. Byron's heroes no longer abolish death; they only damn themselves by inflicting death, like Cain, ". . . who abhor

> "The name of Death so deeply that the thought
> Empoison'd all my life, before I knew
> His aspect—I have led him here, and given
> My brother to his cold and still embrace
> As if he would not have asserted his
> Inexorable claim without my aid."[145]

God has died altogether, though Satan has not, or, if God exists, he is as unjust as he is omnipotent. "Judgment day," wrote Alfred de Vigny, "will be the day on which humanity judges God."[146] "La terre est revolté des injustices et de la création . . . elle s'indigne en secret contre le Dieu qui a crée le mal et la mort. . . . Tous ceux qui luttèrent contre le ciel injuste ont eu l'admiration et l'amour secret des hommes."[147] This, indeed, is Titanism in revolt against an implacable God who only laughs at us.[148] But it is a futile gesture, with no artistic or moral justification beyond itself.

> "Si le Ciel nous laissa, comme un monde avorté,
> Le juste opposera le dédain à l'absence

---

[144] *Philosophy of Right*, pp. 12-13. To an eminent Catholic historian of German 19th-century thought Fichte seemed like a Prometheus of ethics and Hegel a "knowing Prometheus," but for him the act of defiance, the aspiration itself, is crucial, not the essentially poetic character of Prometheus; Balthasar, *op.cit.*, pp. 139-157 and 611-619. Actually a philosophic Prometheus is unimaginable.

[145] *Cain*, Act III, Scene I.

[146] *Journal d'un Poète*, ed. by P. Flottes (Paris, 1949), p. 145.

[147] *Ibid.*, pp. 46-47.   [148] *Ibid.*, p. 146.

Et ne répondra plus que par un froid silence
Au silence éternel de la Divinité."[149]

Silence is the last resort of Prometheus in defeat.

Romantic Religion

Only Nietzsche was able to imagine an active Prometheus in a world without God. For him, indeed, the end of faith meant the beginning of the rule of the Titans. It was a necessary condition of Titanism.[150] However, most romantics were not ready to do without God. Even the youthful atheist, Shelley, felt that, "There is a Power by which we are surrounded, like the atmosphere in which some motionless lyre is suspended which visits with its breath our silent chords at will."[151] To be sure, he disliked the harsh God of the Bible and regarded historical Christianity as an instrument of tyranny. But, like all romantics, he felt a powerful urge to be at one with the One, with the universe. Self-assertion is only one side of Prometheus' character; the other is an intense longing to lose the self in infinity. Apollo the spirit of individuation, and Dionysos the spirit of totality, of self-annihilation, domi-

[149] *Le Mont d'Oliviers.*

[150] *Thus Spake Zarathustra,* tr. by T. Common (Modern Library), pp. 310-320. This difference between Nietzsche and the first romantics has caused Professor Kaufmann in his excellent recent study of Nietzsche to deny that Nietzsche was a real romantic; W. A. Kaufmann, *Nietzsche* (Princeton, 1950), pp. 8-16, 100-105, 113-117, 282-283, and 327-337. He is, of course, quite right in emphasizing this difference between Nietzsche and the early romantics, but a leaning toward a sentimental religious faith is not a genuine quality of romanticism. In many other respects—in the concept of dramatic life, Prometheus, the ethics of genius and individuality, and in his hatred of the philistines—Nietzsche was a romantic. On the other hand, it is an exaggeration to picture Nietzsche as a later edition of early romanticism in every respect. Romantic he was, if the word is given a broad meaning, but not if one tries to show his agreement with the early romantics on every detail, as Karl Joël in his *Nietzsche und die Romantik* (Jena, 1923) tried to do.

[151] *Essay on Christianity, loc.cit.,* p. 87.

nated the romantic stage, long before Nietzsche recognized them explicitly as the two souls of all tragic drama.[152] The yearning for harmony for synthesis, was always at war in Prometheus' soul with the urge for self-distinction and defiance. Indeed, in later years Nietzsche asked himself whether his early concept of Dionysos, as music, as "a metaphysical comfort," as a rest from the burdens of individuality, had not been a romantic one. He decided that it was not, because it had not implied anything Christian.[153] Christian faith had in fact been the end of the need for Dionysos among the early romantics. They fled from their own world. Nietzsche, like Goethe, remained true to the original impulse and came to despise the whimpering weaklings.

At first it was death that was to unite Prometheus with the All. Novalis, the poet of death, even toyed with the thought of creating a new bible, to elaborate the doctrine that all absolute emotion is religious and that, consequently, beauty is the first object of all religion.[154] This aesthetic faith was certainly not orthodox Christianity. Sin, morality, and redemption played no part in it, only immortality through personal love and ecstasy. Nor was personality to be completely sacrificed to totality. God is to be found in ourselves, and we are led to Him by nature, poetry, and love, according to Schleiermacher.[155] The true priest is the poet, like the old *vates*, and miraculously Apollo and Dionysos are reconciled in ourselves,

[152] R. Huch, *Die Bluethezeit der Romantik* (Leipzig, 1899), pp. 82-118; Kluckhohn, *op.cit.*, pp. 125-149; Silz, *op.cit.*, pp. 205-235; Welleck, *op.cit.*, pp. 155-156.

[153] The first statement of the two contesting spirits of tragedy occurred in *The Birth of Tragedy*, the second thought in "An Attempt at Self-Criticism," *Ecce Homo*, pp. 944-946.

[154] *Fragmente, Werke*, vol. II, 179, 180, 217, 241; Dilthey, *op.cit.*, pp. 312-321.

[155] Schleiermacher, *Ueber die Religion*, ed. by M. Rade (Deutsche Bibliothek, Berlin, n.d.), pp. 58-60 and 121-127.

for it is by turning inward that we are made one with the Whole.

What in Schleiermacher turned into aesthetic sentimentality of the worst kind was not enough for more violent natures, like the Schlegels, Schelling, Brentano, and, much later, Dostoyevski, who knew only two extremes, a wild individualism, the cult of the I, or a complete collapse before the cross. Even this submission was, however, often aestheticized. Chateaubriand cared not for the truth but only for the beauty of Christianity. His was a sort of poetic theology which regarded Christianity as a necessity for genius.[156] Faith was justified by its aesthetic results and, among the decadents of the *fin de siècle*, for its voluptuous sensations.[157] This pseudo-Catholicism usually went together with the new "blood and soil" nationalism, the other means of escaping from the "culte du moi," as Barrès was again to discover.[158] This was what Goethe, and after him Heine and Nietzsche hated in romanticism. "Das klosterbrudrisierende, sternbaldisierende Unwesen," Goethe called the new "Christian-patriotic" art.[159] To Heine there were two kinds of men, the Nazarenes, who were life-denying, moralizing cowards, and the Hellenes, who resembled Goethe.[160] It was for this notion that Nietzsche admired him. For him Wagner remained the awful example of what happens to romantics; *Tristan* ends in *Parsifal*.[161] But Heine was in his main beliefs

---

[156] Chateaubriand, *Le Génie du Christianisme, Oeuvres* (Paris, 1874), vol. II, pp. 375-380; G. Boas, *French Philosophies of the Romantic Period* (Baltimore, 1925), pp. 94-102; B. Croce, *European Literature in the Nineteenth Century*, tr. by D. Ainslie (New York, 1924), pp. 2 and 45-51.

[157] Praz, *op.cit.*, pp. 289-411.

[158] C. Buthman, *The Rise of Integral Nationalism in France*, pp. 56-64 and 75-86. C. J. H. Hayes, *The Historical Evolution of Modern Nationalism* (New York, 1950), pp. 184-202.

[159] Quoted in Silz, *op.cit.*, p. 56; Viëtor, *Goethe the Poet*, pp. 150-158.

[160] *Ludwig Boerne, Werke*, vol. VII, pp. 23-25.

[161] *Human-all-too-Human* (II), tr. by P. V. Cohn, *Works*, vol. VII,

a romantic, as was Nietzsche, the champion of "tragic knowledge." However, both were able to resist the lures of "metaphysical comforts," and the two gods of tragedy, Dionysos and Apollo, are at one in their opposition to Christ. This is the real spirit of romanticism. It is life-affirmation, and only a romantic weary of creation, of struggle and drama, sinks into pessimism. When the "unhappy consciousness" loses all energy and seeks solace in oblivion, romanticism is dead. History vindicated Hegel entirely, but this defeat was not the end of the romantic spirit, nor the measure of its achievement.

---

nr. 3; G. de Huszar, "Nietzsche's Theory of Decadence and the Transvaluation of all Values," *Journal of the History of Ideas,* 1945, vol. VI, pp. 259-272; Kaufmann, *op.cit.,* pp. 129-131, 295-341.

CHAPTER III

The Unhappy Consciousness in Society

The Emptiness of Progress

THE "unhappy consciousness" does not just assert itself against the laws of reason and nature. The struggles of Prometheus are only part of the revolt of romanticism against "things as they are." The tragic view of life also embraces history and society; possibly these are even its main preoccupations. Certainly the restless longing of romanticism finds its most vehement expression in its opposition to all historical and social optimism, but the picture of the poet as "a hopeless young man who weeps on a solitary rock" is a gross misrepresentation.[1] It is a picture of defeat that fits very few romantics, and then only after the fight against established social views and institutions has been given up. Most romantics, indeed, were brought to self-recognition as a result of their radical dissatisfaction with their social environment.

The first target of romanticism was the prevalence of utilitarianism, which of all attitudes is the most repulsive to poetry. Godwin's choice of Fénelon as a man useful to mankind would have found little support. In fact, Nietzsche noted that to judge a man according to his utility to mankind is like appraising "the value of a work of art according to its effects."[2] Hedonism he knew to be absurd for anyone engaged in creative work.[3] The very idea of the useful was obnoxious to the

---

[1] D. O. Evans: *Social Romanticism in France* (Oxford, 1951), pp. 29-30. It is, however, true that the French romantics, especially in the years from 1830 to 1848, were politically more active than those elsewhere.

[2] *The Will to Power* (II), nr. 878.

[3] *Beyond Good and Evil*, pp. 529-530.

romantics; it is all that is prosaic, Novalis complained, and Baudelaire found useful persons "particularly horrible."[4] The poets were not concerned like Kant to show that utilitarianism was ethically untenable.[5] It was not even its emotional poverty that distressed them, but rather the fact that utilitarianism was the spirit of the age, that it was the philosophy of a mediocre, undramatic society. "*Utility*," Schiller complained, "is the great idol of the age, to which all powers must do service and all talents swear allegiance. In these clumsy scales the spiritual service of Art has no weight; deprived of all encouragement, she flees from the noisy mart of our century."[6] This protest was repeated over and over again. Utilitarianism is a state of mind that disregards poetry, that denies artistic genius its true place of leadership, and that measures art and artists according to a uniform commercial standard.

However, this hatred of utility is only a part of the artistic rebellion against modern society, a rebellion which found its expression in a new view of history and a new theory of leadership. Just as social theology is a claim for leadership on the part of the guardians of a faith, and liberalism a similar pretension among men of ideas, so romantic social theory is the artists' demand to dominate society. Consequently it began with an attack on the dominant art-denying philosophy of the age, which rebuffed the artist and seemed to render society mechanical and impersonal. Here again romanticism took its position in defense of the aesthetic and actual as opposed to the abstract, the static, and the general.

Not surprisingly, the Enlightenment's faith in progress was obnoxious to the "unhappy consciousness." Complacency re-

[4] Novalis, *Fragmente, Werke*, vol. II, p. 213; Baudelaire, *Intimate Journals*, tr. by C. Isherwood (Hollywood, 1947), p. 67; *L'Art Romantique*, p. 168.

[5] Kant, *Foundations of the Metaphysics of Morals, loc.cit.*, pp. 55-101.

[6] *On the Aesthetic Education of Man*, p. 26 (Schiller's italics).

pels the "unhappy consciousness" in any case, and nothing can be more obvious to the aesthetic mind than the fact that beauty does not progress. Above all, the things that meant progress to both hedonists and rationalists were distasteful to romanticism. Neither mechanical advances, nor universal prosperity, nor an increase in useful knowledge, nor the skeptic's freedom from superstition was at all attractive to them. "While Mechanical Arts, Manufactures, Agriculture, Commerce, and all those products of knowledge which are confined to gross—definite—and tangible objects, have, with the aid of Experimental Philosophy, been putting on more brilliant colours; the splendour of the Imagination has been fading," Wordsworth lamented.[7] To Shelley it seemed that "the unmitigated exercise of the calculating faculty" and "the cultivation of the mechanical arts in a degree disproportioned to the presence of the creative faculty" were responsible for increasing differences in wealth and for the dangers of both despotism and anarchy. The knowledge upon which the age prided itself was false; even the much-heralded liberation from prejudice had "defaced the eternal truths chartered upon the imaginations of men"—that is, the poetic, not the mechanical truths.[8] It is poetry, not knowledge, that makes life worthwhile.

Here the old war between poetry and philosophy is reopened. If Kant did not suffer from the delusions of a fanatical optimism, such as Condorcet's, he still felt that his age was ready to acquire knowledge and that, if not enlightened, it was an age of enlightenment, and that progress was a rational necessity.[9] To this not even the admiring Schiller could

[7] *Convention of Cintra, Political Tracts*, p. 182.

[8] *A Defence of Poetry*, pp. 29-33.

[9] *What Is Enlightenment?* and *Idea for a Universal History with Cosmopolitan Intent, The Philosophy of Kant*, tr. and ed. by C. J. Friedrich (Modern Library, New York, 1949), pp. 116-139.

help replying, "if it be so, why do we still remain barbarians?"[10] Moreover, to Kant, as to all the philosophers, progress meant the advancement of the race as a whole, not the happiness or perfection of every individual. This, to romanticism, was a meaningless abstraction; progress is not progress unless individuals are improved. On the contrary, the romantics felt that the things that had benefited the whole had impoverished the individual. The division of labor, so greatly admired by all practical philosophy, seemed to Schiller to have led to "whole classes of human beings developing only a part of their capacities. . . ." If the community "makes function the measure of man" it is not surprising that each person develops only those qualities which bring him "honour and profit" until "gradually individual concrete life is extinguished, in order that the abstract life of the whole may prolong its sorry existence."[11] A society that disregards the individual in favor of some imaginary whole is an impersonal society, an inhuman society. The trade cycle may have its necessities, Coleridge admitted, "but people are not things—but man does not find his level. Neither in body nor in soul does the man find his level."[12] Men are not things, and any philosophy that places the "system" before the "man" treats him as if he were an object. The result is that man *does* become an expression of a function, almost a thing. That is what Hyperion found in Germany after his return from Greece. An entire people had been torn to pieces. There were laborers, priests, masters and servants, but no men. Germany seemed like a battlefield with dismembered arms and legs strewn about. Every man was forced to put his whole soul and strength into his occupation, and had to strangle anything within him that did not fit his exact title.[13]

[10] Schiller, *op.cit.*, pp. 48-49.   [11] *Ibid.*, pp. 38-41.
[12] S. T. Coleridge, A *Lay Sermon, Political Tracts*, p. 102.
[13] Hoelderlin, *Hyperion* (Part II), *Werke*, ed. A. Brieger (Salzburg, 1952), p. 574. Years later Nietzsche could still belabor this point, e.g., "The Use and Abuse of History," pp. 62-63.

As Schiller had already observed, the individual Athenian was an infinitely superior person to the individual man of modern Europe. With this recognition emerged the full consciousness of man's alienation from society.[14]

No wonder that with such an attitude all talk of progress seemed mischievous. "Oh how deeply I despise this generation which plumes itself more shamelessly than any previous one ever did, which can scarcely endure the belief in a still better future," Schleiermacher exclaimed. "This whole sense of a common material progress" is without value, since the work of humanity is carried out by an "ingenious system" in which each man is forced "to restrict his powers."[15] Baudelaire spoke for all when he observed that, "Belief in Progress is a doctrine of idlers. . . . It is the individual relying upon his neighbours to do his work. There cannot be any Progress (true progress, that is moral) except within the individual and by the individual himself."[16]

Although Rousseau instinctively rebelled against the facile optimism of his contemporaries he resembled them in his indifference to the dramatic nature of history itself. It fell to Herder, the first truly romantic thinker, to reinterpret history in terms of the "unhappy consciousness." "A great scenter of the future," Nietzsche called him, and justly, for it was he who first revolted against the idea of history as a picture of steady human ascent to perfection.[17] With all the violence of a *Sturm und Drang* poet he denounced the present age for its flabbiness, its degeneracy, its artistic sterility.[18] One look at Greece told him how far from perfection the present age was. The dominating force of human history is not the law of progress but inexorable fate. History is only a part of natural his-

[14] H. Popitz, *Der Entfremdete Mensch* (Basel, 1953), pp. 12-36.
[15] *Soliloquies*, pp. 50-53.   [16] *Intimate Journals*, pp. 71-72.
[17] *Human-all-too-Human* (II), "The Wanderer and his Shadow" nr. 118.
[18] R. Pascal, *The German Sturm und Drang*, pp. 217-232.

tory in which each culture, like a plant, has its own preestablished laws of development, its own character, and its own limited life-span.[19] It follows that no general standards for judging past and present are possible. But here Herder was not consistent, for he glorified the creative ages of the past at the expense of his own apparently inactive age. Consistency was, however, not Herder's aim. He saw past and present, as he had seen nature, through artistic eyes.[20] His own age lacked just those qualities which he most admired: energy and creativeness. His main interest was the revival of poetry, and modern life seemed but an obstacle to this end. Its cosmopolitanism had destroyed the primary source of all great poetry, the national soul.[21] Its splendid courts and its polite manners had crushed all originality and vigor.[22] One thing was clear, in any case: Homer and Shakespeare had not been surpassed in the 18th century. What could be more inane than to regard this age as the pinnacle of history? Where was there any progress? Looking back, Herder saw no painless advancement. Such advancement was just a philosophic illusion. He saw in history what he had seen in nature—struggle, violence, and tragedy. If history was God's march through the ages, so was nature; in both cases it was a spectacle of creative, dramatic forces at work.[23] Metaphysics could never grasp this process. To understand history requires an effort of the creative imagination, not of analysis. The historian must live through the past, and recreate it as a personal experience.[24] It is, like writing poetry,

[19] *Auch Eine Philosophie der Geschichte, Werke*, vol. v, pp. 530-539 and 562-564.
[20] A. Gillies, *Herder* (Oxford, 1945), pp. 55-57 and 74-75; T. Litt, *Herder und Kant*, pp. 202-257.
[21] *Auch Eine Philosophie*, pp. 550-552.
[22] *Ueber die Wirkung der Dichterkunst auf die Voelker in Alten und Neuen Zeiten, Werke*, vol. viii, pp. 406-433.
[23] *Auch Eine Philosophie*, pp. 532-533.
[24] *ibid.*, p. 503. This belief has earned Herder the glory of being the founder of modern historicism. F. Meinecke, *Die Entstehung des*

a self-revelation, for history is nature's work, and we too are part of nature. This idea marks a revolution in historical thought. Thus Augustin Thierry, following Herder, could say of his histories that they were dramatic paintings, works of art, from which all philosophic speculation had been excluded. And Michelet announced that he was as old as France, for he had lived her life for two thousand years in writing her history.[25]

In Herder's outburst the tragic sense of life, as well as the cult of creative energy common to all romanticism, found their full expression. But, as always, "the unhappy consciousness" was exposed to two dangers, the scorn of the philosophers, and its own weakness, its longing for some "metaphysical comfort." Herder had not been able to bear the thought of a purposeless nature; in his later years he tried to show that progress does, after all, exist; that history has an aim—the raising of all mankind to true humanity. This was clearly at odds with his continuing belief that each culture was a perfect whole, that no generation is merely a steppingstone for another or for the human race as a whole.[26] His faith in natural evolution was simply imposed upon his picture of history as a scene of endless variety. Kant was not long in noting this confusion. He saw quite clearly that no universal rule of reason or morality could emerge from unaided na-

---

Historismus (Muenchen, 1946), pp. 378-468; *Vom Geschichtlichen Sinn und vom Sinn der Geschichte* (Leipzig, 1939), pp. 46-67. Benedetto Croce, however, insists that Vico, in his struggle with abstract philosophy, as represented by Descartes, was the real founder of modern historical thought; *History as the Story of Liberty*, tr. by S. Sprigge (New York, 1941), pp. 70-77. Probably he is right in terms of dates, but Vico's influence was too small to make him the founder of anything.

[25] R. Picard, *Le Romantisme Social* (New York, 1944), pp. 271-272 and 280.

[26] *Ideen zu einer Philosophie der Menschheit, Werke*, vol. XIII, pp. 338-340.

ture, but only from reason itself. Also, no general principles could be drawn from the events of history alone, without some presupposed rationally necessary end. Herder, he observed, only too justly, had mixed up poetry with philosophy.[27]

Indeed, the yearning for some unifying principle in history did not seem to disturb Herder's awareness of the endless variety of events, as such, and this was typical of some later romantics as well. Tolstoy, for instance, was very similarly torn between his knowledge of the actual incoherence of all historical events and his desire for some idea that might provide a comprehensive justification for this apparent chaos, but he was never able to reconcile these conflicting intellectual impulses.[28] Other historians were more fortunate. Some simply escaped into the past, to Greece, to the Middle Ages, or to the Renaissance, without the comforts of theory. Others let the belief in evolution drown out their sense of the tragic. Progress was no longer conceived as a rational necessity but as organic growth inherent in history, a biological fate. In short, the optimism of the century was the real beneficiary of the insights of the unhappy consciousness, for historicism is the same sort of retreat into totality as religion.

The philosophers, in the meantime, were not silent. Fichte continued to champion the Kantian position. Though he was far less satisfied with his age than Kant had been with his, he too believed in progress as rationally necessary. Again, progress meant the advancement of the race as a whole toward rationality, and not individual development. Like all philosophers he took the "long view" and saw in the evils of the past and present only steps to a better future. Thought alone is universal and immortal, and thought, he felt sure, was

[27] *Rezensionen von Herders Ideen zur Philosophie der Geschichte, Werke,* ed. by E. Cassirer, vol. IV, pp. 179-200; E. Cassirer, *Kant's Leben und Lehre* (Berlin, 1918), pp. 237-246; C. J. Friedrich, *Inevitable Peace,* pp. 65-67.

[28] I. Berlin, *The Hedgehog and the Fox* (New York, 1953).

getting better all the time, until it would "think" humanity into perfection. Not the individual and the transient, but the eternal and immutable life of reason is the center of history.[29] It follows that the philosopher, "the priest of truth," alone fully understands the entire past. Hegel, in fact, said so quite explicitly.[30] For all his consciousness of the dramatic, struggling, and violent nature of history, of the organic development of cultures, and of the unique character of every past event, he still regarded history from a philosophic point of view, that is, abstractly and teleologically. World history is seen as a single whole, a playing-field of universal reason. The lives of individuals and groups are only temporary manifestations of the spirit in its self-development. From beginning to end reason secretly rules the world, and in its final victory it can look down on all the miseries of the past with sly satisfaction, for they were only necessary means to its end, absolute rationality and universal freedom. Good and evil, morality itself, are only accidental features of the spirit's growth in history.[31] Hegel's decision to accept the world was essentially an optimistic act of rational faith. "To recognize reason as the rose in the cross of the present, and thereby to enjoy the present, this is the rational insight that reconciles us to the actual."[32] Reason wants more than tragedy in history; it seeks a justification of God's ways to man, and Hegel found it in the progress of reason.[33]

To the unhappy consciousness, this reasoning is an outrageous bit of casuistry. A monk who has returned to the

---

[29] *The Present Age*, pp. 5-13, 35-67, 77-83, 141-158; X. Léon, *Fichte et son Temps*, vol. II, 394-463.

[30] *The Philosophy of History*, p. 10.

[31] *Ibid.*, pp. 8-79; H. Marcuse, *Reason and Revolution* (New York, 1941), pp. 229-247.

[32] *The Philosophy of Right*, p. 12.

[33] *The Philosophy of History*, pp. 456-457.

world, a Jesuit, is exactly what Kierkegaard called Hegel.[34] Nietzsche could see in this systematized self-satisfaction only "the canonisation of success."[35] The actual can never be palatable to a romantic, and a philosophy which affirms the existing, that finds a rational justification for the evils of life, is doubly obnoxious. To romanticism Hegel was only a bombastic Dr. Pangloss. The artistic consciousness would not be convinced that the passing of the age of poetry into that of prose was a blessing; rather, it seemed to announce the bankruptcy of European culture. Again, a historian of Jacob Burckhardt's moral sensibilities found it difficult to see that misery and violence cease to be evils when seen world-historically.[36] Above all they resented the idea that individual existence was subordinate to history. Hegel had, according to Kierkegaard, forgotten, in a fit of world-historical absentmindedness, what it meant to be an individual.[37] "Life" remains opposed to all systems.

There were two ways in which "life" could assert itself against Hegel. One could return to the life of the past for its own sake, to escape both an unbearable present and the falsifications of philosophic optimism. That was Burckhardt's way. But one could also reject history altogether in favor of immediate life, as Kierkegaard and Nietzsche did. There was indeed in Herder's own appreciation for "the deep irreplaceable feeling of being alive," for the here and now, a very unhistoric feeling that he never developed.[38] But Goethe, who had a far stronger love of life and action, shunned history. Not

[34] J. Wahl, *Etudes Kierkegaardiennes*, p. 485.

[35] "David Strauss, the Confessor and the Writer," *Thoughts out of Season*, Part I, tr. by A. Ludovici; *Works*, vol. I, p. 54; "The Use and Abuse of History," pp. 71-72.

[36] J. Burckhardt, *Force and Freedom*, ed. by J. H. Nichols (New York, 1943), pp. 263 and 362.

[37] *Concluding Unscientific Postscript*, p. 112-113.

[38] *Ideen, Werke*, vol. XIII, p. 337.

.only was he without illusions about progress, but he sensed in the absorption in history the same kind of opiate as in metaphysics. Only if history rouses our enthusiasm and urges us on to action is it justified. In this respect Nietzsche really was Goethe's heir.[39] From a very different conception of life, Kierkegaard too decried history as an "immoral diversion," a way of hiding ourselves from our most important concern, our relation to God.[40] Like Nietzsche, he regarded the present "reflective age" as a corrupt and degenerate period, lacking in all creative energy, and certainly not a cause for satisfaction or progressivist complacency. He too saw in the current preoccupation with history a threat to any remaining vitality. History was becoming an obstacle to overcoming the present. To Kierkegaard religion offered the only hope of escape from this "reflective," leveled, passionless age.[41] Religion, however, was for him something totally unhistorical. To him Hegel's system was not reasonable; it was only a rationalization, an effort to mediate between the irreconcilable elements of real life, between good and evil, the one and the many, heaven and hell.[42] From the point of view of the individual it was unethical and pagan "to concern oneself with the history of the race instead of with one's own existing."[43] To think of the race as prior to the individual is to forget that only the individual can stand before God; such thinking is a disregard for all that matters in concrete living. Not only is historical progress an impossibility, but history can teach us nothing that really matters:

"Whatever one generation may learn from the other, that

[39] Viëtor, *Goethe the Thinker*, pp. 116-135.

[40] *Concluding Unscientific Postscript*, pp. 120-121.

[41] *The Present Age*, tr. by A. Dru (London, 1940), pp. 3-37, 47-49, 60-61.

[42] *Either/Or*, vol. II, pp. 144-149; *Concluding Unscientific Postscript*, pp. 139-141.

[43] *Journal*, s. 1377.

which is genuinely human no generation learns from the foregoing. In this respect every generation begins primitively, has no different task from every previous generation. . . . This authentically human factor is passion.. . . . Thus no generation has learned from another to love, no generation begins at any other point than at the beginning. . . . But the highest passion in a man is faith, and here . . . every generation begins all over again, the subsequent generation gets no further than the foregoing."[44]

This was essentially Nietzsche's view as well, although the passion which had to be defended against history was not faith but creativity. The age being decadent, men must educate themselves in opposition to the present, and get rid of "the abominable flattery of the Time-Fetish" that historicism practiced.[45] To say that Nietzsche despised his own age is an almost hilarious understatement. Most of his writings consist in vitriolic attacks upon the mediocrity, the joylessness, the decadence of modern Europe. But to flee into the past he regarded as an evasion of man's primary object, to live and to create—in his time. Only if history is a means to life, an inspiration to action—that is, if it serves unhistoric ends—is its study justified.[46] Past and present must both be overcome by a form of life that heroically accepts the idea of "eternal recurrences," a purposeless history, and yet not despair.[47]

Neither Nietzsche nor Kierkegaard is really a defeated spirit. Nietzsche continued to believe that man would be surpassed, that some individuals would save themselves out of the general mire. Kierkegaard never doubted that every man ready to become an individual could reach faith. Historical disaster could not crush them, because both saw the

[44] *Fear and Trembling,* p. 130.
[45] "Schopenhauer as Educator," pp. 133-134.
[46] "The Use and Abuse of History," pp. 9-10, 15-16, 24-30, 74.
[47] *The Will to Power* (II), nrs. 1053-1067.

real value of life outside history. But for the aesthete for whom historic culture is everything, who, even if he sees individual man as the center of history, still regards him as only man *in* history, for him absolute despair is a constant danger.[48] Few people have succumbed to historical despair more completely than did Jacob Burckhardt. By admission he was a "poète manqué." His was not only the "unhappy consciousness"; it was also the "frustrated." He was an historian who was forced to admit that poetry occupied a higher rank in the hierarchy of knowledge than history.[49] Like Herder, he tried to make historical writing poetic, a matter of creative sympathy, recreating an entire spirit of a past age in an artistic picture.[50] Like Herder, whom alone among philosophers of history he singled out for praise, he believed in the inner "daemon" of cultures, which the creative historian can reconstruct.[51] But while Herder had still made his journey into the past with some polemical gusto, and even Novalis had looked back to the Middle Ages with the hope of finding there a pattern for the future, Burckhardt wanted only to escape from an intolerable present.

Beauty was for Burckhardt the only immutable standard in a world of flux, and it was to beautiful cultures that he turned for consolation, to the Italian Renaissance and to Greece.[52] There he found the kind of integrated artistic life that he missed so much in his own age. The more he lost himself in the past, the more he detested the present. "I have been reading the Greeks," he wrote to a friend, "and find it easy to feel a real contempt for our century and its pretensions."[53] "The priest of beauty," as he styled himself, was not

---

[48] K. Löwith, *Jacob Burckhardt* (Luzern, 1936), pp. 97-151.
[49] *Force and Freedom*, p. 153.   [50] Löwith, *op.cit.*, p. 189.
[51] *Force and Freedom*, p. 82; W. K. Ferguson, *The Renaissance in Historical Thought* (Boston, 1948), pp. 186-188.
[52] *Force and Freedom*, pp. 86-87.
[53] Letter to F. von Preen, January 8, 1870, *Briefe*, ed. by F. Kaphahn (Leipzig, 1935), p. 311. My translation.

easily consoled.[54] Only in the history of Athens were there "no tedious pages."[55] For the rest he had the decadent romantic's typical sense of degeneration and sin. Destruction in history, as in natural life, implied only the omnipresence of evil, not, as Nietzsche felt, the power of regeneration.[56] In human nature he saw a hell, even in his youth, and in later years it seemed to him that "the devil really ruled the world, as it is written in the New Testament."[57] Not that he believed in God; he believed only in the devil. If beauty had existed, it had left the world of men, for nowhere did Burckhardt see degeneration more actively at work than in modern Europe. The advancement of the "whole," material prosperity, division of labor, and specialization, in these he, like Schiller, saw only the destruction of the whole man, the cultured man.[58] The barbarians produced by such a civilization, he believed, were already at the door. There were no more than some ten years left to the cultured European, he guessed.[59] What men called progress he regarded as mere "domestication."[60] Man had been evened out, standardized, and deprived of energy, but not improved morally. He was the same old animal—only tamed. Needless to add, optimism was anathema to him. He even predicted that a great war between the optimistic Hegelians and the pessimists was about to take place. For himself he chose a position that he called "malism"—which was mere anti-optimism, not a Schopenhauerian Nirvana, nor Nietzsche's tragic "life-in-spite-of."[61]

---

[54] Löwith, op.cit., p. 102.　　[55] Force and Freedom, p. 218.

[56] Ibid., pp. 262 and 361-363.

[57] Letters to H. Schauenburg, March 5, 1846, loc.cit., p. 149, and to F. von Preen, December 29, 1873, p. 358.

[58] Force and Freedom, pp. 99-100, 152.

[59] E.g., Letters to H. Schauenburg, c. September 14, 1849, loc.cit., p. 185, and to F. von Preen, July 24, 1889, pp. 485-486.

[60] Force and Freedom, pp. 149-152.

[61] Ibid., pp. 299-300; Letter to F. von Preen, September 19, 1875, loc.cit., p. 385; Löwith, op.cit., pp. 158-159.

Jacob Burckhardt had succeeded in making a fine art out of disenchantment. He could not escape from history, and yet he could not accept it.

Burckhardt was at least an eminently honest fatalist. The same can scarcely be said for Oswald Spengler, the author one cannot help thinking of when the words fate and decline in history are mentioned. There is so much that seems romantic in *The Decline of the West*—the Faustian posturings, Herder's belief in the unique fate of cultures, the idea that with the end of art the last act of European culture had begun, the calls for "life in the raw," the notion that intuitive perception was the true guide to historical truth, and that history was "living nature."[62] These certainly are the trappings of romanticism, but Spengler was not a romantic, not even an inferior one. His was not an "unhappy consciousness." He was ultimately closer to Hegel than to the latter's opponents. For his real aim was to "give destiny a helping hand."[63] His gospel was not that of defiance but of adjustment. The admitted purpose of his book was to show not only that art was dead but that the coming generation should forget about it, and take up only engineering.[64] His life-feeling was not creative at all but found its expression in an admiration for blood and war, as opposed to commerce.[65] But he had no ideal to substitute for money. Our destiny is merely to destroy, and we cannot alter fate. We can only know its course, and learn how best to adapt ourselves to the inevitable.[66] To destroy illusions is not enough; "malism" was now a positive doctrine, a call for a mixture of resignation and brutality—the two things most hateful to all true romanticism. Spengler is the perfect

[62] O. Spengler, *The Decline of the West*, tr. by C. F. Atkinson (New York, 1939), e.g., vol. I, pp. 6, 21-22, 25, 47-49, and 291-295.
[63] E. Heller, *The Disinherited Mind*, pp. 152-153.
[64] *The Decline of the West*, vol. I, pp. 40-41.
[65] *Ibid.*, vol. II, pp. 469-507.
[66] *Ibid.*, vol. I, p. 159.

example of how the external expressions of romanticism, when deprived of their inner spirit, become the antithesis of the romantic. This is the real danger of romanticism, and its all too frequent end.

Samson and the Philistines

The chief complaint of romanticism against the modern world was its apparent hostility to the arts. "Why be a poet in such miserable times?" Hoelderlin asked.[67] The answer was clear to all romantics: the genius cannot help being himself. The predicament of genius became for them the central social issue, around which an entirely new system of ethics was woven and from which their startling conceptions of social life emerged. Who, then, is the genius? It is important not to confuse him with Prometheus, for he is only the Titan's bastard half-brother. The genius is not a self-created super-man; he is a miracle, a product of nature. Like Samson he owes his peculiar strength to a divine gift, of which he can be robbed. He is only an exceptional man, whose entire glory lies in his difference from other men, not in his ability to transcend himself. That is why Prometheus is an example, an image that one strives to imitate, but the genius is only an idol. Nietzsche, who, like many other Prometheans, often failed to keep the Titan and Samson carefully apart, clearly saw this when he noted that the idolization of genius was just a consolation to the untalented, since a miracle cannot shame one.[68] But the genius, of course, invited idolatry. Who can forget Henry Adams' priceless anecdote about Victor Hugo enthroned before a worshipping claque?[69] Nietzsche felt that Hugo and Richard Wagner at Bayreuth were signs of the degeneracy of

[67] *Brot und Wein.*

[68] *Human-all-too-Human* (1), tr. by H. Zimmern; *Works,* vol. vi, nr. 162.

[69] *The Education of Henry Adams* (Modern Library, New York, 1931), p. 143.

genius in a mass age.[70] But the very notion of genius always invited such demonstrations—for what is an idol if not a natural object that arouses misplaced religious veneration? That is what the genius is, an accident of nature, who expresses a power not its own. He possesses some "afflatus divinus," according to Hamann, or he is the unconscious voice of the collective mind of the nation, according to Coleridge.[71] "A force of nature" emerging from the "inarticulate dregs," Carlyle said of the great man.[72] Schopenhauer saw genius as "working by instinct, like a tree bearing fruit." Moreover, he observed, the difference between the genius and the ordinary man is the most important, real division among men.[73] The genius, then, is absolutely separated from all men, thanks to an endowment which he cannot control. He is thus both an idol and the victim of his situation. If society refuses to admire him, he is a complete outcast, for he cannot be like others, even if he were to choose to become so. On one hand he feels superior to most men, and demands that they recognize his special gifts; on the other, he pities himself because society remains indifferent to him, or even rejects him. Genius, thus, is a social form of the unhappy consciousness.

Prometheus is not so trivial. In a sense Kierkegaard's discussion of the difference betwen the genius and the apostle is the best illustration of the distance between Samson and Prometheus. The genius is limited entirely to the sphere of immanence, the recipient of innate gifts that the whole race eventually appropriates. He exists only for his own sake, with no end beyond his natural activity. There is his greatness, as

[70] E.g., *The Case of Wagner*, tr. by A. M. Ludovici, *Works*, vol. VIII, p. 33; *The Will to Power* (II), nr. 825.
[71] R. Unger, *Hamann und die Aufklaerung* (Saale, 1925), vol. I, pp. 275-305; H. Read, "Coleridge as Critic," *The True Voice of Feeling*, pp. 173 and 178-179.
[72] *Heroes and Heroworship*, p. 150.
[73] *Essays*, tr. by T. B. Saunders (New York, n.d.), vol. IV, pp. 97-110 and 113-114.

well as his smallness. For "it is modest of the nightingale not to require that anyone listen to it; but it is also proud of the nightingale not to care whether anyone listens to it or not."[74] The apostle, on the other hand, belongs to the sphere of transcendence. Anyone can potentially be an apostle, for it is not a matter of any extraordinary gifts but of receiving a mission from God—a revelation that he may not enjoy, but for which he must sacrifice himself. The pagan Prometheus imposed his mission upon himself, the Christian receives it from God; that is a difference, but both seek the same end. Kierkegaard's apostle is a Christian Prometheus in the service of a transcendental ideal. The genius, however, only nurses his talent. The difference between Prometheus and Samson is most obvious when one recalls their respective ends. Prometheus submits only to fate, but Samson is destroyed by his own weakness and by the malice of his inferiors, the Philistines. Prometheus is a religious figure, while the genius is only a natural and social phenomenon.

Uniqueness is not only the defining characteristic of genius; it is also its highest value. The ethics of genius have only one goal, to develop an original personality. Morality was no longer a matter of obedience to a self-imposed law of reason, but of following one's inner "daemon." The individualism of the Enlightenment had demanded that each man follow only his own reason and conscience, or possibly his long-range self-interest. But reason and self-interest were universal, and all perfectly rational men would also be perfectly alike in their conduct. The ethics of the philosophers since Descartes were, in theory at least, both sociable and egalitarian. There is one truth and one reason open to all who will apply themselves. Descartes even made this common understanding the final test of truth, and Kant's ethics depend on a reason inherent in all men.

[74] S. Kierkegaard, "Of the Difference between a Genius and an Apostle," tr. by A. Dru in *The Present Age*, p. 162.

For both, our common humanity, the thing we all share, is our highest good.[75] The value of autonomy was not the satisfaction it brought the individual but the fact that it could lead humanity to agreement in truth and perfection. The ego of Fichte no less than of Descartes is only a cogitating, knowing, legislating ego. It is a generalized ego that possesses no individual characteristics; it is not "the 'I' of flesh and bone, that suffers from tooth-ache, and finds life insupportable if death is the annihilation of the personal consciousness." It is a "counterfeit 'I' " a "theoretical 'I,' " in Unamuno's words.[76] "The ego is free and posits itself . . . as free, because it posits (its) limitations as product of its free activity," Fichte wrote, but all the power of the ego is expended on founding the bases of consciousness and on postulating the objects of knowledge.[77] In ethics it sets itself only universally valid norms and strives to bring men to their destiny of "perfect unity and unanimity."[78]

The immense competence of such an ego appealed to the romantics, but not its aim. They quickly put some flesh and blood on it and gave it unique characteristics.[79] Thus Schelling admired the implication that "man's being is essentially *his own deed*," that he is a self-creation, but he was not ready to let man follow Fichte's universal model. Passion and energy make us good, not reason. The qualities that make us different, not those which unite us, are to be developed.[80] While the Enlightenment and later philosophy looked to reason as the qual-

---

[75] A. O. Lovejoy, "The Parallel of Deism and Classicism," *Essays in the History of Ideas*, pp. 48-98.

[76] *The Tragic Sense of Life*, pp. 28-29.

[77] *The Science of Knowledge*, tr. by A. E. Kroeger (Philadelphia, 1868), p. 220.

[78] *The Vocation of the Scholar*, pp. 167-168.

[79] R. Huch, *Die Blüthezeit der Romantik*, pp. 154-168; P. Kluckhohn, *Das Ideengut der Romantik*, pp. 47-53; *Persoenlichkeit und Gemeinschaft* (Halle-Saale, 1925), pp. 2-12.

[80] Schelling, *Of Human Freedom*, pp. 63, 79-80, 95-97 (his italics).

ity that distinguishes mankind, and so gave it a solidarity transcending the accidents of nature, birth, and environment, the romantics cared only for those qualities which make each person different from every other. For them, men did not gain stature as individuals by conforming to a universal standard, but only by nursing their most distinctly individual traits.

The ethics of genius, of individuality, begin with the belief in the absolute inequality of men, and the romantics seek not the universally human but the incommensurable, the peculiar, in each person. There are no common standards to judge men; there are no universal aims. Thus Nietzsche rejected the individualism of the Enlightenment as a form of collectivism, for it allowed all men the same right to self-expression. True individualism is limited to those who have something remarkable to express and who can live up to his maxim, "Will a self, so that you will become a self."[81] Baudelaire made it the supreme goal "to be a great man and a saint by *one's own standards.*"[82] The ethics of uniqueness rejected both the popular idea of conscience as mere discipline and the rationalist ideal of universality. Only in "the constant contemplation of our own true being" do we become like the Olympians, Schleiermacher observed, and he emphasized that his "only purpose is ever to become more fully what I am." One creates oneself from within, just as an artist creates an original masterpiece.[83] The artist, as Baudelaire insisted, must have something "sui generis."[84] Even in their external habits artists ought not to be like other men, for "they are Brahmins, a higher caste," Friedrich Schlegel wrote.[85] The young followers of Victor Hugo took up the idea with enthusiasm. From their famous *gilet rouge*, long hair, and pale countenance, one generation

[81] E.g. *The Will to Power* (II), nr. 859; *Human-all-too-Human* (I), nr. 366.
[82] *Intimate Journals*, p. 86 (Baudelaire's italics).
[83] *Schleiermacher's Soliloquies*, pp. 25, 71 and 34-35.
[84] *L'Art Romantique*, p. 249.   [85] *Ideen*, p. 31.

for "life in the raw." They have no feeling for organic nature or for the world of natural emotions; they are as much estranged from these as from the rest of the external world. Even the self that must be expressed is something sought and longed for more than a living reality. Ultimately, like all romantics, the existentialist yearns for something more than self, something to be grasped in self-transcendence.

All this gives existentialism an odor of mysticism—or, to be exact, of "mysticism manqué." The experience of self-transcendence, of "existence," ends not in exaltation but in frustration. If, like Buddhism, for example, it knows that no saving truths can be found outside but only within oneself, it does not succeed in reaching even inward truth.[28] Indeed, according to Jaspers, truth is neither revealed nor known; it is a form of being, something hoped for, but never achieved.[29] For him faith, like "life" and "selfhood," remains an unfulfilled hope. Thus philosophy suddenly becomes a "relation to God," but then "God is only another name for transcendence." Revealed religion is resolutely rejected, for Jaspers' denial of any possible absolute is obviously as rude a rejection of Christianity as of the old pretensions of philosophy. Certainly he does not give Bible religion any precedence over other visions.[30] Indeed, Christianity's insistence on exclusiveness, which Camus calls its "spirit of totality," is regarded as one of the sources of Europe's political corruption, its fanaticism.[31] Even the Catholic Marcel is reluctant to make any claim for exclusive truth

[28] This is what drew Aldous Huxley to Buddhism, for instance, *Themes and Variations* (New York, 1943), p. 103; but not all are capable of going the whole way with him and so we are doomed to frustration, Bollnow, *op.cit.*, pp. 26-27.

[29] *The Perennial Scope of Philosophy*, pp. 72-73.

[30] *Rechenschaft und Ausblick*, pp. 216-217; *Perennial Scope*, pp. 31 and 75-117; *Existentialism and Humanism*, pp. 93-97.

[31] Camus, *The Rebel*, pp. 164, 203 and 210-211; Jaspers, *The Perennial Scope*, pp. 93 and 95.

for his faith.[32] In fact, he too is more an aspiring mystic than a churchman. Even those among the existentialists who are not outright atheist cannot attain a stable faith. The unhappy consciousness simply does not lend itself to religious affirmation—even among those who, in their fashion, are believers.

The one thing existentialism does decidedly share with mystic religion is a contempt for "the world"—both for the world of objects and for the self as an empirical reality. In self-transcendence and world-denial are to be found a realm beyond all qualities and all finitudes. There, "existence," the "being of man" independent of all psychological qualities, the pure experience without content, are to be found. However, unlike the true mystic, the existentialist never reaches this state. This quest, like every other, ends in frustration. At best, signs of Being or of God may be seen; certainly He is never faced directly. The existentialist remains in bondage to "the world"— and within it to his "situation," his class, his environment, his age, and his heredity. For Jaspers there are at least some "situations" which drive us to the limits of our experience and when in a shattering encounter with death, sorrow, or guilt we see transcendence. But even on these dramatic occasions we do not really rise above "the world." The world is put in doubt, but we remain tied to it—in a suspended state, having lost the capacity for terrestrial joys, but not having found the mystic's ecstasy.[33]

The dramatic view of life, then, remains, even if only in a refined and pseudo-religious form. Indeed, the dramatic quality of existentialist thought is even more evident in Heidegger than in Jaspers. The crucial experience which opens the possibility of "existence" to us is that of "nothingness." Anxiety shatters the daily world of routine and draws us out of "the

[32] *Men against Humanity*, p. 106; *The Philosophy of Existence*, pp. 29-31.
[33] Jaspers, *Philosophie*, vol. ii, pp. 203-210.

world" and so toward freedom and self-hood.[34] It is important to realize that the sense of nothingness is neither a psychological nor a logical concept. Logicians have objected that nothingness is simply a misuse of a predicate.[35] Others, like Sartre, have tried to give "nothingness" a concrete meaning in describing it as "nausea" at one's own experiences. Actually, for Heidegger, and even for Jaspers, "nothingness" designates a mystical possibility, very close to the idea of a religious "rebirth," for it is in the face of nothingness that we grasp life authentically, that is, we start anew. But then even this is only partial, and we sink back into "the world" which is our fate rather than our home.

The unhappy consciousness is incapable of religion, and dissatisfied with philosophy. As for science, its attitude to it can well be imagined. This last of the three paths to an understanding of the world continues to be anathema to the romantic. Jaspers still supports Goethe against Newton, and he is the most moderate, by far. He at least refuses to deny the importance of science, and he even recognizes a certain ethical value in the method of scientific research.[36] But in general, existentialism is "a turning away from the what of things and science."[37] For the romantic, science can offer at best only a very partial view of reality. At worst, the scientist as an intellectual type is a social menace. "Science," André Malraux feels, "means Bikini."[38] To those "life-philosophers" who are

[34] Heidegger, "What Is Metaphysics," *loc.cit.*, pp. 364-368 and 374-375; *Sein und Zeit* (Tuebingen, 1953), pp. 184-191.

[35] A. J. Ayer's criticism of Sartre's use of the word "nothingness" applies to Heidegger as well, "Sartre," *Horizon*, vol. XII, 1945, pp. 12-26 and 101-110; E. L. Allen, *Existentialism from Within* (London, 1953), pp. 20-22.

[36] *Existentialism and Humanism*, pp. 4-5; *Reason and Anti-Reason in Our Time*, tr. by S. Godman (New Haven, 1952), pp. 27-37; *Rechenschaft*, pp. 204-220; *Origin and Goal*, p. 90.

[37] H. Arendt, "What Is Existenz Philosophy," *loc.cit.*, p. 38.

[38] A. Malraux, "Man and Artistic Culture," *loc.cit.*, p. 84; Aldous

overcome by the "tragic sense of life" science is simply insignificant because it is indifferent to death.[39] Ortega joins Unamuno in casting aside the very notion that science might ever know man. Its disregard of "the ultimate dramatic questions" makes it unimportant.[40]

The futility of science is thus added to the abstractness of philosophy and to the impossibility of religion in the view of the unhappy consciousness. The death of God has left man with no way of rendering the world comprehensible. The coherence of the outer universe has been destroyed, but man, freed from God, has not grown in stature. Nietzsche's superman is nowhere in sight. Instead, man has become fully conscious of his being as a victim—of "the world," of time, of death, of history, of society, of everything external to himself. Because all this is outside himself, it remains incomprehensible and out of man's reach. All philosophy can pretend to be now is an open admission of the failure of all understanding.

Man—Victim and Freedom

The world, indeed all external reality, encloses and defies man. It is in his ultimately futile defiance of these forces, however, that man finds himself and becomes "authentic." This is by no means a victory over circumstances. Man succeeds neither in transcending himself nor in altering "the world," but he may come to a realization and to an acceptance of his situation. Authenticity is the conscious recognition of victimhood, although it is by no means a resignation to that state.

Huxley, too, tends to see the scientist as dangerous and misguided, e.g. *Ends and Means* (London, 1946, pp. 266-269 and 276-277).

[39] M. de Unamuno, *Essays*, pp. 55-56 and 209.

[40] J. Ortega y Gasset, *Toward a Philosophy of History*, tr. by H. Weyl (New York, 1941), pp. 13-15, 178, 182-183, 185-186, 195-197; J. S. Villasenor, *Ortega y Gasset Existentialist*, tr. by J. Small (Chicago, 1949), p. 4.

"Romanticism," writes Alex Comfort, "(is) the belief in
the human conflict against the Universe and against power."
The romantic ethic is based on a radical sense of insecurity,
of common victimhood, of imminent death, and of "the hostility or the neutrality of the Universe."[41] This is of course, the
"silence" that Vigny had already observed, but the romantic
of today does not face it with his stoic attitude of resignation.
Nor has Prometheanism survived. The poet today finds his
hero in Sisyphus, the symbol of futile defiance, not in the
Titan.[42] Even philosophers who, like Marcel, disdain such outbursts against the absurdity of the universe see their task as
opposing "the world" and rising above it.[43] In philosophic
terms, the "absurd," the silent universe, simply becomes the
world of dead matter and of history. For Sartre this implies a
dialectical conflict between the "en soi," which is pure object,
and the "pour soi," man, who is pure freedom. The former
exists only to obstruct man, while man in his struggles against
the "en soi" discovers freedom—and its failures. At no time
can the outer world be integrated into human life. At best it
may be evaded.[44] In this respect, at least, the unhappy consciousness now resembles Christianity more than the romanticism of the last century, which so appreciated the creative vitality of nature.[45]

The fear of nature goes hand in hand with the knowledge
that destruction need not be followed by creation, that death
is absolutely final. The pointlessness of such a death, more
than its power, revolts the unhappy consciousness today. But
if the unhappy consciousness no longer expresses a longing
for death, as did earlier romantics, its aim is not really different; it is still to subordinate death to life. Today, however,

[41] *Art and Social Responsibility*, p. 18.
[42] A. Camus, *Le Mythe de Sisyphe* (Paris, 1942), pp. 163-168.
[43] Marcel, *Men Against Humanity*, pp. 85-89.
[44] Sartre, *L'Etre et le Néant*, pp. 115-149 and 219-271.
[45] Bollnow, *op.cit.*, pp. 37-38 and 48-49.

it has become clear that this is bound to fail. Man is the victim of death as part of his situation in a foreign universe. Just as we must oppose "the world," so must death be defied. By taking death into life we can "live authentically." In that way, death can play an almost creative role in our life. Heidegger holds that a resolute, heroic attitude toward death is our salvation from the false everyday ways of "anyone."[46] Jaspers regards death as one of the "ultimate situations" that open "existence" to us. True being, even genuine philosophy, becomes a conscious acceptance of death.[47] The great spiritual imperative of existentialism might well be, "live so as to prevent death from making your life meaningless at any given moment." Jaspers writes "Philosophy seeks to find a basis on which death is to be sure, not intellectually accepted, but borne in the turmoil of suffering, not with stoicism, but with loving and confident imperturbability."[48] To Camus art offers a similarly unconsoling means of living with death. His "rebellion," like Jaspers' "authentic-being," is ultimately a way of being a victim without self-pity or resignation. "I repeat Prometheus' defiance—but without illusions and hopes. . . . For all the science in the world cannot prove to me that this world is mine."[49]

Victimhood, then, is our lot in the natural world. That, however, is not all. The worst forms of misery are those which men inflict upon each other. Today we are again conscious of the full meaning of evil. Existentialism gives "a real role to evil," one of it adherents notes.[50] The origin of this new awareness is obvious. "Without totalitarianism," Hannah

[46] Heidegger, *Sein und Zeit*, pp. 295-301 and 382.

[47] Jaspers, *Philosophie*, vol. II, pp. 220-229; *The Way to Wisdom*, tr. by R. Manheim (New Haven, Conn., 1951), p. 53.

[48] *The Perennial Scope*, p. 160.

[49] *Le Mythe de Sisyphe*, pp. 130-135, 120-121 and 35 (my translations).

[50] S. de Beauvoir, *The Ethics of Ambiguity*, p. 34. See also J. P. Sartre, *What Is Literature*, tr. by B. Frechtman (New York, 1949), pp. 215-219.

Arendt observes, "we might never have known the truly radical nature of Evil."[51] However, this new sense of evil does not imply a return to the Christian conception of sin. The unhappy consciousness does not believe in redemption. "I share the Christians' horror of evil, but not their hopes," Camus explains.[52] The devil is among us again, but God is not.[53] In a sense we are the victims of even the evil we ourselves perpetrate. It is to be sure, not original sin, but "metaphysical guilt" which, according to Jaspers, we incur simply by being alive. Because we are born into the world and act within some given historical situation, we are bound to share in some of the evil done about us. His conclusion about German guilt is that all who were not killed are at least partially guilty.[54] This attitude is implicit in the new view of evil. Only the absolute victim escapes contamination. Only by suicide can we escape the evil in history.[55]

The universe, death, and evil threaten us everywhere, especially because they are utterly incomprehensible. Knowledge is, after all, the one way to make the world our own, and of this the "unhappy consciousness" despairs. It is, however, not only a matter of intellectual defeat. Ignorance has its comforts. The knowledge of evil, especially, has made it a relief to dispense with the old idea of human nature as something fixed—or knowable. The older romantic idea of self-creation already challenged the religious and philosophic conception of "man" as something definable. As Nietzsche saw, without a Creator, self-creation becomes man's first assertion of freedom, and so his disciples today still argue. To this, however, a far less

[51] The Origins of Totalitarianism, p. ix.
[52] Actuelles I, 1944-1948 (Paris, 1950), p. 213.
[53] A. Malraux, The Voices of Silence, tr. by S. Gilbert (New York, 1953), pp. 540-542.
[54] The Question of German Guilt, tr. by E. B. Ashton (New York, 1947), pp. 32-36 and 71-75.
[55] Von der Wahrheit, pp. 718-719.

ebullient thought has been added. If human nature were unalterably formed by external circumstances, then we really had all better commit suicide in despair. With this in mind, Jaspers urges us not to accept what happened in concentration camps as "the last word" on human nature.[56] In fact, he does not want to believe in the possibility of any "last word" on man or on his nature. Determinism in psychology and in history becomes thoroughly unattractive when the tendency of the inevitable seems so terrifying. Jaspers thus is bitterly opposed to Marx, Freud, and even to anthropology. Their claims to a complete knowledge of man are, to him, degrading in that they reduce man to a mere object of knowledge.[57] Man is always more than can be known of him. Indeed, the principle of causality, when applied to the study of man, cannot reveal the truth about him, and only tends to lower him to the level of things. Here Jaspers is quite at one with the romantic poet, Friedrich Georg Juenger, though he does not care to admit it.[58] In short, it is both depressing and demeaning to try to know man fully. To Jaspers there is even something "totalitarian" in seeking such knowledge. The meaning, not the facts, of human life should concern us.

For Jaspers the belief in self-creation is really a defence of the possible against the actual. Even those who try to find a more positive meaning in the idea of unfinished man admit that self-creation is bound to fail, for we remain tied to our situation. Though we are not determined by the outside world, we are still its victims. In Sartre's "coherent atheism" man is freed from God, the creator, as much as from objective de-

[56] Origin and Goal, p. 148.
[57] Man in the Modern Age, pp. 149-158; The Perennial Scope, pp. 59-61; Reason and Anti-Reason in Our Time, pp. 8-27; Rechenschaft, pp. 221-230.
[58] Existence and Humanism, pp. 68-73; Man in the Modern Age, pp. 146, 158-159 and 199; Origin and Goal, pp. 135-138; The Way to Wisdom, p. 63; F. G. Juenger, The Failure of Technology, tr. by F. D. Wieck (Hinsdale, Ill., 1949), pp. 51-56, 64-65 and 126.

terminants and from causality. This, to him, means that man becomes his own "project," that he "transcends" himself in planning his future being. From these premises Sartre, moreover, tries to deduce an ethical meaning. It is our "responsibility" to choose ourselves, and so to be free.[59] Epistemologically this is, of course, pure nonsense. The indeterminate state of human nature has nothing to do with freedom in the social sense. In any case, no norm, no "responsibility," can be deduced from this, or any other fact, about the nature of man. Moreover, Sartre does not believe in the realization of freedom at all, but only in the absence of rational causes. That we will fail in every attempt to be ourselves is quite certain, and our only real chance to prove our independence is to resort to "a death freely chosen."[60] Here there is none of the joy of self-creation that Ortega, for instance, as a representative of an older tradition can still feel. For him it is a matter of dramatic struggle, an artistic enterprise, like composing a novel, a proof that history dominates nature.[61] For the existentialist, however, freedom from a Creator or a settled nature implies no positive achievement. We cannot overcome, alter, or escape our "situation." Authenticity consists in realizing this and in facing up to it. Our "situation," however, continues to victimize us as much as do death and evil.

In most cases "situations" are historical. In Jaspers' words: "For good or ill, the individual is born into a situation; he has to take what is tradition and reality. No individual and no group can at one stroke, or even in a single generation change the conditions by which all of us live."[62] Sartre reduces man's

[59] L'Etre et le Néant, pp. 561-638; L'Existentialisme est un Humanisme (Paris, 1946), pp. 17-25, 33-39 and 94-95.
[60] S. de Beauvoir, The Ethics of Ambiguity, p. 32.
[61] Toward a Philosophy of History, pp. 108, 199-200, 203, and 217; J. S. Villasenor, op.cit., pp. 95 and 98.
[62] The Question of German Guilt, p. 35; Philosophie, vol. II, pp. 201-203.

freedom even more, because for him social situations are so important. In addition to the "human situation" of "death and mutability," he ceaselessly emphasizes class, nationality, and age as part of the external limits that enclose us. Liberty and victimhood respectively depend, moreover, on the number of situations to which we are exposed. The Jew, for example, is the victim of two situations: that of having the human situation thrust upon him, and then, of being "thrown into . . . abandoned to . . . the situation of a Jew."[63] In short, the non-existence of human nature and man's unknowability mean only that we are not "made." We remain prisoners of external conditions and are limited to making our own a fate we know to be nothing but an imposition from without, which we can "clarify" but never know; defy, but never alter.

Of all "situations," none is more impenetrable to the un-happy consciousness than history. Nowhere is Hegel's descrip-tion of the "alienated soul" more apt. History is a foreign intrusion upon the "self." Here again it is not only causal in-determinism that makes certain knowledge impossible, but such knowledge is itself not really very important since it is so remote to the "self." Not only are there no "laws of his-tory"; history itself is something eternally strange to us. The impersonal history of philosophy is meaningless to the "liv-ing" individual. The real battle is still the same as it was for Nietzsche—against historicism, against progressivism and evo-lutionary optimism. The whole philosophy of transcendence is a polemic against historicity. If it accepts history as at all rel-evant it is as something that can be internalized.[64] Objective history is as obstructive to "existence" as it was to Nietzsche's idea of "life." Only if we can make the persons and events of the past subjectively our own, can they have any existential im-

[63] *Anti-Semite and Jew*, tr. by G. J. Becker (New York, 1948), pp. 78-79 and 89.
[64] H. U. von Balthasar, *Apokalypse der Deutschen Seele*, vol. III (Salzburg-Leipzig, 1939), pp. 396-402.

portance. If they are inspiring, they can call us to "existence" now.[65] It is the present evocation of their memory, not their objective past, that matters. Assimilation as part of one's own life, not knowledge, is the end of historical studies. History can arouse and edify us, but it remains only a limited part of our personal reality.[66] In Heidegger's philosophy the entire breadth that Herder once imparted to the word history is lost. To him it does not even matter that man is part of world history. Only the subjective meaning of the fact that each person has a past, "a" history, is of interest.[67] Jaspers looks only for "meaning," not for facts, in his study of man's history.

Today even Hegelians, usually of the left persuasion, admit that there is a gap between "lived" and "thought" history, even though they are far from rejecting history as an objective "whole."[68] Their dream is to re-romanticize Hegel and to strip Marx of his materialism. For instance, Sartre regards Marxian determinism as reactionary because it deprives the worker of any motive for action. A rational, determined history, like a fixed human nature, is an intolerable limitation. History is meaningful only as part of our private situation, and within the context of our battle against that situation. As a barren system of causes and effects, it is altogether beyond us. For all his semi-Marxian verbiage Sartre believes, as Jaspers and every other romantic does, that the unique in history and creation cannot be understood causally. It follows that Hegel's and Marx's belief in an objectively comprehensible history is excluded. Only our individual visions of historical reality count. From the worker's "situation," history looks entirely different than it does from the bourgeois'. Thus Hannah Arendt, like

[65] Bollnow, op.cit., pp. 111-112.
[66] E.g., Jaspers, Philosophie, vol. ii, pp. 393-403.
[67] Sein und Zeit, p. 382-397.
[68] R. Caillois, "Le Monde Vécu et l'Histoire," in L'Homme, le Monde, l'Histoire (Cahiers du Collège Philosophique), (Grenoble et Paris, 1948), pp. 10-11.

Sartre, is led to assert that "the workers" were never anti-semitic because they "see history in terms of their struggle with the bourgeoisie." The bourgeois, according to Sartre, sees history as an expression of individual wills, again as a result of his particular situation.[69] The fact is that there is for existentialism no "general" history, and ultimately there are as many histories as there are human situations from which history can be seen and assimilated.

If a "general" history exists at all, it is either something entirely alien to the individual or simply a tale of personal failures.[70] For romantics today there can be no historical progress, because personal life does not progress. A purely material and scientific progress has never been appreciated by romantics. Aldous Huxley can still remind us that progress is something that may occur on the level of the species, but never on that of the individual.[71] In words reminiscent of a Schiller or a Wordsworth, Gabriel Marcel writes, "It would be no exaggeration to say that the more progress 'humanity' as an abstraction makes toward the mastery of nature, the more actual individual men tend to become slaves of this very conquest."[72] Stephen Spender recalls that even among the "pink" artists of the Thirties progress was more of a "desperate hope" than a real belief.[73]

Today, however, there is more than a mere disdain for the idea of progress. No laws of history are wanted any longer, for we do not really care to predict the future. Historical ig-

[69] H. Arendt, *The Origins of Totalitarianism*, p. 25; J. P. Sartre, *Anti-Semite*, pp. 35-37; *L'Existentialisme*, pp. 136-141; "Matérialisme et Révolution," *Situations III* (Paris, 1949), pp. 155-160, 194-195 and 209; S. de Beauvoir, *The Ethics of Ambiguity*, p. 147.

[70] R. Aron, "Remarques sur les Rapports entre Existentialisme et Marxisme," *L'Homme, le Monde, l'Histoire*, pp. 183-184.

[71] *Themes and Variations*, pp. 175-176. On other aspects of Huxley's romanticism, see D. Daiches, *The Novel in the Modern World* (Chicago, 1939), pp. 188-210.

[72] *Men against Humanity*, p. 41.   [73] *The Creative Element*, p. 32.

norance, like an indeterminate human nature, seems the only alternative to despair. It is only because we know nothing about the future, according to Marcel, that we are able to place a "wager" on it, and so keep going.[74] Jaspers too preaches that hopelessness must be eschewed, since, after all, we do not know the future.[75] If the distance between the individual and "general" history is made the basis of our attitude to history, then Toynbee's and Spengler's accounts of the rise and fall of civilizations become as empty as the old faith in progress. In fact, Huxley and Malraux have made a point of showing the remoteness of these theories from "lived" history, which allows them to salvage some extra-historical values and achievements from the march of destiny which has now become so threatening. The individual is thus disentangled from history. For both, art is the great symbol of human activity apart from history. The creative process is outside history. History can tell us nothing about it.[76] Jaspers can even find in the "exceptional individual," as such, a reminder of "the eternally non-historical ground of life."[77] Huxley has drawn up an impressive list of instances in our lives which remain untouched by history. Death, suffering, mystical religion, sleep, and sex are "enclaves of purest non-historicity."[78]

The negative aspects of this separation of the individual from history, however, outweigh its obvious attractions. The dreadfulness of the present age lies just in that it forces us all into this inherently foreign world of history. We have been "brutally reintegrated into history," Sartre reminds his fellow-intellectuals.[79] Freedom from history does not mean that his-

[74] *Men against Humanity*, p. 9.
[75] *Existentialism and Humanism*, p. 84.
[76] Huxley, *Themes and Variations*, pp. 61-64, 161-164, 208-209; Malraux, *The Voices of Silence*, pp. 614-629, 635 and 407-416.
[77] *Von der Wahrheit*, pp. 764-765.
[78] *Themes and Variations*, pp. 65-82.
[79] *What Is Literature?* p. 215.

tory cannot defeat us; our "situation" can crush us even if we feel ourselves to be outside it. The "historically-minded" have today triumphed over the "personally-minded," and they have made a world which rejects aesthetic and subjective values. Progress, or some sort of historical necessity, is the basis of all totalitarianism. The "wave of the future" has swamped every non-historical or non-social form of existence.[80] The intensity and prevalence of the unhappy consciousness today is not surprising in view of the crimes justified in the name of suprapersonal, historical reason. It is this which enrages the Christian Marcel no less than the atheist Camus, and so unites them. "Hitler," the latter remarks, "was history in its purest form."[81] In his beautiful defence of the eternally human values of indignation against revolutions justified by historical reason, we find again Kierkegaard's disgust at Hegel's bland systematization of evil. Totalitarianism has only intensified the romantic's sense of apartness from history. But in this extreme alienation lies also an admission of futility, for history is now too far from us to be even understood. It has joined the world of nature, death, and evil as one of the great external threats to our individuality, and as such it is beyond comprehension.

In addition to all these cold external powers, there is one more mighty abstraction to crush the individual—society. To a degree this is the old malady of poets, and many artists see themselves doomed to living in an "age of prose" today. But from the strict point of view of "existence," too, every natural community appears as mere mass keeping "the self" down.[82] The conflict between the isolated "one" and the social "many" becomes the one fundamental social situation for both the aesthete and for the existentialist. From this point of view all

[80] Huxley, *Ends and Means*, pp. 66-69; *Themes and Variations*, pp. 50-51.
[81] Camus, *The Rebel*, p. 150; Marcel, *Men against Humanity*, pp. 4-5.
[82] Bollnow, *op.cit.*, p. 48.

modern society is profoundly unsatisfactory. It is, however, worth noting that the cult of genius has lost much of its vigor. In the subdued and discouraged temper of the present it is a rather more modest battle between "the artist and society" or "the exception and the masses." Nevertheless, the sources of discomfort under both democratic and totalitarian conditions today are much the same as they were in the last century. Thus E. M. Forster can send up only two cheers for democracy; for, "estimable is mateyness, and the man who achieves it gives many a pleasant little drink to himself and to others. But it has no traceable connection with the creative impulse, and probably acts as an inhibition on it."[83] The trouble with democracy is that it tries to enforce "mateyness," which is bound to harm aesthetic life, for artists are important just because they are *not* average.

There are, of course, more serious complaints than this one. Materialism and progressivism, "the nonsense of democracy," still drive the artist into isolation, Spender feels.[84] But for him, as for Forster, solitude is an essential aspect of all artistic creativity. The creative vision owes no allegiance to society, just as it is outside history. After the illusions of the Thirties, Spender now regards society, as such, as a "destructive" element, and he now sympathizes with those poets who fled from it. "Genius had renounced or moved outside society, and any acceptance of a social concept that threatened individual isolation (was) destructive to its unique vision."[85] Spender accepts this as inevitable today. Indeed, he senses a general longing for "genius" to free us from society.[86] Not all artists are ready to see this as a permanent predicament. To Malraux it seems that this too is part of the death of God. Only when the artist and the "bourgeoisie" ceased to share a common tran-

---

[83] *Two Cheers for Democracy* (New York, 1951), pp. 92-93.
[84] *The Creative Element*, pp. 18-19.
[85] *Ibid.*, p. 12.
[86] *Ibid.*, p. 13.

scendental faith was it necessary for the former to shun society.[87] Sartre, with his penchant for semi-Marxist terms, speaks of the artist as "unclassed," deprived of a proletarian public by the dogmatism of the communists, and alienated from the "bourgeois" class of "oppressors," the class, in Malraux's words, "that left Verlaine and Gauguin abandoned in hospitals."[88]

The dramatic efforts of many intellectuals during the Thirties to join the masses can be explained only as a last effort to escape their social loneliness. It was usually an act of desperation. It is no ordinary feeling of isolation that makes a writer like André Gide note in his diary, after seeing a Chaplin movie: "Unique case where one can share the popular opinion. And no misunderstanding about it. You and I laugh at the same thing. It would be a shame to miss this possibility of communion. *It is good to be able not to scorn what the crowd admires.*"[89] However, the yearning for a return to the community ended in frustration. Today fear of the masses has widely replaced it. Ortega y Gasset speaks for more intellectuals now than ever before. It is he who from the first insisted on the total discrepancy between the intellectual and every other kind of person.[90] To him society in general is an evil, and he rejects liberalism because it forgets the conflict between the "one" and society.[91] This, of course, is the real quarrel between the liberal and the romantic attitude. For the latter, society is not something man-made; it is a foreign body which the individual simply "finds" there confronting him

[87] *The Voices of Silence*, pp. 483-496.

[88] *What Is Literature?* pp. 101 and 241-265. *The Case for De Gaulle, A Dialogue between André Malraux and James Burnham* (New York, 1948), p. 66.

[89] *The Journals of André Gide*, tr. by J. O'Brien (New York, 1948), vol. II, April 19, 1927, p. 397 (my italics).

[90] "Der Intellectuelle und der Andere," *Betrachtungen Ueber die Technik* etc., tr. by F. Schalk (Stuttgart, 1949), pp. 136-137.

[91] *Concord and Liberty*, p. 24.

against his will.[92] It is to this point of view that the "unhappy consciousness" always returns. We live, Huxley feels, on three levels, "the individual, the abstract and the conventional." These three never really meet. Man and society are separate entities, each enclosed in its own "watertight compartment," so that the relationship is necessarily one of "incommensurability."[93]

Nothing separates existentialism more from traditional philosophy than its appreciation of this "incommensurability." Indeed, social isolation is here made into an integral part of philosophy. For Jaspers the "exception" is as essential and as permanent a category as it was for Kierkegaard, but to this is added a sense of an unavoidable tension between the "self" and society, for society always regards the individual as a function and thus excludes transcendence and self-realization.[94] My "social I," that makes me part of "we all," is never my real "self." For that "self" is never what I achieve; that is only my value to society. In that light I remain undifferentiated and far from "existence."[95] Conventional life is always superficial, and to lose oneself in it is to fall into nothingness. To Jaspers it therefore seems that nothing less than some great act of loving charity can save us from an excessive horror of society, while still keeping us at a distance from it.[96] Society is, then, part of that "world" that draws us all down. But within society the "exception" is exposed to special difficulties. All societies tend to become mere masses, and the "exceptional man" is he who tries to combat this trend. He is above society by virtue of his uniqueness, yet within it, since he opposes its inclinations in the course of expressing his selfhood. He is, therefore a savior of society too. However, if Jaspers is far from

[92] *Ibid.*, p. 33.
[93] *Themes and Variations*, pp. 173-175, 166 and 56.
[94] *Philosophie*, vol. II, pp. 369-370.
[95] *Ibid.*, pp. 29-33.
[96] *Ibid.*, pp. 382-389.

worshiping genius, his "exception" is not Kierkegaard's apostle either. In naming three typical "exceptions" he can think only of Hoelderlin, Kierkegaard, and Nietzsche.[97]

Jaspers at least believes that, though it is a bitter necessity, the "self" must somehow accommodate itself to society. Heidegger, however, sees in social life a "fall" in a sense that has clearly been borrowed from Christianity. The decline into the average, the commonplace, is a depravity from which we must forcibly save ourselves.[98] Only a dramatic sense of our ultimate, least social experience, death, can pull us out of the social mire.[99]

"I tried to state the condition of the isolated self as the universal condition of all existence," Spender writes in his autobiography.[100] The "unhappy consciousness," whether poetic or reflective, always tends to express and to generalize its own condition. The ethics of individuality have in a dejected age become those of isolation.

Ethics: How to Live without God.

At first sight nothing could seem less promising than an attempt to devise an ethic for isolated individuals. Existentialism has, so far, done nothing to dispel this impression. Nevertheless, the unhappy consciousness longs for fellowship and continues to seek not only a social world for itself but also some system of values which will permit it to make relevant social judgments and decisions. But from the very first the unhappy consciousness really knows that it cannot succeed, for God is dead, and all the highest values went with Him. Moreover, existentialism has in its preoccupation with victimhood come to deny the reality of all those human relationships upon which systems of morality are explicitly or implicitly based.

[97] *Von der Wahrheit*, pp. 748-760, 762 and 831.
[98] *Sein und Zeit*, pp. 126-129.   [99] *Ibid.*, pp. 305-310.
[100] *World Within World* (New York, 1951), p. 231.

Where there is no common human nature and no natural community among men, it is difficult to imagine any ethics. For existentialism, human relations are either a matter of open hostility or of superficial and casual contacts. Some admit the possibility of genuine communication, but that involves only lonely souls calling to each other in a social void.[101] In any case, there is no spontaneous emotional ground for human relations. That, after all, is what estrangement, at its worst, really means.

For 19th-century romantics there had been two possibilities, either total solitude or the closed circle of like-minded friends. The end of both was, however, the same—to promote self-realization and individuality—and this continues to be the purpose of all social relations for romantics. Heidegger's "Mitsein," Marcel's "intersubjectivity," and Jaspers' "communication" are all ways of finding the "self" in others.[102] As for the position of total solitude, it is today best represented by Sartre. For him "the other" is always a rival simply because he is not "self."[103] All concrete human relations are forms of conflict.[104] Our consciousness of "the other" is always an effort to reduce him to an object. We "look at" him, and are in turn "looked at" by him. In every case we are regarded as mere objects, not as we see ourselves, as subjects.[105] Being together as "we" is never an integral part of our consciousness. "We" becomes a real experience only as "we object," where "we" have been made into things together by a third party.[106] Only in oppression do we find association. The origin of Sartre's affection for the oppressed classes and for revolutionary politics becomes quite clear here. Only in some

[101] Bollnow, op.cit., pp. 49-51.
[102] Heinemann, op.cit., pp. 146-147.
[103] Allen, op.cit., pp. 62-67.
[104] L'Etre et le Néant, pp. 428-431.
[105] Ibid., pp. 310-368.
[106] Ibid., pp. 484-503.

dramatic act of revolt against a common enemy do we find each other bearable. At all other times, "Hell is other people," as one of his characters says.[107] Sexual perversion, masochism, and sadism provide the usual pattern for our behavior. Either we try to force "the other" to be a mere thing, or we make that our own condition.[108]

By no means do all existentialists share Sartre's gloomy view of human relations. Heidegger, for instance, regards "being together" as an essential part of our condition (Dasein). But this has nothing to do with the actual presence or absence of others. It is merely our consciousness of others, manifesting itself as "care" about them. Potentially "the other" is, however, a danger to us in our quest for "being," for our relations with him may degenerate into a mere routine, and so become a means of evading our obligation to reach authentic selfhood.[109] Here we find the core of all existentialist ethics. It is simply the notion that authentic selfhood is the sole and the highest value. For Sartre "others" matter only to the degree that they obstruct it. To Heidegger they are indifferent as long as they do not do so. For Marcel and Jaspers, "the other" may be a positive help in achieving it. In no case is "the other" an absolute end in himself.

Certainly Gabriel Marcel does not share Sartre's view of "the other." For him "we" is a real possibility, the result of making a gift of oneself. It is to open oneself to others, to place oneself "at their disposal." Communion with others is possible by "calling out," to a fellow traveller, by self-sacrifice, by an act of charity.[110] But what it is not is also quite obvious. It is neither an act of reason nor a spontaneous feeling. That is why it does not break through the inherent tension between

[107] In Camera, tr. by S. Gilbert (London, 1946), p. 166.
[108] L'Etre et le Néant, pp. 431-484.
[109] Sein und Zeit, pp. 117-126.
[110] The Philosophy of Existence, pp. 73-76 and 25-29.

the "I" and the "other." It is a Christian's way of reaching "existence," or a dramatic effort to extend one's subjectivity. This is equally true of Jaspers' celebrated doctrine of "communication," which Marcel admires so much. This, too, is a quasi-religious experience of two lonely souls finding selfhood in each other.[111] Communion with God is, in fact, transferred to the human level—an impression that is strengthened by the assertion that death and absence do not end "communication."[112] Far from being the antithesis of solitude, communication is in fact based upon a loneliness that it preserves, for self-realization requires aloneness as much as it needs communion. Nor can it provide a basis for any general ethic. "Communication" is always a unique experience, beyond all generalizations, apart from all social forms.[113] It is ultimately a part only of the mystical road to "existence," a task, more than a realization of a relationship. It demands "a leap," an intense spiritual effort—like communion with God—and as such it is a rarity, especially today.[114]

If the only two possible kinds of human contact are a duel or an act of religious devotion, then ethics become superfluous. It is futile to demand that,

> "You shall love your crooked neighbor
> With your crooked heart."[115]

Rules of morality are not applicable to mystical experiences. The death of God has, moreover, added other difficulties. Whatever the relations of "the self" to "the other" may involve in terms of effort, we have no outside guides to help us in building or in judging them. As for all romantics, the sole

[111] *Philosophie*, vol. II, pp. 60-64; *The Perennial Scope*, pp. 166-167 and 180-183.
[112] *Philosophie*, vol. II, pp. 221-222.
[113] *Ibid.*, pp. 97 and 427-429.
[114] *Ibid.*, pp. 51-52; *The Way to Wisdom*, pp. 24-25.
[115] W. H. Auden, *Collected Poetry* (New York, 1945), p. 198.

ethical question asked is, "How shall I live in relation to my-self?" Today, in the absence of God, the only answer is, "In any way I choose." To choose oneself becomes the first law, then, of a new moral code, of the ethics of authenticity.

In Heidegger's case there really is only one imperative: to face death resolutely and so achieve genuine selfhood. This alone saves us from the fall into the commonplace.[116] For Sartre the question is rather more complex since, unlike Heidegger, he does not regard death as the only important "situation" we face. How is one to deal with the numerous social and political situations that surround one? What does it mean to be "doomed" to make one's own values, since God has not created them? In essence Sartre's answer is the same as Heidegger's. Make a virtue out of necessity, and do it consciously and bravely. To be authentic then means that we must "choose" our situation, as well as being simply committed to it.[117] Since we are fated in any case to find no prefabricated values we must *never* accept any from outside. In short, the act of choosing is what separates the "authentic" man from the "sub-men" who have "annihilated subjectivity" by acts of "bad faith" in allowing others to provide them with values.[118] In practice this always seems to mean that only dramatic, violent, and exceedingly unconventional behavior is to be condoned. For instance the "class war" provides the contemporary author with his situation, and with the object of his choice.[119] Again, Simone de Beauvoir finds the Marquis de Sade an exemplary character because he

[116] *Sein und Zeit*, pp. 252-267, 289-301 and 382; Bollnow, *op.cit.*, pp. 69-73 and 90-92; M. Grene, "Authenticity: An Existential Virtue," *International Journal of Ethics*, vol. LXII, 1952, pp. 266-274.

[117] *L'Etre et le Néant*, pp. 605-608 and 638-642. This he feels, is particularly necessary for social victims, such as Jews.

[118] *Ibid.*, pp. 85-111; Beauvoir, *Ethics of Ambiguity*, pp. 45-46 and 47-51.

[119] Sartre, *What Is Literature?* pp. 276-277.

tried to make an ethic out of his situation as a sexual pervert, and so "broke through the banality of everyday life."[120] Sartre reproaches Baudelaire for having failed to do this, for having misbehaved without asserting that his actions were also ethically valid.[121] For "the genuine man will not agree to recognize any foreign absolute."[122]

Ultimately there must, it seems, be as many systems of value as there are situations, that is, people. This implication of the ethics of authenticity appears in all existentialist writers, even those who have no liking for the outrageous. Even the Christian Gabriel Marcel finds conformism of any kind detestable, and abjures all general moral rules—for the good old romantic reason that every case is unique.[123] The mild-tempered Jaspers is not above raising the ideal of the heroic "lonely doer."[124] In Ortega, indeed, the ethics of authenticity become ridiculous. Freedom means only the freedom to be oneself.[125] Society is the creature of inauthenticity, and thus to be quite disregarded.[126] It follows that a man who is meant to be a thief, but who decides to be honest, is false to himself, in fact, immoral. Conversely, a "great man" is *ipso facto* above common morality.[127] Again, in the novels of André Malraux, individual heroism alone illuminates an utterly bleak world, but it is the heroism of despair that knows that it will inevitably meet disaster.

For all its pugnacious sound, the ethics of authenticity remain those of complete futility. They do not allow us to alter

[120] *Must We Burn De Sade?* tr. by A. Michelson (London, 1953), pp. 13 and 81.
[121] *Baudelaire*, tr. by M. Turnell (New York, 1950), pp. 50-52.
[122] Beauvoir, *Ethics of Ambiguity*, p. 14.
[123] *Men against Humanity*, pp. 304 and 18.
[124] *Man in the Modern Age*, pp. 170-173.
[125] *Toward a Philosophy of History*, p. 57; Villasenor, *op.cit.*, p. 102.
[126] *Concord and Liberty*, p. 108.
[127] Villasenor, *op.cit.*, pp. 110-111 and 117.

our "situation," only to assert it.[128] They do not bring us closer to our fellow men. Yet the "unhappy consciousness" longs for some measure of human solidarity. The ethics of authenticity, however, are at best an instrument of personal liberation. They provide no basis for stable freedom, nor for community. The effort of French thinkers to use it as a rationalization for their revolutionary sympathies has, therefore, ended in the most childish inconsistencies. It is now argued that though we do not share a common nature, we do live in a "human situation" which enables us to act together.[129] Moreover, it now seems that in the very act of choosing an action I assert its general validity.[130] But since this is an "outside" value for every other person, this can hardly make any difference. Nevertheless, it is asserted that these general implications of my choice commit me to a responsibility for all mankind—especially in matters of politics. Thus because I desire my freedom, I at once desire the freedom of all mankind. Actually, however, it is hard to see that this responsibility can mean anything but a subjective sensation, since all values are only emanations of personal states, and valid only for their originators. Responsibility can no more be a universally valid norm than Ortega's "thiefhood" could be. Logically and ethically this new discovery of mankind is nonsense. It does, however, correspond to a real experience. Freedom as "absolute solitude (and) total responsibility" was a sensation felt by many intellectuals in the resistance movement.[131] It was for them the first experience of social solidarity, yet it also provided an opportunity for dramatic revolt. Thus Sartre writes:

[128] For instance, the "authentic" Jew can do nothing about antisemitism, Sartre, *Anti Semite*, p. 151.
[129] *L'Existentialisme est un Humanisme*, pp. 67-71.
[130] *Ibid.*, pp. 24-28 and 71-79.
[131] Sartre, *Baudelaire*, p. 69.

"Jamais nous n'avons été plus libres que sous l'occupation allemande. Nous avions perdu tous nos droits et d'abord celui de parler; . . . à cause de tout cela nous étions libres. Puisque le venin nazi se glissait jusque dans notre pensée, chaque pensée juste était une conquète . . . chacun de nos gestes avait le poids d'un engagement. Les circonstances souvent atroces de notre combat nous mettaient enfin a même de vivre, sans fard et sans voile, cette situation déchirée, insoutenable qu'on appelle la condition humaine. . . . Et le choix que chacun faisait de lui-même était authentique puisqu'il se faisait en présence de la mort. . . . Ainsi la question même de la liberté était posée et nous étions au bord de la connaissance la plus profonde que l'homme peut avoir de lui-même. Car le secret d'un homme, ce n'est pas son complexe d'Oedipe ou d'infériorité, c'est la limite même de sa liberté, c'est son pouvoir de résistance aux supplices et à la mort. . . . (Ceux) qui eurent une activité clandestine . . . ne combattaient pas au grand jour, comme des soldats, traqués dans la solitude, arrêtés dans la solitude, c'est dans le délaissement, dans le dénuement le plus complet qu'ils résistaient. . . . Pourtant, au plus profond de cette solitude, c'étaient les autres, tous les autres, tous les camarades de résistance qu'ils défendaient. . . . Cette responsabilité totale dans la solitude totale, n'est-ce pas le dévoilement même de notre liberté?"[132]

The maquis has become the symbol of the one form of valid social action even among English writers.[133] The romantic can find meaning in social life only in such "extreme situations" as the war and the Resistance offered the French intellectuals. However, at all other times authentic action means action directed only at the self and, logically, no social rules can be derived from it. There is no reason to suppose

---

[132] "La République du Silence," *Situations III*, pp. 11-13.
[133] Comfort, *Art and Social Responsibility*, p. 23.

with Camus that when a slave revolts he is asserting the freedom of mankind rather than just rebelling against his personal oppressor.[134] Authenticity does not lead to cooperation; in fact, it militates against it. Jaspers alone remains consistent in insisting that though communion is possible only among free persons, this is a freedom that is not at all social. Its end is mystic union and selfhood. Indeed, he feels that freedom cannot be grasped sociologically at all.[135]

Recently the helplessness of this philosophy of meaninglessness in the face of the hard ideologies of totalitarianism has become clear to many romantics. In the case of Sartre and his followers, it led to an ill-digested claim of affinity to Kant, Fichte, and Hegel.[136] Jaspers has, indeed, since 1933 tried to narrow the gap between "existence" and reason, and today, in his concern for politics, he feels that a return to the philosophic tradition of Plato and Kant is our first need. "Vernunft," not just the immoderate quest for "existence," is now to be the real basis of philosophy.[137] But it is too soon to say where this will lead him. Aldous Huxley long ago noted the difficulties that his generation faced after the Twenties. The philosophy of meaninglessness had freed them from conventionality, especially from sexual conventions, but that was not enough. It was followed by despair and by an acceptance of "tough" ideologies. Only people who were personally highly creative, Huxley concludes, could afford such a mood at all.[138] It is to the values of creation, to aesthetic idealism, that those who find the bare ethics of authenticity insufficient are

[134] The Rebel, pp. 20-25; R. Wollheim, "The Political Philosophy of Existentialism," The Cambridge Journal, vol. VII, 1953, pp. 3-19.
[135] Philosophie, vol. II, p. 57; Rechenschaft, pp. 304-307.
[136] E.g., Ethics of Ambiguity, pp. 16-17.
[137] Allen, op.cit., pp. 100-101; Bollnow, op.cit., pp. 113-114; K. Jaspers, "The Importance of Nietzsche, Marx and Kierkegaard in the History of Philosophy," tr. by S. Godman, Hibbert Journal, vol. 49, 1950-1951, pp. 226-234; Von der Wahrheit, p. 969.
[138] Ends and Means, pp. 273-276.

now returning. This or a return to traditional philosophy seem to be the only available alternatives.

Certainly the attractions of violent action have now diminished for many intellectuals, and at present even the despair over our absurd fate seems to be less intense. Camus, for one, admits that he is less despondent today and that he has emerged from the nihilism of the interwar years to recognize the creative values of art.[139] Moreover, the "unhappy consciousness" is quite aware of its reasons for turning to art. What was implicit in 19th-century romanticism has become perfectly clear today. Camus knows that it is the impossibility of living without either God or the rationalist values that has driven him to the values of creativity.[140] Spender speaks openly of poetry as a substitute for religion.[141] André Malraux regards art as the sole surviving value, occupying the place that reason and justice did in the last century.[142] Even Gabriel Marcel finds a positive basis for hope in artistic creation, rather than solely in his religious faith.[143]

For these romantics art has also a liberating function. "From art," Spender writes, "society may even learn to some extent to escape from its own prison."[144] His revulsion against Marxism was, above all, disgust at its literary principles, and the subordination of art to political purposes. The real value of art for the romantic is that it allows him to remain outside "abstract" society, and yet to contribute to it in a significant way. As a defence against "absurdity" in the universe and in society, art acquires an ethical value. In short, we are

[139] *Actuelles II, 1948-1953* (Paris, 1953), pp. 9-12 and 35-36; *The Rebel*, p. 237.

[140] *The Rebel*, pp. 103-104, 114 and 195, *Actuelles II*, pp. 39-49.

[141] *The Creative Element*, p. 176.

[142] *The Voices of Silence*, pp. 525-530 and 540-542 and 635. See also his novel *The Walnut Trees of Altenburg*, tr. by A. W. Fielding (London, 1952), p. 96.

[143] *The Philosophy of Existence*, pp. 20-21.

[144] *The God that Failed*, p. 267.

with Shelley's Prometheus again. Painting, Malraux observes, is the true expression of man's revolt against his fate and his victory over destiny. It alone links us to an enduring quality in man, across the changing ages and cultures and within an indifferent universe. Today, moreover, it has a specific social meaning too, as an indictment of a tainted world.[145] As the sole living value it indeed imposes a social duty upon us. Having abandoned violent revolutionary action, Malraux has now turned to "cultural democracy." The first task of politics, he explained to an earnest and obviously puzzled James Burnham, is to make art available to all through the widest possible display of good reproductions.[146]

Camus goes even farther. He not only shares Malraux's sentiments; he gives them an even more specific social meaning. Artistic creation is for him both a form of metaphysical rebellion and the eternal ally of the oppressed. As Comfort puts it, the function of art is to provide "voices for all those who have not voices."[147] Workers and artists, writes Camus, are natural allies, the only two genuine aristocracies. The first task today is to allow workers to become creators.[148] In England, Sir Herbert Read, and now Comfort, have been preaching this gospel for some time. "To hell with culture," Sir Herbert cries, by which he means that a culture limited to professional artists and existing apart from daily work is worthless.[149]

For the aesthetic idealist the death of God is not fatal. In creativity, in art, and in work he has found a new source of universal and social meaning. Art provides values that are emo-

[145] *The Voices of Silence*, pp. 317, 320 and 359, 600-602 and 630-642.
[146] *The Case for De Gaulle*, pp. 68-69.
[147] *Art and Social Responsibility*, p. 38.
[148] *The Rebel*, pp. 179-180, 185-187, 222-245.
[149] H. Read, *The Politics of the Unpolitical* (London, 1943), pp. 47-73; *Poetry and Anarchism* (London, 1938); A. Comfort, *Art and Social Responsibility*, p. 31.

tionally satisfying and that have an evident social purpose, but as a basis of politics this sort of romanticism remains as useless as it was in the 19th century. For to create beauty is the sole duty art can recognize—and this remains a task very much outside that of the "citizen."

Political Anarchism: The End of Revolution

The ethics of authenticity recognize no duty to "others." The ethics of beauty demand nothing but creativity. Neither, it would seem, permits a generally valid *system* of ethics. Their relevance for politics would appear to be, if anything, even less. Yet the modern romantic is not overtly indifferent to politics, although political life involves forms of action which he detests and wants to avoid or transform. Indeed, it is hardly surprising that those who find their values solely in creativity should be apolitical. Sir Herbert Read, and now Comfort, openly declare their anarchism. However, anarchism or, to be more precise, a dislike of politics, prevails in existentialist thought as well. What, after all, is more entirely of "the world" than politics? However, "the world" of today is not that of the early days of romanticism. No one now feels justified in waving politics aside with one gesture as a Schlegel so easily could. Moreover, the sporadic desire to find self-expression in political activity still animates romantic souls. The Byronic impulse is by no means dead. The difficulty is that it has led to involvements of a rather more complex kind than Byron's Greek venture. The participation in, and subsequent disillusion with, totalitarian movements has reinforced the unhappy consciousness. Not only God and Marx but all political hopes are dead. That is what Koestler meant when he noted that the "pink" decade was followed by a "Yogi" decade.[150] For the romantic, politics remain futile,

[150] A. Koestler, *The Yogi and the Commissar* (New York, 1946), p. 7.

and this keeps alive the old paradox of "the politics of the unpolitical."

For the old-fashioned anarchist there is a very clear conflict between "the man" and "the citizen." All political institutions are only so many means of transforming the former into the latter. All are "intervening abstractions" that prevent us from recognizing each other as individuals.[151] From this point of view there is naturally little to choose between democracy and totalitarianism. All modern governments are pernicious. The totalitarian variety reaches the "epitome of a barbarism" that is inherent in all the "megalopolitan" societies of our day, for all power structures manipulate, rather than express, the spirit of a people.[152] And this is unavoidable.[153] Only artists can provide leadership that is expressive, and not repressive.

This is an extreme attitude, but it lies at the heart of all contemporary romanticism. One of the accusations that Ortega brings against liberalism is that it forgot the violence inherent in politics.[154] It follows that to him all political activity seems degrading, especially for the intellectual, whose function he sees as the very opposite of that of the politician. His great fear is that politics will absorb the whole man today.[155] This thought terrifies all romantics. Thus both Huxley and Gabriel Marcel feel that the very essence of totalitarianism is the reduction of men to mere citizens.[156] The use of the word "citizens" is significant, for citizens are just what the subjects of totalitarian regimes cannot be. It is only in

[151] A. Comfort, The Novel and Our Time (London, 1948), p. 19; The Pattern of the Future (London, 1949), pp. 27-28.

[152] Read, Politics of the Unpolitical, p. 13; Comfort, Art and Social Responsibility, pp. 16, 24 and 84.

[153] Read, Politics of the Unpolitical, pp. 31-33.

[154] Concord and Liberty, p. 26.

[155] Ibid., pp. 51-52; Toward a Philosophy of History, pp. 70-71.

[156] Huxley, Themes and Variations, p. 86; Marcel, "Préface" à La Vingt-Cinquième Heure de V. Gheorghiu (Paris, 1949), p. 5.

the eyes of a romantic that the citizen and the subject seem alike, that citizenship is onerous and law a coercive force, indistinguishable from arbitrary rule. These feelings are evident even in the most moderate, accommodating romantics. For instance, it is a great cause of dejection for Jaspers that no one today can escape politics or the state, however much he may wish to.[157] For not only is there something "dreadful" in the sphere of the state but "communication" can never take place there. Politics may, he recognizes, serve as a means of self-realization to some individuals. In general, however, the world of power relations and of public life excludes "existence" and threatens the individual.[158] This is especially true today, when politics have become a matter of leaderless masses. Still, Jaspers dolefully insists, one must concern oneself with this mess. Today, sobered even more by the experience of Nazism, he tries to adopt a rather more positive attitude toward political action. He has come to believe, for instance, that it is possible for the individual to achieve an inner balance between authority and freedom.[159] He has also adopted a rather conventional conservative liberalism in which Hayek, Lippmann, and Roepke have been his avowed guides.[160] In the Thirties, however, he lamented that politics had ceased to be exciting: "Thus the political destiny of all would seem to be a lack of destiny, for destiny only exists when selfhood grasps life, takes life over by its activity, realises itself, and dares."[161]

There we have as clear an example as any of a basic distaste for all politics combined with a desire to exploit the political

[157] Jaspers, *Existentialism and Humanism*, pp. 77-81; *The Question of German Guilt*, p. 62.
[158] *Man in the Modern Age*, pp. 87-94; *Philosophie*, vol. I, pp. 102-105 and 386-389; *Rechenschaft*, p. 294.
[159] *Von der Wahrheit*, pp. 797-799.
[160] *The Origin and Goal*, pp. 157-193 and 281-283.
[161] *Man in the Modern Age*, p. 102.

world as a means for self-expression. As is only too well known, many intellectuals have tried far more actively than Jaspers to explore the possibilities of such politics. Not the least ironic aspect of this situation is that often it is "the party" that rejects these aspiring revolutionaries, for it often knows sooner than they do the full incompatibility of romanticism with all discipline—especially with the totalitarian variety. The experiences of many leftist intellectuals have been told often enough now to be universally known. The encounters between some German romantics and the Nazis were no less instructive. Heidegger attempted to give his philosophy a Nazi slant, simply by translating his ultimate value, self-realization, into the right of the German people "to will itself."[162] However, these expressions of political enthusiasm lasted for only a year, for Nazi politics, quite obviously, were a part of that despised everyday routine existence in which no one "wills himself," as anyone familiar with the pages of Sein und Zeit could have told their author.[163] In many ways the story of Gottfried Benn, the expressionist poet, is even more interesting, and sadder. To him it seemed that the Nazis would give "form"—a purely

[162] M. Heidegger, Die Selbstbehauptung der Deutschen Universitaet (Breslau, 1934), p. 22.

[163] Whether Heidegger's philosophy is or is not compatible with Nazism has become the subject of a heated debate. Those who feel that romantic despair "leads" to totalitarianism tend to regard him as a "bad influence" and so an aid to the Nazis. E.g., K. Loewith, Heidegger: Denker in Duerftiger Zeit (Frankfurt am Main, 1953), pp. 49-55; "Les Implications Politiques de la Philosophie de l'Existence Chez Heidegger," tr. by J. Rovan, Les Temps Modernes, vol. II (2), 1946, pp. 343-360. However, interpretation in terms of oblique inferences is never convincing. The entire romantic spirit of Heidegger's philosophy is apolitical, and especially remote from the life of a totalitarian state or party. One must simply separate the man from the philosophy in this case. P. Kecskemeti, "Existentialism, a New Trend in Philosophy," Modern Review, vol. I, 1947, pp. 34-51; A. de Waehlens, "La Philosophie de Heidegger et le Nazisme," Les Temps Modernes, vol. II (5), 1947, pp. 115-127; E. Weil, "Le Cas Heidegger," ibid., pp. 128-138.

aesthetic concept—to the German people, and as a poet he wanted to participate in this good work. To his infinite surprise the Nazis not only rejected his services but persecuted him as a "decadent" artist, so that he was among the first to emigrate in an "aristocratic way," by joining the army.[164] Today Benn has turned his back on all politics, on the usual romantic grounds that they are anti-artistic. Now he limits himself entirely to the aesthetic sphere, as the only sphere that can leave us above time, above history, and, one might add, above our own political follies.[165]

In spite of these and so many similar instances, this is still the age of Garine, the hero of Malraux's *The Conquerors*, who joins the Chinese uprising in order to give his personal life some meaning, only to find himself in hopeless conflict with the demands of a revolution methodically planned and organized in Moscow. For, whatever the objective implications of revolutions may be, they can still be a source of personal inspiration to some romantics. "Revolution," to Simone de Beauvoir, "is an end in itself."[166] That, for instance explains why a non-communist magazine of the left, such as Sartre's *Les Temps Modernes*, does not devote a single page to the concrete reforms of socialist governments, but dwells only upon revolutionary situations, colonialism, and the class war. It represents the politics of "extreme situations" and of dramatic violence, in much the same way as Sartre's ethics express them. Politics are defined as revolution, in fact, as "transcending the present toward the future." The man who tries only to maintain something already in existence has no political life, it is claimed. Moreover, this transcendence must be self-projection toward others, indeed toward all humanity.[167]

---

[164] G. Benn, *Doppelleben* (Wiesbaden, 1950), pp. 49-73 and 77-126; *Ausdruckswelt* (Wiesbaden, 1949), pp. 5-31.
[165] *Doppelleben*, pp. 187-206.
[166] *Existentialisme et la Sagesse des Nations*, p. 81.
[167] *Ibid.*, pp. 78, 87 and 88-89; *Ethics of Ambiguity*, p. 91.

This, however, has nothing to do with any form of institutional or organized action. Indeed, Simone de Beauvoir has given us a very clear account of the difference between violence as part of a direct, personal act of vengeance, for example, and a death sentence imposed by a court of law. The former is, in her eyes, justified by its immediacy, its emotional meaning. The latter, however, is entirely repugnant to her, because it is social and abstract, and always remote from the individuals involved. "We may kill, but not judge," she concludes.[168]

That such an outlook should be utterly incompatible with the ideology and practices of the Communist Party should seem obvious enough.[169] It is not, however, apparent to Sartre and Simone de Beauvoir, who seem to live in hopeful expectation of finding their haven there. The unhappy consciousness consists in just this: that it cannot bear its self-created estrangement from all stable social organizations. In the last century it ended by forcing itself into the church or into militaristic nationalism. Today it is left with two choices: to live on the fringes of some unreceptive totalitarian party or to recognize its situation of revolutionary futility. Such acts of self-awareness are what really distinguishes the unhappy consciousness today. As the philosopher Merleau-Ponty, one of Sartre's former collaborators, puts it, it has become impossible to be either pro- or anti-communist.[170] "The tragedy of our generation," Camus adds, "is to have seen a false hope."[171] The end of 19th-century revolutions and class wars in barbaric societies is clear to him, as it is Comfort.[172] With them have gone all utopian hope. The time of the apocalypse is past, we are

[168] *Existentialisme et la Sagesse des Nations*, pp. 125-165.

[169] R. Aron, "Remarques sur les Rapports entre Existentialisme et Marxisme," *loc.cit.*, pp. 165, 180-181, 190-191, 193-195.

[170] M. Merleau-Ponty, *Humanisme et Terreur* (Paris, 1947), pp. xvii; Camus, *Actuelles I*, pp. 48-52.

[171] Camus, *ibid.*, p. 236.

[172] *Authority and Delinquency*, pp. 86, 89 and 93-94; *Art and Social Responsibility*, pp. 29-30.

in the era of mediocre organization"—and not only mediocre, for *all* governments are criminal today, too.[173]

For Camus and all genuine romantics it has become vital to separate their revolutionary urges from the historic and organized revolutions of our time. It is thus not just violence, but "comfortable" violence, violence from a distance, above all, reasoned violence that has become detestable.[174] Rational revolutions are, moreover, not only cruel; they are anti-artistic.[175] But above all, the logic on which ideological revolutions base themselves is emotionally repugnant to the romantic—both to a radical like Camus and to a conservative like Gabriel Marcel. "I am not opposed to logic," the former notes," but to ideology which substitutes a succession of reasons for every living reality."[176] Marcel adds that the real horror of totalitarian atrocities lies in their being "a barbarism based on reason."[177] In America, too, Hannah Arendt has made this point. To her the "logicality" of totalitarian ideology is so important a factor that she would call totalitarian government, "logocracy."[178] Abstract logic never appealed to a romantic.

To sum up, then, politics, whether they take the form of law and stable institutions or of ideological and organized revolution, are incompatible with romanticism. All politics are mere barriers to genuine personal relationships. If there is such a thing as a romantic political theory today, it consists in rejecting all historically possible forms of political life. There, as everywhere else, the spirit of futility is dominant, for this uncongenial political world cannot be fled or altered. Indeed, it can hardly be understood. The actual is too foreign to the

[173] Camus, *Actuelles I*, pp. 48-52.
[174] *Ibid.*, pp. 184 and 200.
[175] *The Rebel*, pp. 77-78 and 215-223.
[176] *Actuelles II*, pp. 660-61.
[177] *Men against Humanity*, p. 73.
[178] *Totalitarianism*, ed. by C. J. Friedrich (Cambridge, Mass., 1954), pp. 133-134.

unhappy consciousness to be grasped. The world of power and of social institutions is neither interesting, acceptable, nor comprehensible, because it is too distant from the individual. Such changes as might be made by the application of external power do not concern the romantic, for only internal life and the free expression of creative instinct really matter, and there politics are meaningless.

The State of Man: Technology and the Mass Order

History and politics are, then, incomprehensible, nor can either provide meaningful experiences for the individual except on rare "extreme" or dramatic occasions. Their only significance lies in their impact upon the inner life of the individual. The romantic, therefore, does not analyze the present historical situation in terms of causes and effects, which he regards as inhibiting concepts, nor indeed, in any objective terms. All he asks is, "What does the outer world mean to the individual today?" The outer world is always taken as something essentially strange and hostile to the self. The vital thing about the present, to the unhappy consciousness, is that the external world has reached new heights of strangeness and danger, for it is now composed of two forces, technology and the masses, the material and human incarnations respectively of all that is impersonal, abstract, and general. To the unhappy consciousness "the world" is always a prison, but today it appears more so than ever. All the particular manifestations of the age, such as totalitarianism, are not really independent occurrences; they are only reflections of the general condition of this threatening world. Romanticism from the first was a protest against an entire civilization, and that is what it has remained. Whether expressed in open polemic or in an apparently calm description of the "human situation" today, romanticism always presents an indictment of a culture that disregards the emotional and aesthetic needs of the individual.

In its general approach, the unhappy consciousness does not differ materially from its 19th-century predecessor. For the latter the "trivial, Unhappy City, the desert of the average," to use Auden's phrase, was already the focus of resentment, and he is quite at one with them in his hatred of the world of the "churls," of the urban masses.[179] That man has become a mere function of the division of labor has been the chief complaint of romantics since Schiller's time, and never more so than today. That is the real sin of technology. That is what Comfort means when he speaks of "the industrial abolition of humanity," and protests against "megalopolitan cities" inhabited by mere "onlookers" incapable of any creativity, because they can only mutely obey Captain Bligh in the form of a fragmented, mechanized order.[180] Camus echoes these sentiments in his complaints that production, not creation, dominates our activity.[181] The demands of functional society have obliterated the difference between man and thing, Marcel objects, in much the same words that Coleridge once used.[182] Or, as the most embittered enemy of technology, Friedrich Georg Juenger, puts it, man and thing differ only as long as both are not covered by the concept of function.[183] For it is not just the machine, but the subordination of the individual to the demands of the division of labor on which technology depends, that is so horrifying to the romantic.[184]

To this a new evil has been added. The great intellectual disaster of the age, for many people, is that universal knowledge has become impossible. The fact that no one today can

[179] The Enchafèd Flood, p. 26; "Introduction" to Baudelaire, Intimate Journals, pp. 13-28.
[180] Art and Social Responsibility, pp. 20, 27 and 31.
[181] The Rebel, pp. 189-190 and 240.
[182] The Philosophy of Existence, pp. 1-3.
[183] Maschine und Eigentum (Frankfurt-am-Main, 1949), pp. 128-129.
[184] The Future of Technology, pp. 59-60 and 74-78; Camus, The Rebel, p. 262.

feel, as Aristotle, St. Thomas Aquinas, and even Voltaire well could, that they knew all that was to be known, has provided a new inspiration to the unhappy consciousness. For, though the hope of universality has gone forever, the idea of partial knowledge remains unpalatable—hence the hatred of specialists, of the "barbarian engineer," of the "limited scientists," in fact, of all who possess complex knowledge but who want to know no more than their "field." They symbolize, as much by what they *do* know, as by what they may *not* know, our fragmented world of knowledge. That is why they arouse such unreasonable resentment in the romantic mind.[185]

Moreover, this sense of what has been lost increases the unhappy consciousness' awareness of the difference between the intellectual and "the others." Thus, for all the romantic's dislike of science, the "creator" of scientific and technical knowledge is well distinguished from the mere consumer of its products.[186] True science is, after all, as Jaspers has it, "an aristocratic affair."[187] What the romantic hates most is the blind submission to machines, the accommodation to functionalism, that characterizes those "sub-men" of the technological world— the masses, who are the most "other" of all human types. It is they who have destroyed the possibility of any creation, even in science.[188] For they, and the technological order to which they belong, today form "the world" that represses the unique individual. Thus even those who, like Jaspers, try to dissociate themselves from the wildest attacks on technology speak of its "demonism," and hail Burckhardt as a prophet. For to the

[185] E.g., J. Ortega y Gasset, *Mission of the University*, tr. by H. Nostrand (Princeton, N.J., 1944), pp. 57-58.

[186] E.g., Jaspers, *Origin and Goal*, pp. 101-102 and 104-105; Marcel, *Men against Humanity*, pp. 41-43.

[187] *Man in the Modern Age*, p. 137.

[188] *Ibid.*, pp. 117-120 and 127-143; Huxley, *Ends and Means*, pp. 269-270; Juenger, *The Future of Technology*, pp. 84-87; Marcel, *Men against Humanity*, pp. 53-54.

existentialist philosopher, technology and the masses are the enemies of contemplation, just as to the aesthetic romantic they seem to threaten creation. Technology makes "existence" impossible.[189] In many ways the complaints against technology resemble those once made against rationalism and utilitarianism. To Marcel, for one, technology, is only the modern expression of these forms of thought.[190] It is even noted that technology and reason have the same pernicious effect on individuality. Both make us all alike, and in the romantic mind it is but a short step from such uniformity to universal collectivization.[191] Like reason, too, technology is useless to us in our most serious moments—when we are dying for instance.[192] One recognizes Kierkegaard's scorn for rationalist philosophy in this.

In politics, technology means the totalitarian state, Society and the state always tend to look like machines to the romantic, and none more so than totalitarian regimes. Almost all romantic writers, moreover, seem to accept Burnham's prediction of the coming rule of technocrats, though they hardly share his composure in facing such a prospect.[193] Like him, they see in totalitarian government the triumph of the machine and the machine-man. Huxley, for instance, writes that machine techniques are the greatest danger to our liberties, for the cult of efficiency is the root of totalitarianism. This, he now claims, is the message of his earlier novel *Brave New World*. That is rather odd; for, however artificial and mechanical is the life described there, it is not a picture of a totalitarian state. It is not at all comparable to the vision of Orwell's *Nine-*

[189] *Origin and Goal*, pp. 97-98, 122-125; *Man in the Modern Age*, pp. 82-84.

[190] "Préface" à *La Vingt-Cinquième Heure*, pp. ii-iii.

[191] Ortega y Gasset, *Toward a Philosophy of History*, pp. 150-151; Juenger, *The Future of Technology*, pp. 97, 125-131 and 144-145.

[192] Marcel, *Men against Humanity*, p. 71.

[193] E.g., Camus, *The Rebel*, p. 185; Marcel, *Men against Humanity*, p. 188.

teen Eighty-Four. It presents a rationalized technological nightmare, repugnant to the child of nature, which is a typically romantic theme, but it is not a political novel and it offers no insights into totalitarian systems. It is revealing, too, that Huxley regards Jeremy Bentham and his brother Samuel, with their plan for a rational prison, as the founders of the efficiency-mad state.[194] Bentham has ever been hateful to romantics.

To the unhappy consciousness, the machine-world, as a prison for the individual, and totalitarianism are one and the same thing. In its view, both have merged with all those forces in civilization which earlier romantics deplored long before totalitarianism had appeared. But the romantic of today is not interested either in understanding what distinguishes one political form from another or really in the causes of totalitarianism. He seeks only to "clarify" the situation of the self in the world. In society "the one" is threatened by the mechanical order and by those who are devoted to it, the masses. The great question is, "What and who are the masses?" It is typical that even those romantics who talk most about them are unable to provide a clear definition. The one thing that emerges clearly is the meaning of the masses for the self. But accounts of their objective origins and nature are rare indeed. Are they the average, the mediocre, the Philistines, the poor, the people, the majority, the workers, the non-classes? What is their relationship to totalitarianism? Are they something new, or have they always been around? No one quite knows. Only one thing is certain: that they stand everywhere, abstract, negative, and opposed to the self and its aspirations.

To Jaspers the real issue today is the struggle of "possible existence" against the masses, and of selfhood against the mass order.[195] Huxley notes that dictators love crowds because they

---

[194] *Themes and Variations*, pp. 43-45, 48-49 and 202-207.
[195] *Man in the Modern Age*, pp. 45-57 and 74-75.

fear transcendence which can be reached only in solitude.[196] The masses, Marcel observes, have no "substantial being," no "ontological dignity." They are Heidegger's "anybody."[197] As Jaspers repeats over and over again, they are dangerous, for the individual loses his selfhood in their midst. The real tragedy of the present is, in fact, that the eternal struggle between the "exception" and the mass tendency of society has been resolved in favor of the latter. "Joint enterprise or perish" has become the rule. But it is still only the "exception" who can make history, produce a work of art, or invent something new.[198] And in our age he is crushed.

All this sounds much like the 19th-century romantic's song about the plight of individuality and originality and about a vulgar society. This is not surprising, for the masses have simply replaced the average and the Philistine. In his search for a definition of the masses, Jaspers, for example, rejects as too vague the idea that they are the public. The masses are a permanent life order—the rule of the average within any given group. At the level of averages there can be no spiritual life. The mass man has no self, and is incapable of freedom.[199] This theory of the masses as the eternal average Jaspers owes to Ortega y Gasset. In fact both he and Marcel acknowledge their debt to the Spanish philosopher.[200] Indeed, whatever his

[196] *Ends and Means*, pp. 71-74.

[197] *Men against Humanity*, pp. 104-105 and 195.

[198] *Man in the Modern Age*, pp. 40-43, 53-58, 127-129 and 175-196; *Origin and Goal*, pp. 96-125.

[199] *Existentialism and Humanism*, p. 92; *Man in the Modern Age*, pp. 40-41 and 117-18.

[200] Jaspers, *Origin and Goal*, p. 281; Marcel, *Men against Humanity*, pp. 103-104. Fear of a technological-mass society of course preceded Ortega's work. During the Twenties many books appeared describing the horrors of such a civilization. Many of these were also anti-American, since the United States was held to represent the forces of technology and mass life. The best known of these books were probably Georges Duhamel's *America the Menace*, tr. by C. M. Thompson (Boston, 1931) and Lucien Romier's *Who Will Be Master?* tr. by

shortcomings as a metaphysician might be, Ortega has made a major contribution to contemporary romantic social theory. Not only was he the first to identify the rule of the masses as the chief feature of the present age; he also at once linked fascism and communism to this phenomenon. The man of the mass is he who has no self, and likes it; who is perfectly happy to say that he is "just like everyone else." He is the man who refuses to make an effort. People like that, of course, have always comprised the great majority of mankind, but until now they had been well-suppressed by their betters. Today, freed from all external authority, they have asserted themselves and try to rule, in spite of their manifest inferiority.[201] Moreover, urban life increases their number. Congested cities physically prevent the growth of the individual, and so increase the number of mass-men. However this ought not to make us think that the masses are simply the poor. On the contrary, they are the barbarians from every group of society. In short, Nietzsche's fears have come true—without any signs of a super-man. Nor do Ortega and his followers believe that anything can be done to elevate the masses. They are, Marcel finds, beneath education; they can only be trained. He can see no end to them, and to the "fanaticized consciousness" that moves them and expresses itself in totalitarianism.[202] Ortega at least sees some ways in which the élite might still separate itself from the masses. In modern art, which he detests, he nevertheless finds an avenue of escape. Because of its esoteric qualities it separates the élite of initiates from the excluded masses.[203]

M. Josephson (New York, 1928). It is to Ortega's credit that from the first he rejected the theory of the "Americanization of Europe." To him the whole world suffered from the same disease, the masses.

[201] *The Revolt of the Masses* (Mentor Book, New York, 1950), pp. 7-91; *Toward a Philosophy of History*, pp. 56 and 72-76.

[202] *Men against Humanity*, p. 8.

[203] *The Dehumanization of Art*, tr. by H. Weyl (Princeton, N.J., 1948), pp. 5-7.

In romantic minds, the average and the Philistine have always been more or less identical. Today the masses are recognized as the new Philistia. Thus Hannah Arendt speaks of the totalitarian society as "the masses of co-ordinated Philistines" come together from every corner of society.[204] To more aesthetically inclined romantics, the absence of artistic taste among them demonstrates their descent from the Philistines as well. The masses are mere pleasure seekers, the extension of the 19th-century public. To Jaspers the difference between the "good" theatre and the "vulgar" cinema shows the decline of popular taste into a mere thirst for sensation.[205] The masses are not "the creators" of folk art. The proletariat has no art, Comfort notes, because it has been perverted by the cinema and the radio.[206] Marcel holds that the people have been ruined by bourgeois frivolity.[207] Malraux writes that the "arts of delectation," the art popular today, is the direct successor of 19th-century "official art." The masses today, like the bourgeoisie then, do not seek transcendence in art but momentary enjoyment.[208] To the artist, both are equally abhorrent. Stuffiness has been replaced by trash, and Philistia by the masses.

What, however, is the social significance of the masses, quite aside from their "averageness" and lack of aesthetic sensibility? Here no very definite answers are forthcoming. This is natural, since man's situation is, for the romantic, never primarily social. One thing, though, is certain: the masses are *not* the people. Romantics always had a fondness for simple, natural folk who provide them with "local color." The masses have nothing in common with these. They are the product of the decline of community, of faith, and of

[204] *The Origins of Totalitarianism*, pp. 330-331.
[205] *Man in the Modern Age*, pp. 129-133.
[206] *Art and Social Responsibility*, p. 60.
[207] *Men against Humanity*, p. 82.
[208] *The Voices of Silence*, pp. 514-530 and 601-602.

tradition. Domesticated, but uprooted, Jaspers calls them.[209] "Earthly but not rooted," Marcel comments.[210] Hannah Arendt feels that the destruction of the national community by imperialism was an essential preparation for the totalitarian mass state. On the whole, this is only a repetition of the 19th-century romantic's cry for roots. The fate of the man who, estranged from the earth, lives on a "Cartesian globe" is still bemoaned.[211] But roots, then as now, remain something necessary for "the others." Certainly the other-worldly existentialist and the "exception" do not propose to settle down. This is aestheticism, too, then.

Actually, there are only two genuinely sociological theories to account for the masses. One regards the masses as the antithesis of the classes; the other is Le Bon's simple racist élitism. Of these two, the second enjoys a vast prestige among romantics. This is not altogether surprising. There is always an inclination in romanticism to shift back and forth between mysticism and materialism, and this tendency can be observed in romantic social thought as well as anywhere. To explain the appearance of the masses, romantic writers have grasped at the simplest of material facts. The increase in the world's population is accepted without further analysis as a cause of mass life.[212] Again, urbanization is held to be somehow responsible for the rise of the masses and for totalitarianism—this in spite of the fact that Britain and the United States, though by far the most industrialized and urban of all nations, are singularly unafflicted by totalitarianism. Miss Arendt, for instance, finds an explanation for the rise of the masses and of totalitarianism

---

[209] *Origin and Goal*, pp. 111 and 115-116.

[210] *Men against Humanity*, pp. 69-71.

[211] F. G. Juenger, *Maschine und Eigentum*, p. 190.

[212] For the undue effect of increases in the population, see e.g., H. Arendt, *Origins of Totalitarianism*, pp. 304-305; Huxley, *Themes and Variations*, pp. 235-272; Jaspers, *Man in the Modern Age*, p. 38; Ortega y Gasset, *The Revolt of the Masses*, pp. 35-37.

in Lenin's theory of imperialism. Again, Sartre and his school, as we saw, identify all politics with the class war. Above all, almost all romantics have found in Le Bon a prop for their attitudes toward the masses, and an explanation of totalitarianism. All that Le Bon really said was that any number of men acting together tend toward irrationality and that, therefore, popular government is impossible. To him all groups were equally mad. A jury was as much a "crowd" as an enraged gang. Moreover, he assumed that the character of crowds was determined by race. All this he believed in true 19th-century fashion to be "scientific" fact.[213] Actually, of course, Kierkegaard knew as much as Le Bon ever did about how individuals change when they become part of a collectivity, but he had no scientific pretensions and he wisely refrained from drawing simple political conclusions from complex emotional realities. Nevertheless, it is to Le Bon that everyone turns today to confirm their fears about the irrational masses.

This identification of the masses with the irrational crowd is particularly popular among those who suffer because Marx is dead. For them the wickedness of the masses at least explains the success of totalitarianism and the failure of socialism. Koestler, for example, turned directly from Marx to Le Bon.[214] Especially illuminating, in this respect, are Emil Lederer's and Hannah Arendt's theories of the masses and of their contribution to totalitarianism. Both try to revise Marx with the aid of Le Bon. Lederer continued to believe with Marx that all societies, so far, have been class structures. The classless society, however, for which Marx had longed was a horrible mistake. It was the mass society, or rather, no society at all, since with the collapse of classes, society itself had dis-

[213] G. Le Bon, *The Crowd*, tr. anon. (London, 1896). See also the excellent account of Le Bon's theories by H. E. Barnes in the *Encyclopaedia of the Social Sciences*.

[214] A. Koestler, *The Invisible Writing* (London, 1954), p. 263.

integrated. Le Bon's irrational masses are the successors of the classes. Totalitarian regimes merely reflect, institutionalize, and maintain mass life on which their power is based. The state is always an expression of class, or mass, existence.[215] This is essentially Hannah Arendt's view, as well, except that she regards the nation state as equally important in preventing society from dissolving into an amorphous mass. She has also added such psychological factors as the sense of uselessness in describing the nature of the masses. But this is only a part of their lack of class and national functions.[216] For her, as for Lederer, the impossibility of believing in the proletariat has led to a view that relegates the majority of men to a life of reasonless ferocity, which only some artificial restraint, such as class bonds, can control. With the end of Marxian certainties society has become strange, irrational, and unmanageable, and a new form of "unhappy consciousness" has been created, which again feels that the "world" is beyond salvation.

These theories about the masses suffer from all the defects of Marxian class theory, but they at least treat the masses as a concrete, new social phenomenon, and try to show how they become totalitarian. This is more than the pure romantics are capable of doing. Jaspers speaks of Nazism as the dissolution of old loyalties and as a loss of faith, but that is hardly adequate.[217] Marcel just assumes that Western civilization has ceased to care for the individual, and never will again. Totali-

---

[215] *State of the Masses* (New York, 1940). For a Marxian refutation of Lederer, see F. Neumann, *Behemoth*, pp. 365-369. The extent to which Lederer's view coincided with orthodox conservatism has been stressed by G. Briefs, "Intellectual Tragedy," *The Commonweal*, vol. 33, 1940-1941, p. 25.

[216] *The Origins of Totalitarianism*, pp. 250-298 and 301-318. For a criticism of the whole mass-class theory, see L. O'Boyle, "The Class Concept in History," *Journal of Modern History*, vol. 24, 1952, pp. 391-397.

[217] "The Fight against Totalitarianism," *Confluence*, vol. 3, 1954, pp. 251-266.

tarianism is merely the mark of this condition. Freedom in such a regime can never be achieved through political action. Only through transcendence can the individual find liberation. But that is true freedom under any conditions. The whole problem, as he, in fact, admits, is not political, at all, but spiritual.[218] The situation of man in the modern world, like everything else, can be felt but not understood. There romanticism rests.

The state of the world today encourages the growth of the unhappy consciousness. It is now the most prevalent of all intellectual conditions, and the one to which the most imaginative and subtle spirits are drawn. And who is to say that they are "wrong"? To be sure, they can offer us no coherent account of nature, man, history, or society. They do not even try, for the defeat of the spirit lies in just this: that everything has become incomprehensible. But, then, the strangeness of "the world" is constantly pressed upon us. The romanticism of defeat is the simple submission to this "otherness" of nature and society. All that the unhappy consciousness can do now is preserve its own integrity against the encroachments of a hostile world. Its shortcomings, both practical and intellectual, are obvious enough, but one question remains. Is anything else possible?

[218] *Men against Humanity*, pp. 14-15.

CHAPTER V

Christian Fatalism

Social Theology and Social Alienation

IF THE ABSENCE of all faith creates the unhappy consciousness, one might suppose that Christianity could assuage its restless longing. This, however, is no longer possible, for the real source of romantic feeling today is the loss of all social allegiance, and Christians, too, feel this estrangement from modern history. In any case, it is not the function of religion to reconcile men to history in the way that Hegel envisaged. However, since the origin of romantic alienation is now social and not solely religious in character, only some new secular doctrine could present itself as an alternative. That is why romantics who can no longer endure their predicament tend to seek self-immolation in totalitarian movements. To be sure, Catholicism often was a haven for tired romantics in the 19th century. But many treated religion as only another, perhaps the supreme, manifestation of the poetic spirit. Nor did religion bring them to a genuine acceptance of historical life. It usually meant a transfer of culture-longing from Greece to the Middle Ages, and of course the church represented at least a symbolic union with that remote age. To that extent one can speak of at least a partial return to history, and an abandonment of the complete isolation of pure romanticism, which did mean a new sense of cultural continuity. However, tradition rather than faith drew the exhausted "genius" to Christianity, and since he saw this tradition everywhere in decay, his dislike for the modern world was in no way lessened. On the contrary, the converted romantic helped to increase the tension between Christianity and the main currents of modern thought and life. If today there flourishes a Christian fatalism which sees an un-Christian Europe doomed to internal decay because it has abandoned its spiritual basis, this is due partly to the infusion of romantic forms of thought into Christian social theory. Certainly at present there is a Christian social despair that is analogous to the unhappy consciousness, and in no sense an answer to it. The Christian feels as rejected and despised in the post-Christian era as the romantic does in the world of Philistines.

Christian faith has never been conducive to a complacent acceptance of secular culture. Not only does faith, like aesthetic sense, spring from an a-historical and a-political source of human feeling; it also stands as a constant challenge to and condemnation of the world of sin, error, and frivolity. If Christianity finds its origins in events within history, it also stands above them. Consequently, cultural conditions, however much they may appall the Christian, can never bring him to the utter despair of the unhappy consciousness. He may and does join the romantic in despairing of technological, scientific, urban mass society, but this spectacle means something different to him. First of all, he sees its cause in the decline of faith, not in the absence of aesthetic impulses. Moreover, he himself remains secure in his faith; he observes the disaster of others. In short, even the most extreme Christian fatalist who is certain of the imminent end of Western culture, and even of the coming of Anti-Christ, can never share the total estrangement of the romantic. On the other hand, he is not in a condition to offer the romantic a new hope.

For romantics such as Dostoyevsky, for instance, not the least attraction of Christianity was that it seemed opposed in every way to modern cultural standards, especially those prevalent in Western Europe. This extreme position of social dissatisfaction is by no means typical of Christianity as such. However, the French Revolution shocked Catholics especially into a new social and cultural awareness. The reaffirmation of their faith came as a result of social changes that seemed to them catastrophic, and consequently it expressed itself as a form of culture consciousness. If for a century there had been hardly any specifically Christian social theory, there now arose in opposition to the Enlightenment and to the Revolution a Catholicism that was primarily concerned with the state of European society. The central fact for the theorists of the "reaction" was their somewhat belated realization that Christian faith had ceased to dominate social and intellectual life. Their faith, therefore, asserted itself as a belief in Christian civilization and tradition rather than as a solely mystical experience. Nowhere is this more evident than in the writings of Maistre, Lammenais, and later of the Spanish author, Donoso Cortes. The implications of this culture consciousness were, moreover, very serious for these Christians. The identification of Christianity with a dying social order meant that faith itself was about to disappear from the world, and in this calamity they saw the very end of the world, the approach of the prophesied coming of Anti-Christ, and the Apocalypse.

Nothing could be farther from the Enlightenment than this eschatological consciousness. It represents the absolute antithesis of both its belief in reason and its notion of progress. The notion of progress, of course, is never acceptable to Christians, since it ignores the human burden of sin. Cultural despair, however, is not inherently Christian. The feeling of being lost in history has its origins in the war against the Enlightenment, against secularization, indeed against the whole world that had conspicuously abandoned Christian habits of thought. Who can fail to sympathize with this despair? Where the romantic feels expelled from society purely as an individual, the Christian sees the entire edifice of theology, of church establishment, and of centuries of tradition dissolving before his eyes. While one may well feel that the romantic suffers only from the excesses of self-pity, the Christian's plight is real enough. Yet the analysis that he offers in explanation, not of his situation but of the state of Western society as a whole, is not adequate, for it is the expression of his own unhappy position in it, not of those who do not share his difficulties. Nevertheless, Christian fatalism has grown, especially under the stress of recent events. In our time Stalin and Hitler fill many Christian minds with the forebodings that Robespierre and Napoleon once inspired. Moreover, the most diverse thinkers have come to share the belief that Europe must inevitably die of irreligion. It is no longer a view shared only by a number of ultra-conservative Catholics. With the increasing distaste for the Enlightenment everywhere, Christians of every kind have come to accept the views that once were peculiar to its extreme opponents. In a less consistent and perhaps inarticulate way it is a particularly widespread mood. This rather than the mere fact that Christianity can no longer salvage the unhappy consciousness lends Christian fatalism its real interest. Among Catholics, for instance, the democratic Jacques Maritain is at one with the authoritarian Henri Massis, and a close reasoner like Monsignor Knox agrees with the imaginative Max Picard. The English writers Belloc and Christopher Dawson share with the German Romano Guardini the concern for European culture. Again, the Russian Berdiaev and the Protestant Emil Brunner, the English theologian Nicholas Micklem, the "Christendom" group of the Church of England, and even a poet, T. S. Eliot, all are certain that Europe is doomed and all see the doom as a matter of inexorable decline throughout the years of secularization.

The decline of orthodoxy too, not just of faith, is fatal in this view. The unconventional Christianity of a Kierkegaard or even of Gabriel Marcel today is of a romantic, and thus different, order. If the romantic and the Christian share the culture consciousness of the outcasts—so foreign to the secure

Enlightenment philosopher—the culture the Christian sees dying is that of tradition, of a bygone social order. The romantic, however, finds every external social bond suffocating, though in his loneliness he may dream of some imaginary culture which would suit him. The Christian fatalist is more definite, and sees in specific historical events the gradual and unavoidable decay of both faith and culture. This stark theory is, of course, not the only possible religious interpretation of our time, but in its extremity it is both consistent and representative of a venerable tradition of Christian social analysis, now applied to unprecedented experience. The terrifying conclusions that it reaches about the modern world are based on an extremely ancient method of historical interpretation. At its simplest it is the assumption that every social event is ultimately based on some specific religious belief, and that to understand history we need only find the short iron chain of cause and effect that ties every political act directly to an item of faith. Conversely, it is argued that all religious beliefs must sooner or later find an exact reflection in social history. The historical fate of mankind is, therefore, determined by the "truth" of their own and their ancestors' religious faith. It follows that religion must be examined in terms of its political implications, and that certainly the only thing that matters in politics is its effect on religious faith. Thus the Enlightenment is still described as a religious heresy, as are totalitarian ideologies, while totalitarian movements are seen as counter-religions. Indeed, the anti-Christian character of the Enlightenment and now of totalitarian ideologies is their defining aspect, and to draw careful distinctions between such purely secular phenomena becomes unnecessary, for only the degree of irreligion matters. It is this inclination that persuades the Christian fatalist to identify rationalism and Protestantism if he is Catholic, or to see no real difference between a secular democracy and a totalitarian state. This reasoning creates a picture of modern history as a simple and uniform stream, and only tends to increase the fatalistic despair that inspired the vision. It is not only that history is seen solely as a religious drama; it is the picture painted by believers who feel that they have been excluded from the play. The difficulty is that this reasoning is, theoretically, not helpful as an explanation of contemporary culture, for it is the absolutizing of views and observations that were, perhaps, valid once but are not so today. Religion has in various cultures and in the past in the West been a very powerful cultural determinant, though it never was the only one. Certainly, it has not played that role in Europe for centuries, long before the Enlightenment.

This form of fatalism not only has its roots in an outworn view of culture in general; it is also the offspring of that venerable approach to politics known as "political theology." This theory, at its simplest, assumes that all political ideas and institutions ought to be based upon direct revelation and that political truths are a part of general theology. In practice this means that political theology depends on simple analogical reasoning. Thus in patristic times there were attempts to justify the rule of the Roman Emperor as the political counterpart of monotheism.[1] Today it is claimed that the Molinist doctrine of Grace, which makes man an active "co-worker" of God in achieving salvation, must express itself in political democracy. If man is not passive in his relations to God, he must not be deprived of the right to participate in politics.[2] Christian theorists who oppose this type of reasoning have tried to show that, when the monocratic analogy was discarded after the Arian controversy, every kind of political

[1] E. Peterson, *Der Monotheismus als Politisches Problem* (Leipzig, 1935).
[2] E. Alexander, "Church and Society in Germany," tr. by T. Stolper in J. N. Moody et al. *Church and Society* (New York, 1953), pp. 494-495.

theology was proscribed.[3] Thomist scholars feel that the "common good" is the proper standard for political judgment, and that man as a rational social being has, in accordance with this standard, a wide field of independent choice.[4] However, just as Stahl once tried to show that monarchy was the only form of government consonant with Protestant theology, and as the French theocrats tried to show that it alone conformed to Catholicism, so today there are those who defend specific social institutions as theological truths. Their scope, to be sure, is broader. General social structures, not only state forms, are involved. *Social* theology has replaced purely *political* theology, and the Christian cultural fatalism of the present is thus best described as a social theology. Social traditions and the organic state are still deduced by its adherents as necessary consequences of the doctrine of human solidarity in sin and creation. A hierarchy of spiritual values is still held to imply social differentiation, and the fact that God has not endowed all with equal gifts, a divine justification of social inequality.

Among the many possible Christian philosophies of politics, political theology is by no means the most popular. If it can claim adherents among both Protestants and Catholics, it also has opponents in both camps. It is certainly not *the* Christian political theory, *par excellence*. It is only the form that was revived as the first Christian response to the French Revolution and that has flourished most remarkably since then with the general decline of Enlightenment optimism. In fact, however, neither it nor any other political theory ought to be called, simply, Christian. Not only has almost every political system been defended, in all sincerity, in the name of Christianity, but many theologians deny that any sort of Christian politics is possible at all. To them the very idea of combining

[3] E. Peterson, *op.cit.*, pp. 96-100.
[4] H. Rommen, *The State in Catholic Thought* (St. Louis & London, 1950), pp. 99-122.

Christianity and politics is clearly self-contradictory. It would therefore be extremely rash to treat Christian political ideas as if they formed a single, well-defined body of thought. However, there is a way of looking at politics that can quite reasonably be identified as Christian. If there is no systematic theory, there is at least a constant effort to analyze and evaluate social life in terms of the divinely revealed origin and end of man, even if no agreement as to the exact meaning of the Christian revelation can be found. It is not the great variety of answers that such inquiries are bound to yield, but their common purpose and inspiration that matters. Even those who reject the belief that Christianity has a direct political message agree that the Christian has a special vantage point from which he can and must judge society.[5] With all the theoretical possibilities open to Christians, social theology is only one among many, but it is the most direct response to the Enlightenment and to secularization in general. It is also the clearest form, among Christians, of that intense anxiety for the fate of European culture that has grown throughout the last century and that reached its climax since the First World War.

Today social theology does not flourish so much as a system of positive ideas but as a critical and analytical method. For instance, such notably Thomist thinkers as Maritain, Rommen, and the Anglo-Catholic theologian Canon V. A. Demant employ the analytical concepts of political and social theology, while they entirely reject its validity as a constructive system of ideas. They, and many others, employ social theology as a method of interpreting political ideas and institutions, for since these are always explicitly or implicitly based on some theological doctrine, or at least a conception of God, one must

[5] Thus Karl Barth insists that "there is clearly no cause for the Church to act as though it lived in relation to the State in a night in which all cats are gray." *Church and State*, tr. by G. R. Howe (London, 1939), pp. 31-32.

always look for the theological basis upon which they rest.[6] For example, Carl Schmitt, in his analysis of the political theories of romanticism, opens his discussion by demonstrating the origin of these theories in theological occasionalism.[7] Professor Erich Voegelin studies all post-mediaeval political thought as an offspring of the alleged "Gnosticism" of Joachim of Floris.[8] In the realm of political action, the French Revolution has often been regarded as an expression of Protestantism. Today Nazism and Communism are traced respectively to Lutheranism, Eastern Orthodoxy, or Judaism. On the positive side, Calvinism, with its concern for worldly righteousness, is said to have saved Britain, Switzerland, Holland, and the U.S.A. from Germany's and Russia's sad fate. In fact, the entire modern age is nothing but the outcome of secularization, and totalitarianism is its final blossoming. As Nathaniel Micklem notes, "all political problems are at bottom theological."[9] His Catholic compatriot, the historian Christopher Dawson, adds that "the political problems of the modern world are in the last resort religious," and that totalitarianism is the "culmination of the secularizing process in the West, and "the unification of our culture on a purely materialistic basis."[10]

From the religious point of view, the great danger of political theology has always been its inclination toward pragmatism. It begins by arguing that only true theology can produce sound politics; it ends by asking whether this or that theology is politically desirable. Because it sees church, society, and state as parts of the same direct revelation, it tends to judge one in terms of the other.[11] At its simplest it is the method of Bonald and

[6] H. Rommen, op.cit., p. 93.
[7] Politische Romantik, pp. 115-152.
[8] The New Science of Politics (Chicago, 1952), pp. 107-189.
[9] The Theology of Politics (London, 1941), pp. xv and 38.
[10] Religion and the Modern State (London, 1935), p. 44.
[11] W. Gurian, Die Politischen und Sozialen Ideen des Franzoesischen Katholizismus, 1789-1914 (M. Gladbach, 1929), p. 62.

Maistre, who "considered religion in politics and politics in religion."[12] But in any of its forms it judges not only social actions in terms of their effect on faith, but also religion in terms of its historical results. This sort of religious pragmatism is actually an old idea. It has often appealed to people of little or no faith, such as Machiavelli, Rousseau, or Saint-Simon, who looked at religion entirely from the outside. In recent years Charles Maurras, who did not even believe in God, supported Catholicism as an instrument of order, and Arnold Toynbee advocates a return to Christianity as the sole means of saving Western civilization. This is simply to make "religion the handmaid of civilization," an idea that no Christian may entertain.[13] However, there have been strong elements of pragmatism in all social theology. Even those social theologians who most perfectly recognize the absolute primacy of the spiritual, still discuss religion as an historical phenomenon, as a cultural force. In the end all make estimates of its social utility.

The pragmatic attitude really received its great impetus from the Gallicans who identified church and state from the first. Bossuet already noted that some religion, true or false, was essential for a stable political order, and that the long duration of Catholic kingdoms was a proof of the truth of that religion.[14] Among the supporters of the *ancien régime* after the Revolution, Catholicism was regarded as an historical and political necessity, rather than simply as an end in itself.[15] It also became an instrument of nationalism, for the destinies

[12] Bonald's letter to Maistre, March 30, 1819, in J. de Maistre, *Oeuvres* (Lyon, 1886), vol. xiv, pp. 335-339.

[13] V. A. Demant, *Theology of Society* (London, 1947), pp. 126-127.

[14] Gurian points to the 18th-century court preacher Fauchet as the first churchman to employ such reasoning. *Op.cit.*, p. 18. In fact, Bossuet already used it, which only strengthens Gurian's point that this theory originates with Gallicanism. Bossuet, *Politique Tirée des Propres Paroles de l'Ecriture Sainte*, Liv., vii, Arts. 2 and 3.

[15] "Vive le roi, vive la foi" was the real basis of emigré Catholicism.

of the church and the French nation were regarded as inseparable. Since Maistre's day "group romanticism," the faith in the unique nation, in cultural individuality, has been common among social theologians. To be sure, they have always stressed their opposition to pagan nationalism, to a nationalism that recognizes no principles above itself.[16] But the idea of a national mission in the service of religion is a common one, and one which coincidences of nationality and religion have doubtless furthered. The belief in "Gesta Dei per Francos" is older even than Gallicanism. T. S. Eliot, one of the earliest English admirers of both Maurras and Massis, insists that a Christian culture must be national in spirit.[17] A German theologian thinks that Germany was endowed by Luther with a special religious vocation.[18] An Anglo-Catholic author felt Britain to be the instrument of providence in the last World War.[19] The disciples of Dostoyevski, however much they may detest Bolshevism, still proclaim the religious virtues of the "Russian idea," and its destiny to save a rotting West.[20] For that matter, the whole over-concentration on "the West" is only religious nationalism extended in cultural scope. Today social theology is comprehensive in scope. It now identifies Europe and Christendom.[21] But its pragmatism remains. Its argument rests on

[16] C. J. H. Hayes, *The Historical Evolution of Modern Nationalism*, pp. 84-119. Massis, for instance, distinguishes the romantic nationalism of Barrès from the classical theory of Maurras on this basis. *Jugements* (Paris, 1923), pp. 171-252.

[17] "The Action Francaise," *Criterion*, vol. 7, 1928, pp. 195-203; "A Reply to Mr. Ward," *ibid.*, pp. 84-88; "The Literature of Fascism," *ibid.*, vol. 8, 1928-1929, pp. 280-290.

[18] H. D. Wendland in H. G. Wood et al., *The Kingdom of God and History*, p. 177.

[19] V. A. Demant, *Theology of Society*, p. 137.

[20] N. Berdiaev, *Towards a New Epoch*, tr. by O. F. Clarke (London, 1949), pp. 39-40, 53-70, 73-75, 92-94, and 105-117.

[21] Thus, for example, Romano Guardini claims that the Nazis were anti-Christian, *because* they were anti-European, the two being essentially one. *Der Heilbringer* (Zuerich, 1946), p. 48.

an historical law, namely, that religion is, as a matter of established fact, the most vital force in shaping culture and that no civilization can survive without religious inspiration. In fact, it defines culture as a system of shared beliefs and values, upon which everything else is built.[22] "If I know what your understanding of life is, I can tell you what sort of state, science, art and economic and social order you will create," the Swiss theologian, Emil Brunner, writes.[23] Social theology as an analytical method continues to reduce the Christian's sense of the primacy of faith to an explanation of history. An article of faith is transformed into a sociological hypothesis.

It is, however, not the pragmatic use of religious faith that is alone of interest today. That is, after all, an old problem. The contribution of social theology to the analysis of contemporary life lies in its extreme fatalism, for social theology from the outset completely denies that political life has any autonomy. Politics are regarded as a mere reflection of deeper spiritual forces, and thus quite incapable of social creativeness. Consequently, all political errors in general, but totalitarianism especially, are only signs of far greater disturbances. They are not only of no significance in themselves, but quite impervious to improvement by other forms of political action.[24] Today,

[22] C. Dawson, *Religion and Culture* (London, 1948), pp. 48-49.

[23] *The Theology of Crisis* (New York, 1948), p. xviii. Twenty years later Brunner drew the logical conclusions from this premise when he proclaimed that "the totalitarian state is not the invention of a handful of criminals . . . but Western humanity's own product, the ineluctable consequence of its own positivism . . . this is the inevitable result of man's loss of faith in a *divine* law, in an eternal justice." *Justice and the Social Order*, tr. by M. Hottinger (London & Redhill, 1945), p. 16 (italics supplied).

[24] Thus Christopher Dawson writes: "(It) is not the politicians who are primarily responsible for the crisis. The scientists and the technicians, the philosophers and the theologians and the men of letters have played a larger part than the politicians themselves in producing those great changes of culture which have transformed the modern world and ultimately led to the present crisis. . . . (The) making of Europe and the successive changes of Western culture are mainly

totalitarian rule is only one expression among others of a general crisis, specifically the rapid degeneration of an increasingly secularized culture. If, as Christopher Dawson notes, religion alone is the key to history and culture, then it follows that Christianity is indeed the indispensable core of Western civilization.[25] No one can, moreover, very well deny that Europe has become increasingly secular in character. To social theology, the conclusions from these propositions seem obvious. All the social and political disasters of the age are only symptoms of the death throes of a culture from which the spirit has all but departed. In short, social theology is a systematic form of cultural fatalism.

Christian Hope and Social Despair

Because social theologians see a religious significance in all political events, they tend to regard every reverse in political fortune as a cosmic disaster. This inclination constantly threatens to throw them into a state of despair that is, in fact, forbidden by their faith. However, since the French Revolution and the spread of liberalism and socialism, an ever-increasing number of Christian observers have been convinced not only of Europe's moribund condition but of the approaching end of all history. Cultural death from irreligion, or even the advent of the kingdom of Satan built on false religions, have been predicted, solely on the basis of political analyses. The most brilliant disciple of the Theocratic school, Donoso Cortes, spelled out in detail the reasons for the tragedy. Like all theologians of society he held that "every political or social truth necessarily resolves itself into a theological truth," and every religious error must end in social disaster. Liberalism,

---

the result of spiritual and intellectual forces which are not political in origin, though they have their consequences on the political plane." *Understanding Europe* (London, 1952), pp. 187-188.
[25] *Religion and Culture*, pp. 48-50.

because it is anti-theological, "is impotent to give any impulsion to civilization, for every form of civilization is only a reflection of theology." Socialism, indeed, has a theology, a completely abominable one, which gives it the strength to defeat liberalism, and so heralds the end of Europe.[26] Today these prognostications have become even more alarming, for it is recognized that not just a critical period, but the final crisis of mankind, may be at hand. Thus Peter Wust, a Catholic theologian, insists that it is just because Christian society has fallen from so high a spiritual level as that of the Middle Ages that its descent is the worst yet known in history. "For the first time there arises the danger of collective annihilation of religion." The old saying, "corruptio optimi pessima," is as applicable to groups as to individuals. The necessarily simultaneous elimination of religion and culture is about to bring an age far worse than any pre-Christian pagan era.[27] What is one to do but despair?

It is nevertheless a little difficult to accept the idea of any kind of Christian fatalism, or even of complete resignation. Christianity is clearly not compatible with any historical determinism, for this would contradict the doctrine of the freedom of the will. Again, mystical pessimism of the Oriental variety is unacceptable, for the duty to love one's neighbor involves at least a minimum concern with temporal life. In any case, such withdrawal from all social life has no appeal to social theologians who, by definition, are preoccupied with life in this world. Indeed, no despair at all is permitted Christians. The call to hope cannot be evaded. However, social

[26] *An Essay on Catholicism, Authority and Order,* tr. by M. V. Goddard (New York, 1925), pp. 4-5, 75-79, 159-171, 204-208.

[27] P. Wust, "Crisis in the West," *Essays in Order,* ed. by C. Dawson et al. (New York, 1931), pp. 107-108 and 114. That the "post Christian" age will of necessity be worse than that of ancient paganism is also emphasized by Canon V. A. Demant, in his *Religion and the Decline of Capitalism* (London, 1952), p. 180. See also J. Pieper, *op.cit.*

theology, because it sees social decline and religious disaster as one, is a positive invitation to hopelessness. Still, the doctrine of hope must somehow be salvaged, in spite of the signs of the times. Thus, so entirely orthodox a Catholic as Monsignor Ronald Knox, observing the world of the atomic bomb, is forced to agree that, "The Christian virtue of hope has nothing whatever to do with the world's future. . . . (Hope) in the theological sense is concerned only with the salvation of the individual believer and the means which will help him attain it."[28] A Christian does not sin if he expects the world to blow itself up in the near future, and Monsignor Knox reminds us that the first Christians lived in daily expectation of the world's end. But he warns that a pretense of hope must be kept up lest we lose our morale and fall into total despair. In short, he clearly recognizes the great danger, as well as the appeal, which social despondency has for Christians.

This qualified doctrine of hope seems a long way from the historical optimism of a Bossuet, who saw in every historical event a new proof of the benevolent design of providence. Indeed there are few Christians today who share the classical composure of the great bishop.[29] How unlike him is Dawson's view of history, for instance, when he recalls in Augustinian tones that: "Christ came not to bring peace, but a sword, and the Kingdom of God comes not by the elimination of conflict, but through the increasing opposition and tension between the Church and the world. The conflict between the two cities is as old as humanity and must endure to the end of time."[30] Dawson admits that these considerations are a

[28] *God and the Atom* (London, 1945), pp. 104-107.

[29] There still are, of course, theologians who accept Bossuet's philosophy of history, especially in America, but theirs is becoming a minority view. A rare example of Bossuet-like confidence is to be found in J. Schrembs' essay of the same title in *The Catholic Philosophy of History*, ed. by P. Guilday (New York, 1936), pp. 3-41.

[30] C. Dawson in H. G. Wood et al., *The Kingdom of God and History* (Chicago and New York, 1938), p. 216.

response to the events of recent years. In a companion essay a Protestant theologian, Edwyn Bevan, again reminds us that the early Christians expected life in this world to get constantly worse, and that the experience of the present age should lead us to a return to their apocalyptic hopes. For, though it is clear that the world is in a very bad state, God remains the Lord of History.[31] Even Monsignor Knox admits that the end of the world may be occurring "according to schedule," but that, since only few Christians have the fortitude to recognize this and yet remain undaunted, the great majority of believers ought not to indulge in such speculations.[32]

By seeing religious meaning in the events of history, social theology comes to attach so high a religious value to Western civilization that its cultural fears must be translated into supra-historical hope. Just as conservative liberalism has abandoned the faith in progress, so Christians today reject the cosmic complacency of Bossuet. In neither case has a loss of confidence led to a measured skepticism in regard to philosophies of history. In turning against itself, hope in historical life has ended in despair of the world.

The New View of the Apocalypse: A Philosophy of History

The revival of apocalyptic expectations among the orthodox is particularly startling since it is not sanctioned by tradition. The Catholic Church has long repudiated the hope of an early second coming which the early Christians cherished, for these expectations threw doubt upon the doctrine that Christ founded the church.[33] Again Bossuet's belief in a slow evolu-

---

[31] *Ibid.*, pp. 46-47, 68-71.
[32] *Op.cit.*, pp. 104-105 and 133-143.
[33] R. L. Shinn, *Christianity and the Problem of History* (New York, 1953), p. 183. Mr. Shinn also observes that the opposition to millenarianism really begins with St. Augustine's "ecclesiasticism," the notion that the church is the City of God, pp. 29-62. It is also with St. Augustine that the uncompromising rejection of worldly life is mitigated. In him, as J. N. Figgis said, "the world renouncing and

tion of God's design in history postpones its fulfillment indefinitely. In any case, the historical despair of the present does not even resemble the milleniarism of the past, for it is derived from the deductions of social theology and from political analysis especially, while the ancient prophecy was mystical in its origin and in its entire character. The milleniarism of the past was not inspired by changes in cultural and social life, yet these provide the entire foundation for the apprehensions of modern social theology. Among the early Christians, milleniarism expressed itself in the most complete social quietism. "I secede from the populace," Tertullian announced.[34] Among contemporary Christians the end of history is anticipated as a response to social and cultural events, and to an intense preoccupation with these. At its roots is the method of social theology, the belief in the inseparability of social and religious experiences. Thus the social crisis of the present is not regarded as only the product of religious error but in itself an event of primary religious import, for it seems to proclaim the end of Christianity. This new apocalyptic vision actually represents a departure from accepted thought. One might well call it the "post-providential" theory of history. It rejects the conclusions of Bossuet's philosophy but not its premises. This becomes particularly evident when one recalls that there are other alternatives to both providential optimism and pessimism.

---

world accepting temper both meet." *The Political Aspects of St. Augustine's "City of God"* (London, 1921), p. 67. Compared to his predecessors, his is a distinctly "world accepting" view. At least he thought social institutions worth discussing and evaluating. Tartullian, the milleniarist, spoke of them only to revile them. C. N. Cochrane, *Christianity and Classical Culture* (London and New York, 1944), pp. 213-214, 222-224, 227-230, and 245-247. C. Dawson, "St. Augustine and His Age," in M. C. D'Arcy, S. J., at al., *A Monument to Saint Augustine* (London, 1930), pp. 43-77.

[34] Quoted in J. Baillie, *What Is Christian Civilization?* (London, 1945), p. 16.

Protestantism was never committed to the theory of Bossuet; though today it is no less crisis-conscious than Catholicism. It is among those Protestants, like Brunner, who in their approach to natural theology are closest to Catholicism, that political fatalism predominates.[35] There is, however, a significant movement in Protestant theology that denies that history has any theological meaning. To Karl Barth, for instance, neither natural theology nor historical theology are acceptable. The distance between man and God, time and eternity, cannot be bridged by any human action. Nothing that happens in history, the realm of human life, can have any Christological significance. Paradoxically this attitude, which because of its emphasis on human depravity and the principle of "sola gratia" has been regarded as theological pessimism, does not involve any historical fatalism, as Barth has frequently noted. He refuses to have any part of Christian anthropology, Christian psychology, a "Christian interpretation of our time." These subjects lie entirely outside the concerns of Christian theology. Similarly, he finds it absurd to speak of Christian civilization or a "post-Christian" age, since the world has never been Christian at all and will never become so by its own efforts. The world is always ill, sometimes more obviously so than at others, as in the case of Nazi Germany, but neither the present age nor any other era need surprise the Christian.

[35] For purposes of social theology, the word "Catholic" is here used to indicate both Roman and Anglo-Catholics, since the differences are, in this realm, not significant.

The extent to which Protestantism has adopted the attitude of social theology to the alleged crisis of civilization can be gauged from the statements issued by the World Council of Churches at Amsterdam in 1948: "The world today is experiencing a social crisis of unparalleled proportions. The deepest root of that disorder is the refusal of men to see and admit that their responsibility to God stands over and above their loyalty to any earthly community. . . ." "Report of Section III, 'The Church and the Disorder of Society,'" *Man's Disorder and God's Design, The Amsterdam Assembly Series* (New York, 1949), v. III, p. 189.

From the Christian point of view, things in the world remain much the same at all times.[36]

In philosophic terms the same view has been developed in Karl Loewith's critique of all philosophies of history in general. The modern "over-concentration on history" seems to him devoid of both the natural wisdom of antiquity and of the supernatural faith of the New Testament. A Christian history is nonsense, since salvation is in no way bound up with any historic groups, neither nations nor civilizations. As an historical movement, Christianity has, in any case, been a failure—the world has not altered since Alaric's day. Bossuet was, in Loewith's eyes, rather more a churchman than a theologian, describing the progress of "the church triumphant," not the faith which lives apart from the world.[37] As far as the world is concerned, Christ's coming has made no real difference and history is what it always was, a "story of action and suffering, of power and pride, of sin and death. In its profane appearance it is a continuous repetition of painful miscarriages and of costly achievements which end in ordinary failures—from Hannibal to Napoleon and the contemporary leaders."[38] An unconventional Catholic philosopher, Erich Frank, adds that "in this world, it is always Caesar who is bound to be victorious, while Christ will forever be crucified."[39] The world for all the apparent changes it undergoes

[36] Barth's objections to all natural theology are to be found in his reply to Emil Brunner's "Nature and Grace," which he simply entitled "No." Both are included in *Natural Theology*, tr. by P. Frankel, ed. by J. Baillie (London, 1946); note particularly pp. 74-76 and 108-109. His rejection of the present crisis mentality he expressed at Amsterdam. "No Christian Marshall Plan," *The Christian Century*, 1948, v. 65, pp. 130-133. As to the illness of the world, it is his constant topic; in reference to Germany it can be found in *The Only Way*, tr. by M. N. Neufeld and R. G. Smith (New York, 1947), p. 3.

[37] *Meaning in History* (Chicago, 1949), pp. viii, 138-139, 185 and 191-199.

[38] *Ibid.*, p. 190.

[39] *Philosophic Understanding and Religious Truth* (New York, 1945), pp. 128-130.

remains fundamentally the same. Providence has only a spiritual, not an historical meaning, giving cause for neither hope nor despair in history.

This balanced, if discouraging, philosophy remains entirely unacceptable to those latter-day disciples of Bossuet who, though they have lost his optimism, accept his identification of faith and history and his ecclesiasticism. The vagaries of historic life cannot fail to impinge deeply upon their religious conceptions, just as these religious conceptions determine their interpretation of every historical incident. It is therefore not surprising that apocalyptic hope based on political despair has its origins with those social theologians who witnessed the collapse of Bossuet's world. The Theocrats not only saw the roots of the French Revolution in religion, or rather in heresy; they also recognized in it a divine significance, a punishment, or even the end of the world. To Bonald and Maistre, France seemed to have a divinely ordained mission to lead Europe, and her defections meant the end of civilization, and so of religion. Bonald, therefore, declined to commit himself to the belief that France was dead, because it would mean the absolute end, and he reproached Maistre for suggesting this conclusion. But even Bonald finally saw the apocalypse in the turmoil of Restoration politics.[40] Maistre knew very well the trend of his ideas. To save his orthodoxy he denounced all such "illuminism," but he never rejected the obvious implications of his premises.[41] The less circumspect Lamennais, how-

[40] Bonald's letters to Maistre, October 7, 1814, December 2, 1817, March 30, July 10, 1819 and n.d. 1819, Maistre, *Oeuvres*, vol. xiv, pp. 299-308, 319-323, 338, 341-350.

[41] *Soirées de St. Petersbourg*, vol. ii, pp. 213-242. It is interesting to observe that Monsignor Knox follows the same maneuver. First he ridicules the entire trend of apocalyptic thinking, especially the "professional students of prophecy." Then he turns to the truest Christians, whose faith he knows will not be endangered by despair, and admits that to them the end of the world must be clear and that they need no fictions to keep up their spirits. No less than Maistre and Lamen-

ever, did not hesitate to take this final step. While he still shared Maistre's political sympathies, he wrote him about his disdain for the political life of the Restoration. These disorders held a clear religious message for him: "It seems to me that everything is getting ready for the great final catastrophe; . . . Everything is extreme today, because there no longer is a middle way between faith and nothingness; the world no longer exists."[42] He took heart in observing the purity of the church as it prepared for the last day.

Contemporary social theologists no longer limit themselves to observations on national decline; they see the end of an entire culture, but its religious meaning is for them the same as that which the Revolution held for the Theocrats: "The events of the last few years portend either the end of human history, or a turning point in it. They have warned us in letters of fire that our civilization has been tried and found wanting."[43] These words of Christopher Dawson follow his denunciation of a technological age which, having turned from God, is now turning against mankind itself. However, he continues to believe, like all social theologians, that history is a rational process leading to a preordained end. The perplexities of the age, therefore, are a great discouragement to those who wish only to achieve temporal successes. To the Christian, "who sees the end of history as dawn and not as night," they are ultimately not a cause for despair.[44] Apocalyptic hope is

---

nais, he feels that historical events can reveal a divine message—in this case the end of the world. Op.cit., pp. 104-105 and 133-143.

[42] Lamennais' letter to Maistre, January 2, 1821, Maistre, Oeuvres, vol. XIV, pp. 369-372 (my translation). It has been well noted that Lamennais, both before and after his break with the church, shared the Theocrats' belief in the inseparability of the religious and social orders. Gurian, op.cit., pp. 112-113.

[43] Religion and Culture, p. 215.

[44] Beyond Politics (New York, 1939), pp. 121-136. The apocalyptic mood is by no means limited to Catholics. Mr. Dawson's Protestant compatriot, the theologian Edwyn Bevan, in response to the war ex-

today the answer to cultural failure, and the Christian duty to hope is observed, in spite of social fatalism of the most extreme kind.

Heresy: The Origin of Totalitarianism

The very essence of fatalism in social theology is that all political mistakes are the expression of the most deep-seated theological errors. Needless to say, a misfortune of the magnitude of the French Revolution had to be traced to the greatest of all religious errors in history. And indeed, from Maistre to the Papal Encyclical of 1885, *Immortale Dei*, there had been no doubt in Catholic minds that the Protestant Reformation was the real source of this and of all subsequent evils, caused by "the deplorable passion for innovation." Protestantism had perverted philosophy and false philosophy in action was the real basis of all modern political disasters.[45] Only "the doctrinal intolerance of the Church has saved the world from chaos," Donoso Cortes wrote, and with the revival of every heresy known to man, chaos had returned.[46] His friend the French publicist, Louis Veuillot, knowing that the Catholic opposition to republicanism, liberalism, and socialism constituted a war of religion, even called upon the Pope to lead a new crusade. To him all ordinary political and social measures seemed futile, since the issue was obviously not a temporal one.[47]

---

pressed identical feelings in his *Christians in a World at War* (London, 1940).

[45] "Immortale Dei," M. Oakeshott, *The Social and Political Doctrines of Contemporary Europe* (Cambridge and New York, 1947), p. 50. To Maistre, Protestantism was as much a civil as a religious heresy. Revolt was its natural condition. The "sansculottism of religion," he called it. *Reflections sur le Protestantisme* and *Lettre sur l'Etat du Christianisme en Europe, Oeuvres,* vol. VIII, pp. 63-97 and 485-519.

[46] *Op.cit.*, p. 31.

[47] W. Gurian, *op.cit.*, pp. 218-223.

To less conservative Catholics today this analysis is entirely unacceptable. Thus Rommen notes that many Protestant countries, notably Prussia, far from being radical in their political life, are, in fact, very stable and conservative.[48] But the theory, which, as Rommen points out, has always been a favorite among political theologians, is still accepted by many social theologians today. At the very least, contemporary social theologians argue, the Reformation opened the door to secularism by disrupting the unity of Christendom, and secularism is the immediate cause of the crisis today. Thus Dawson: "Protestantism, liberalism and communism are the successive stages by which our civilization has passed from Catholicism to complete secularism. The first eliminated the Church, the second eliminated Christianity and the third eliminated the human soul."[49] Totalitarianism, then, is ultimately due to the Reformation. The real depth of this political disaster can be understood only when it is recognized as something too old and too universal to be capable of any merely human solution.

On the whole, however, there is a more popular religious explanation for the rise of totalitarianism in Germany and Russia. It is the attempt to find the roots of totalitarianism in the religious history of just these nations, not in the Reformation as such. In the case of Germany, it now appears that the nation was never fully part of the West. The Latin influence was never able to fully overcome the barbarian Teutons.[50] Christianity came late to them and was never able to eradicate older influences.[51] Throughout the centuries the Germans have

[48] H. Rommen, op.cit., pp. 110-111.

[49] Religion and the Modern State, pp. 147-148. Hilaire Belloc made the same point in his plea that Europe must return to the Church if it is to save itself from communism. The Crisis of Civilization (New York, 1937), pp. 131-191.

[50] A. Kolnai, The War against the West (New York, 1938), pp. 559-562 and 565-582.

[51] The following quotation from a British historian speaks for itself: "(The) Germans have always resisted Europe; the influence of Rome

retained their hostility to Western culture. Lutheranism was merely a resurgence of these feelings, the manifestation of atavism.[52] It was not only a Germanic perversion of Christianity; it was not Christianity at all. In spite of its "Christian polish," Lutheranism was really a pagan revival of earlier anti-Roman, anti-Western instincts.[53] Even those who do not deny the religious character of Lutheranism insist that it is a form of "Eastern mysticism," and so a rejection of the West as much as of Rome.[54] But whether it is paganism or mysticism that was the real sin of Luther, it is clear to social theologians that the effects of Lutheranism are directly political, and that they explain the anti-Western aggressiveness and lack of public rectitude apparently common to Germans of all ages. The Germans' excessive sense of sin leads to indifference in politics, and so to submission to tyrants at home; their isolation from the West, to expansion abroad. Nazism is thus only an instance in a long chain of religio-social events, an inevitable application of the most ancient instincts and beliefs to the

in the shape of Christianity came to them late and incompletely. It came in the person of one of the greatest Englishmen—Boniface, the Devonshireman slain by the proto-Nazis of the eighth century." A. L. Rowse, *The End of an Epoch* (London, 1947), pp 183-184. Also C. Dawson, *The Judgment of Nations* (New York, 1942), p. 30.

[52] G. Moenius, "Le Germanisme contre la Romanité" in H. Massis' *Allemagne d'Hier et d'Après-Demain* (Paris, 1949), p. 110.

[53] Kolnai, *op.cit.*, p. 127.

[54] H. Massis, *The Defence of the West*, tr. by F. S. Flint (New York, 1928), pp. 15-69. Massis represents, in more orthodox form, the thesis of Charles Maurras that the church and the "Latin" nations have alone given order and civilization to Europe. All else is barbarism. Massis, although never a member of the Action Française, has remained a great admirer of Maurras to the very last, but he continued to be entirely orthodox in his Catholicism, unlike the latter. It is this which makes him a valid representative of this extreme form of social theology, since in Maurras' case it is more than doubtful whether he was concerned with theology, especially Christian theology. Massis' final appreciation of Maurras is to be found in his *Maurras et Notre Temps* (Paris, 1951).

modern age.[55] This inevitability is the result of the inseparability of religious and political movements, of the civil nature of religions, and the political bases of religion. Fundamentally the "German problem," as a whole, is a religious one.[56]

No one would deny that there have been important differences, if not between Protestant and Catholic political thought, between the Augustinian and Thomist conceptions of the state. To the former the state was the creature of human sin, made necessary only to prevent worse sin. The latter sees the state as the emanation of man's social nature, a nature not completely maimed by sin.[57] The state, thus, would exist even if man had never fallen, although its coercive activities would not be required.[58] Luther, it is well known, took the Augustinian position in this matter. It is also true that Luther —though he, and especially Melanchthon, did believe in a law that expressed itself in all men's conscience and that was a "higher law" limiting the will of princes—took a far dimmer view than St. Thomas or Calvin of the practical likelihood of its really restraining anyone. Luther felt a particularly strong aversion to all political authorities. The only people who really mattered to him were "a poor little heap of Christians" lost in a basically pagan world, who had no need for either political

[55] Massis, *Allemagne*, pp. 10, 13, and 19-20.

[56] "En son fond le problème allemand est un problème spirituel, un problème religieux. Aucune politique réaliste ne saurait l'oublier." H. Massis, *Allemagne*, p. 99.

[57] A. Passarin d'Entrèves, *The Medieval Contribution to Political Thought* (Oxford, 1939), pp. 17-43.

[58] These differences are as marked today as ever. One need only compare Niebuhr's dictum that "political morality must be morally ambiguous" because it must deal wickedly with wickedness. *The Children of Light and the Children of Darkness* (New York, 1944), pp. 72-73. Again Brunner asserts flatly that human evil makes the state necessary. *Justice*, p. 175. The Thomist view can be found in Rommen, *op.cit.*, pp. 62-65 and 221-229; Demant, *Social Theology*, pp. 215-216; J. Maritain, *Scholasticism and Politics*, tr. ed. by M. J. Adler (New York, 1940), pp. 89-143; Yves Simon, *Philosophy of Democratic Government* (Chicago, 1951), pp. 3-5.

or ecclesiastical organizations. He believed, like most mediae-val political thinkers, and his own contemporaries, that no violent resistance to secular authority was permissible. By this, however, he was very far from claiming that a Christian must rejoice in everything that "the powers that be" did.[59] Luther's was, undoubtedly, a world-denying and so, from the political point of view, anarchistic attitude. However, even his "other-worldliness" can be exaggerated. He had never been a hu-manist, to be sure, but even as a monk he had taken a more kindly view of the new learning than did many of the other brothers. Again, later when the humanists were everywhere under attack in Germany, especially from his own extremist followers, Luther took a decidedly moderate attitude. Cer-tainly he was not among those who wanted to abolish all learning. His "irrationalism" was not really a matter of intel-lectual or social concern at all; it was centered on one issue, that human reason cannot understand God and His ways, that He remains unknown to us.[60]

There has, moreover, always been a great diversity of opin-ion, among Lutherans themselves as well, about what Luther

[59] J. W. Allen, *The History of Political Thought in the Sixteenth Century* (London, 1941), pp. 15-34. Allen strongly emphasizes the unpolitical nature of Luther's thought as well as his dislike for all state power, and especially state churches. Professor Friedrich strongly em-phasizes his positive utterances on behalf of natural law. C. J. Fried-rich, *Inevitable Peace* (Cambridge, Mass.), pp. 98-103. On the other hand the German theologian Karl Holl representing the "orthodox" school strongly opposes such "modernism." While he denies that Luther believed in anything like mediaeval natural law, he admits that Luther believed in "natural conscience." He argues that though Luther battled tyranny, he insisted that the state originated in God's will, not in man's natural needs. On the whole I find this view the most convincing. K. Holl, *Gesammelte Aufsaetze zur Kirchen-geschichte* (Tuebingen, 1921), vol. I, "Luther," pp. 206-244 and 367-382. See also, P. Smith, *The Life and Letters of Martin Luther* (Bos-ton, 1911), pp. 157-167.

[60] R. Thiel, *Luther* (Wien, 1952), pp. 240-249, 490-495, 579-588 and 596-604.

really meant, for he altered his opinions as circumstances required. What does seem to stand out quite clearly in his social ideas is that he hated tyranny and that a state church was the last thing he wanted to set up. From all this it becomes entirely incomprehensible why social theologians should see in Luther the origin of Nazism. Yet Christopher Dawson writes of his influence as such that the war between Western democracy and Nazism was one "between two opposite conceptions of natural law and consequently of public morality."[61]

The reasoning behind such statements as this is an intellectual determinism that longs to see a closed system of continuity, in spite of all the differences in time, in place, and in spirit. Thus Maritain sees "anti-intellectualism" as a constant strain in German thought from Luther to Klages, and so to Hitler.[62] Here every form of irrationalism is simply reduced to the same level to suit the conveniences of theory, a rather odd procedure indeed for one who himself professes a profoundly mystical faith. It is not surprising to find one critic of this theory remarking that "the intention of human ideas is disregarded for the sake of finding a handsome collection of scapegoats."[63]

What Luther actually said and did is, to social theology, of infinitely less importance than the potential consequences of his thought. Yet on such matters as toleration Luther was, if not consistent, certainly more generous than Calvin or the

[61] C. Dawson, *The Judgment of Nations*, p. 52. That the difference between German and "Western" political life is due to the rejection of natural law in German political theory is a rather old theory, which had its advocates even in Germany. Ernst Troeltsch expounded it after the First War; he did not seek the origins of this idea in Lutheranism but in the peculiarities of German thought since the Romantic era—a rather more defensible notion. See his essay, "Naturrecht und Humanitaet in der Weltpolitik" in *Deutscher Geist und West-Europa* (Tuebingen, 1925), pp. 3-27.

[62] *Scholasticism and Politics*, p. 4. Also V. A. Demant, *Social Theology*, p. 225; N. Micklen, *op.cit.*, pp. 45-47.

[63] J. Barzun, *Romanticism and the Modern Ego* (Boston, 1944), p. 15.

Catholic Church of his day.[64] One might well argue that religious toleration and the separation of church and state are of far greater political relevance than ideas about natural law or rational theology. The fact that social theologians ignore the argument is significant only because it points to the basis of dogmatic intolerance upon which their whole outlook rests. For in fact religious toleration is not easily translated into social or political tolerance, and the effect of religious doctrine and policy on subsequent secular behavior is remote in this, as in all other, cases. This of course is the stumbling-block of social theology. Indeed, there are few theories that assume more and explain less than this one. How can it account for the democratic and peaceful political life of the very Lutheran Scandinavian countries? How does it demonstrate the psychological changes by which the excessive other-worldliness of a Luther is transformed into the furious·activism of the S.A. man? Why must even his critics admit that Barth and his followers, who still deny the idea of a natural law, stood up best to the inducements of "German Christianity"?[65] And that is not all. Not only is there a manifest failure to demonstrate the relation of one form of religious faith to a great variety of political actions; there is also no attempt to account for the fact that people who differ in ideas about natural law may well share the same attitudes to the immediate problems of political life, while many who agree on the former disagree on the latter. Thus the politics of the Thomist Maritain are a lot closer to those of the Protestant Niebuhr than to those of his erstwhile associate Massis.[66] Brunner's program is much

[64] J. W. Allen, op.cit., pp. 24-27 and 73-102; P. Smith, op.cit., pp. 214-228.

[65] R. Niebuhr, "We Are Men not Gods," The Christian Century, v. 65, 1948, pp. 1138-1140. Rommen, op.cit., p. 63, n.

[66] For the bitterness of the quarrel between Massis and Maritain on matters of politics, one need only see Massis' denunciations, Maurras et Notre Temps, vol. I, pp. 156-177.

like that of Dawson or Demant, but it in no way resembles that of his fellow Protestant, Tillich. The list can be extended much farther.[67]

At first sight it would seem that this analysis, whatever its usefulness in the case of German totalitarianism, would be entirely inapplicable to communism, which has no religio-national origins at all. However, the "primordial Slav" has been set up beside the "eternal German" to explain Bolshevism. It is moreover suggested that the prophetic fervor, the apocalyptic spirit and Messianic hopes of the Jewish prophets animated Marx, who was, after all, born a Jew.[68] Since there is no evidence that Marx ever lived in an even moderately Jewish environment, nor that he had any contact with the religious beliefs or writings of Judaism, it can only be assumed that religious instincts are genetically transmissible, a view not commonly accepted.[69] Even if the religious origin of Marxism is not often discussed in these terms, Russian Bolshevism is frequently regarded as the result of either the mystic withdrawal from the world on the part of the Orthodox Church or of its Erastian position. Sometimes, both are blamed together! Bolshevism is only a return to the anti-Western and un-Latin spirit of old Russia that Peter the Great had in vain tried to transform.[70] Others argue that the Bolsheviks are only continuing Peter's efforts of Westernization by violent means.[71]

[67] By no means are all theologians given to forgetfulness of these facts. Dr. Walter Lowrie, in his explanation of the Barthian doctrine of "sanctification" by religion, points to the diversity of character and behavior developed by the same religion and the similarities among men of the most divergent faiths. *Our Concern with the Theology of Crisis* (Boston, 1932), pp. 198-199.

[68] H. Belloc, *op.cit.*, pp. 185-186; C. Dawson, *Religion and the Modern State*, pp. 86-96.

[69] I. Berlin, *Karl Marx* (London, 1948), pp. 23-24, 97-98 and 253.

[70] H. Massis, *The Defence of the West*, pp. 70-158. *Découverte de la Russie* (Montreal, 1944).

[71] C. Dawson, *Understanding Europe*, pp. 84-122.

Both views insist that autocracy is natural to the Russians as a consequence of their religio-political history. Even the expansionism of the Soviet régime is only a new form of the Messianic mission to purify the West that had long been preached by the Orthodox Church. As in the case of Lutheranism, no direct relations can, of course, be shown between the Orthodox Church and the Bolsheviks, as individuals, or between Eastern Christianity and communism as intellectual movements. Militant atheism can suddenly be accepted as the logical consequence of mysticism, provided that both are to be found within the same nation.

That the writers who most fervently support these views should themselves be strong nationalists is not surprising, but the real failure of these efforts to find the origins of totalitarianism in the history of nations does not follow from that. Their inadequacies are factual and logical. The national and religious bases of communism are obscure, to say the least, since the Party has drawn its support from people of every nation and every kind of religious and un-religious background.[72] Moreover, the religious history of Russia itself does not lend itself to simple deductions. One must be on one's guard against the romantic theologians, like Berdiaev, who over-emphasize the effects of religion on Russian culture and on the so-called "Russian soul." For him Russian Bolshevism is the outcome of such traits as asceticism, dogmatism, self-sacrifice, and a real sense of the hereafter, which he sees as permanent aspects of the Russian religious character. In its apocalyptic hopes Bolshevism is moreover only continuing the old feeling for Moscow as the Third Rome that inspired the Russians since the fall of the Byzantine Empire.[73] Such easy

[72] G. Almond, *The Appeals of Communism* (Princeton, N.J., 1954), pp. 210-216. There a fairly large number of interviews with ex-communists showed that a religious background was, if anything, more common than an unreligious one among communists.

[73] N. Berdiaev, *Les Sources et le Sens du Communisme Russe*, tr. by

analogies are of course congenial to all social theology, as to all fatalisms. In addition to an unrealistic tendency to reduce communism to a purely Russian phenomenon, they also simplify Russian history. To more rationalist historians, it appears clear that the whole idea of the Third Rome was a politically inspired fabrication of the Tsars. Nor does the religiosity of the Russian popular soul impress them too greatly. The peasantry was given more to ritualism than to profound piety—as it was everywhere else. Most important of all, there was no simple, single line of religious development in Russia that can be called orthodoxy. The church itself was torn by schisms in the 17th century and thereafter there appeared an ever-increasing number of sects.[74]

The history of religion in Russia, as well as of Europe, in fact, tends to show that the effect of political events on religious doctrines is as powerful as that of religion on politics. The real tragedy of Luther's life was that he felt himself to have a mission only to that "poor lost heap of Christians," but was step by step forced to become the advisor of princes and the founder of an ecclesiastical institution. With these changes his doctrine underwent noticeable changes. Again, Calvin was forced to amend his doctrine as the result of political events in France. In Russia—very much as in Britain—the growth of intensely spiritual sects followed the submission of the church

---

A. Nerville (Paris, 1951), pp. 7-25. It is of course quite true that Marxism was transformed by the Russian intelligentsia, but this was the most Western, least religious group in Russia itself, cut off for centuries from the "popular soul." Moreover, this is a fact of small importance today, since Bolshevism now finds followers everywhere. See J. Plamenatz, *German Marxism and Russian Communism* (London, 1954), pp. 191-249 and 306-351, for an account of the Russian revision of Marx prior to the Revolution.

[74] P. Miliukov, *Outlines of Russian Culture*, Part I, "Religion and the Church," tr. by V. Ughet and E. Davis, ed. by M. Karpovich (Philadelphia, 1942), pp. 1-2, 15-17, 27-39, 40-121, and 141-147.

to the state.[75] No one would argue from these circumstances that religious beliefs are determined by political events. What is evident is that history is not a simple process of the embodiment of religious ideas in political acts. Historical change is a matter of multiform interactions, not of plain lines of cause and effect.

The weakness of social theology, as an interpretation of history, reveals itself finally in its inability to account for contemporary events. No theory of religious development can explain the rise of totalitarianism in some countries and its absence in others. Unless one is ready to agree that Mussolini and Franco are in no way totalitarian, but, on the contrary, saviors of the West, it becomes evident that Latin and religious nations are today as susceptible to totalitarianism as Eastern and irreligious ones.[76] The fact remains that Fascist Italy, especially, was in every respect a more totalitarian society than such largely secular or Protestant nations as Britain, France, or the Scandinavian countries, even if it never reached the extremes of Nazi Germany. This objection must be directed, moreover, not only against the theory of the anti-Western nature of totalitarianism but also against the idea that secularism is the real root of totalitarian politics. This theory is on the whole more popular than the notion of a merely national-religious origin. Protestants tend to reject the latter in any case. Thus Emil Brunner denies that the present conflict is one between East and West, since communism has its origins in Western secularism and has its adherents in such ultra-Western nations as France and Italy.[77] Again, Maritain attaches to the irrationalism of Lutheranism a secondary though

[75] G. Vernadsky, A History of Russia (New Haven, Conn., 1951), pp. 124-126.

[76] Chefs (Paris, 1939), pp. 3-175.

[77] Communism, Capitalism and Christianity, tr. by N. P. Goldhawk (London, 1949), pp. 26-27; Die Kirche zwischen Ost und West (Stuttgart, 1949), pp. 21-22, 25-26, 36.

by no means negligible importance, and puts the chief blame upon "anthropocentric humanism."[78]

The End of an Age

As a form of political fatalism this "secularist" theory is even more extreme than that of the "nationalists." The latter at least believes that there are still sources of social and religious vitality in the "Roman," "Western" part of the world. If it is secularism—and admittedly secularism is now universal —that lies at the root of the trouble, then all is lost. If, in T. S. Eliot's phrase, our society, "worm-eaten with liberalism," is sinking into paganism, and if we must either "have God (and he is a jealous God)" or "pay (our) respects to Hitler or Stalin," then, on their own showing, social theologians have no grounds for hope.[79] If not the end of the world, we are at least faced with the death, by suicide, of the modern age. "We are looking at the liquidation of the modern world," Maritain writes, and many Christians echo his sentiments.[80]

It seems rather easy for Christian writers to announce the end of the age since, after all, it never was to their liking. The popular expression, "an age of faith," could hardly be applied to it. Humanism, to the extent that it is not severed from Christian faith, has found its defenders among Christians, but rationalism and its progeny remain anathema. It must, however, be noted that under the impact of totalitarianism, Christian thinkers have shown a far higher regard for those political and intellectual liberties against which they "conducted a vain

[78] *The Twilight of Civilization*, tr. by L. Landry (New York, 1944), p. 4.
[79] *After Strange Gods* (New York, 1934), p. 12; *The Idea of a Christian Society* (New York, 1940), p. 64.
[80] *Christianity and Democracy* (New York, 1945), p. 12. The following titles are instructive: Maritain's *The Twilight of Civilization*; N. Berdyaev's *The End of Our Time*, tr. by D. Atwater (London, 1933); R. Guardini's *Das Ende der Neuzeit* (Basel, 1950). There are a great many more with similar names and messages.

rearguard action," since the Enlightenment.[81] It is not really that they have grown any fonder of the philosophic premises of modern liberty, but only that their successors seem so obviously worse. Rationalism, liberalism, capitalism, and socialism are not only still rejected; they are also regarded as the necessary precursors of totalitarianism. They are not only wrong in themselves, but also so many steps down the ladder to the totalitarian tragedy. Of course, not even the most embittered enemy of the modern age would claim that humanism or liberalism are themselves totalitarian. The argument of Christian fatalism is not that simple. What it does is to judge them, and all secular ideals, in terms of their potential evils, of their remote results. The cardinal fault of "anthropocentric humanism," and of all morality not based directly upon religious dogma, is that it is bound to fail. Nothing but religious faith is capable of keeping society from falling into radical evil, for it is taken as an established historical law that religion is the only dynamic, the only effective, force in culture. Non-religious ethics, however, undermine religion on one hand and, on the other, are unable to provide a viable substitute. Without Christianity there can, in the West, be neither culture nor genuine community life. Christianity alone offers Europe "the culture-transcendent presuppositions of every culture."[82] "Europe will be Christian or it will not exist at all," Romano Guardini flatly states, and that indeed is the core of the argument.[83]

Emil Brunner is especially vehement in his denunciation of

[81] H. Butterfield, *Christianity in European History* (London, 1952), p. 52.

[82] E. Brunner, *Christianity and Civilization* (London, 1949), vol. I, p. 11. Christopher Dawson's entire work is devoted to an exposition of this idea, and it is, therefore, hopeless to assemble passages on this point. *Religion and Culture* and *Understanding Europe* are perhaps the most important in emphasizing these thoughts.

[83] *Der Heilbringer*, p. 47. "Europa wird Christlich, oder es wird ueberhaupt nicht sein."

Stoicism, which he, quite rightly, sees reincarnated in modern rationalism, especially in the Enlightenment. His argument, which is the same that Bossuet put forward long ago, is that neither Stoicism nor Epicureanism can provide the cohesive force necessary to a stable society.[84] Brunner, moreover, claims that Stoicism acts positively against community feeling, since it urges the wise to withdraw from society. Actually this is something of a misrepresentation; the Stoic doctrine urges the wise to be indifferent to the transient preoccupations of society, not to leave it to its own devices. This is to give each person the courage to do his tasks without concern for the immediate consequences. Stoicism is above all the ethic of the unpleasant duty. In no sense is it an invitation to irresponsibility. Other theologians might well take note of Tillich's remark that because the "Stoic has a social and personal courage" his is "the only real alternative to Christianity in the Western world."[85] There is, of course, the obvious objection to Stoicism, that while it preaches the innate rationality of man, it cannot account for the widespread existence of folly, a paradox that the Christian doctrine of sin solves. But the ideal of the wise man is anything but an inducement to social escapism.[86]

Social theologians do not really concern themselves with these issues. Their entire attack is based on pragmatic not on intellectual grounds. Stoicism has bad social consequences. It is not useful. A sterile "clericalism of the reason," "artificial

[84] They lacked, Bossuet wrote, "la stabilité raisonable qui constitue les Etats," *Politique*, Liv. VIII, Art. II.

[85] *The Courage to Be* (New Haven, 1952), pp. 9-10.

[86] *Ibid.*, pp. 11-17. Possibly Ernst Cassirer's phrase is the best description of neo-Stoicism, "the promise to restore man to his ethical dignity." *The Myth of the State* (New Haven, 1946), p. 169. The compatibility of the ideal of the wise man above society and the demands of social duty are especially evident in Seneca. R. W. and A. J. Carlyle, *A History of Mediaeval Political Theory in the West*, vol. I (New York, 1950), pp. 19-32.

and hypercritical," Maritain says of Kant.[87] And Brunner sums up the case: "Mere ethics has never displayed real dynamic. You cannot cure a demon-ridden technical world with moral postulates. In contrast to mere ethics and morality Christian faith has the dynamic of passion, of surrender and sacrifice, it is capable of turning men to the eternal end, of unmasking demonic sin and thereby leavening it, which no enlightened education is capable of doing."[88]

"Mere ethics" and "mere humanism" are socially impotent. That is the essence of the argument against the modern age. "Wisdom," T. S. Eliot writes, "is no substitute for faith," for humanism can appeal only to "a small number of superior individuals" and it cannot give them "the power necessary to influence the mass of mankind."[89] Reason, moreover, Brunner argues, makes men feel self-sufficient, autonomous, and so devoid of communal feeling. In politics that means "atomistic liberalism or its consequence collectivism."[90] That is the real trouble, for it is not only the futility of rationalist ethics but their long-term effects that must be judged.

There is, moreover, a Gresham's law of ideas according to which one intellectual error must of necessity be followed by a multitude of even greater sins. It is much like the argument about Lutheranism. There is an inevitable sequence of ideas from the first steps of humanism away from religion to its own destruction by forces both anti-Christian and anti-humanistic. Nietzsche thus, by revealing "the antinomy that was inherent in humanism" from the beginning—that is, its Christian origins and its anti-Christian trend—destroyed it, as it had to be de-

[87] *Scholasticism and Politics*, p. 14.
[88] *Christianity and Civilization*, vol. ii, p. 15.
[89] "The Christian Concept of Education," *Malvern, 1941: The Life of the Church and the Order of Society* (London, 1941), pp. 201-213. Also "The Humanism of Irving Babbitt," *Selected Essays* (New York, 1950), pp. 419-428.
[90] *Justice*, p. 68; *Christianity and Civilization*, vol. i, pp. 91-105.

stroyed. "Each fresh victory of the humanistic spirit undermined the foundations of its own vitality," namely Christian
dogma. Nietzsche was only the end result of this process, according to Dawson.[91] From him on, the road to totalitarianism
is clear. Nietzsche's fault was that he "did not grasp that man
has no choice except between two roads: the road to Calvary
and the road to the slaughter-house,"[92] Maritain writes. The
consequences of this are to be found in the works of Nazism,
since, "the trouble with all forms of noble and lofty counter-
humanism is that inevitably men end by substituting for them
the meanest forms."[93] Like Lutheranism, which it resembles so
little, "rationalism which denies God" turns itself into the irrationalism of Nazism. No less certainly does it lead to Marx
and the rulers of the USSR, for Soviet communism "both as
an idea and a way of life" is part of rationalistic humanism,
even if it is "a spiritual catastrophe thereof."[94]

This intellectual descent from religion to totalitarian ideology is reproduced exactly on the scene of political life. That is
implicit in a theory which regards each action as the direct
expression of some general theological, or anti-theological, pre-
supposition. Liberalism is in politics what humanism is in the
realm of philosophy. It too is merely a transitional stage. The
liberals of the last century were still "sublimated Christians,"
unconsciously living off the accumulated spiritual and moral
capital of the Christian civilization which they slowly killed
by severing it from its religious bases.[95] But, as Donoso Cortes
had observed from the first, the "religious weakness" of liberal-

[91] "The End of an Age," *Criterion*, vol. IX, 1929-1930, pp. 386-401;
Religion and Culture, pp. 8-10.
[92] *Scholasticism and Politics*, p. 4; *The Twilight of Civilization*,
pp. 8-10.
[93] *Ibid.*, p. 8.
[94] *Ibid.*, p. 11.
[95] Dawson, *Beyond Politics*, pp. 101-104; *The Judgment of Nations*,
p. 31; Demant, *Religion and the Decline of Capitalism*, pp. 59-88;
Theology of Society, p. 64.

ism was bound to lead it to destruction by socialism. And Dawson today echoes his premonitions: "Once society is launched on the path of secularisation it cannot stop in the half-way house of Liberalism; it must go on to the bitter end, whether the end be Communism or some alternative type of totalitarian secularism."[96] Communism especially is "the culminating point of the secularising process in modern civilization." For it merely develops more rigorously "the Liberal dogma" that only the temporal sphere exists.[97] The only reason that all Europe is not yet communist is due to the existence of some reserves from the "pre-naturalist and pre-positivist" era, since totalitarianism of all kinds is only the "dynamic heir" of these philosophies.[98]

As far as Russian Bolshevism is concerned, this argument is particularly weak. In the beginning of the present century, when Western secular ideas were gaining an ever-increasing number of adherents among Russians, a genuine religious revival was also taking place. There was a strong movement within the Orthodox Church to free itself from the state; there were such spiritualist sects as the "Stundites"; and there was, above all, the enormous influence of Tolstoy.[99] If Russia was careening down the path of secularism, secularism was far less noticeable there than in the West. Can one think of any great European novelist, either then or now, producing a figure like Father Zossima? In short, wholesale secularization was hardly the prelude to communism in Russia. Moreover, one might well object that nothing like a "liberal era" ever existed in Europe as a whole. In fact, the countries in which totalitarianism has flourished are notable for never having passed through this "transitional stage." Neither Russia nor Germany

[96] *Religion and the Modern State*, pp. 64-65.
[97] Demant, *The Religious Prospect* (London, 1939), pp. 56-82 and 110.
[98] Brunner, *Die Kirche zwischen Ost und West*, pp. 21-22, 25-26.
[99] Vernadsky, *op.cit.*, pp. 212-213.

were in the 19th-century classical examples of liberalism, to say the least. Indeed, the prevalence of mystical religions, which social theology emphasizes so much, is supposed to have prevented the development of humanistic-liberal ideas in these countries. It is odd that so many Catholic social theologians should see these two antithetical forms of thoughts leading to the same political end.[100] It can be argued that Lutheranism, by preventing the rise of liberal politics, contributed to totalitarianism, only if it is assumed that liberalism prevents such an outcome. Since, however, liberalism too is suspect, it is difficult to see the relevance of this assumption. However, this seemingly incomprehensible conclusion is inherent in social theology. Not only does it insist that religion alone explains all subsequent forms of behavior; it also believes that there is but one set of social truths to be directly derived from religious dogma. All other forms of social thought and action are more or less alike in being false.

This is particularly important for the critique of democracy. To social theologians, democracy, far from being the answer to totalitarianism, is only another form of secularism, and part of the same web of errors as the former. A few of the democratic states, because they have retained implicitly some of their Christian habits, remain superior to totalitarianism, but to the degree that they fall into pure secularism they are in all essentials no different from them.[101] The prospect of "totali-

[100] Maritain insists that Nazism and communism are alike because both are "irrational tidal waves," Nazism from the first and Marxism because it is "reason that decapitates reason." Both are the outcome of the tragic wheel of rationalistic humanism. The wheel, one might recall, has always been the symbol of fatalism. *Scholasticism and Politics*, pp. 4-12. Among those who hold both Lutheranism and secularist humanism responsible for totalitarianism are Dawson, Demant, Maritain and Micklem, to name only the most obvious.

[101] It is only on religious grounds that Maritain has hopes for the U.S.A. and Brunner for Switzerland, Holland, and Scandinavia. Maritain, *Christianity and Democracy*, pp. 19-21; Brunner, *Justice*, pp. 86-87.

tarian democracy" is upon us. Dawson regards the Roosevelt New Deal as the American equivalent of European totalitarianism, and in Britain he sees an "Anglo-Saxon" form of totalitarianism daily gaining ground. It is not castor oil and concentration camps that make totalitarianism; there is also a "democratic totalitarianism" which relies on "free milk and birth control clinics" to achieve its ends.[102] In either case the totalitarian element is the suppression of religion, not just by violence but by "the sheer weight of state inspired public opinion and by the mass organization of society on a purely secular basis."[103] Democracy as such is a negative idea, T. S. Eliot adds, for there are only two positive forms of society available, the Christian and the pagan-totalitarian. At best, democracy can hope to be apathetic "without a philosophy of life, either Christian or pagan; and without art"; at worst it will be totalitarian, built on "the puritanism of hygienic morality in the interest of efficiency."[104] To students of politics the relation of birth-control clinics and hygiene to totalitarianism may seem a bit obscure, but it must be recalled that for social theology it is not specific political forms that matter. Since totalitarianism is defined as anti-Christianism in the first place, any kind of social policy that seems incompatible with Christianity can thereafter be regarded as a form of totalitarianism. Therefore Eliot is quite consistent when he ends these remarks with the observation that the problem is not political at all, but religious in character, and that only a religious revolution is capable of saving Western culture.

If the question is to be regarded politically at all, it is one of justice, and justice is possible only where the supremacy of the spiritual realm is clearly recognized. To Emil Brunner the very idea of political sovereignty represents a form of "social

[102] *Religion and the Modern State*, pp. 23-24, 45-58 and 106-108.
[103] *Ibid.*, p. 57.
[104] T. S. Eliot, *The Idea of a Christian Society*, pp. 21-22.

atheism," since it obliterates this principle.[105] Only where a real duality between church and state exists, with an ultimate appeal to the former, can justice or any reasonable political life exist. Without the guidance of religious dogma, political life is bound to be dominated by some subordinate secular principle, whether it be the economic liberalism of the last century or the purely political ideologies of totalitarianism. "(Without) a basis in dogma concerning the purpose of political action, politics seeks to administer the life of the community under the direction of some deracinated subsidiary element of the community's real life, until a demonic reaction is produced. . . . Politics can remain in health only so long as it is concerned to co-ordinate the activities of men with respect to the natural hierarchy of human needs and power; and this means that it must be somehow conscious of man as ultimately spiritual."[106]

The task today is obviously not simple political action or to uphold one set of secular principles against another. It is to oppose secularism itself, which today means totalitarianism, by a return to the Christian hierarchy of values and to Christian natural law. It is because of this that Brunner feels that it is "disastrous that the struggle against the totalitarian State . . . should be carried out in the name of democracy, while the problem of the totalitarian State has practically nothing to do with the problem of democracy." In short, to oppose democracy to totalitarianism is simply to confuse the real issues involved. Similarly there is in economic life no genuine difference between capitalism, socialism, and collectivism. All three are only aspects of the same error, even "twins," according to Brunner, both because "capitalist anarchy" has to end in collectivism and because neither recognizes guiding prin-

[105] *Justice*, p. 71.
[106] W. G. Peck, "The Validity of Politics" in *Prospect for Christendom*, ed. by M. B. Reckitt (London, 1945), p. 166.

ciples of a supra-material kind. Neither one is compatible with natural law.[107]

From a Christian point of view, writes Canon Demant, there is nothing to choose between liberalism and socialism. As for collectivism, it is only "atomism packed tight," a revenge upon the disruptions of capitalist economics. However, like the latter it remains an "unnatural order" in which the natural hierarchy of values is reversed. As such, socialism, communism, and capitalism remain much more similar to each other than to a Christian order which subordinates material to spiritual ends. If collectivism cannot reintegrate society because it remains secular in orientation, the free market economy was the original mistake. Canon Demant explicitly rejects the contention of such liberals as Professor Wilhelm Roepke that it was not in the economic realm that liberalism failed, but in the rest of the social fabric, which then forced distortions upon the operation of the free market. For him any economic system that attempts to act autonomously upon its own imperatives is "unnatural" and disruptive.[108]

T. S. Eliot extends the argument even further, to culture as a whole, especially to artistic and intellectual activity. Neither, he insists, can prosper without dependence upon some religion, even a false religion being preferable to none.[109] But at the highest levels of both religion and culture there must also be tension between the two. "Totalitarianism," he writes, "is a

[107] The Theology of Crisis, pp. xxii-xxiii; Justice, pp. 72-79 and 156-169; Communism, Capitalism and Christianity, pp. 10-11; Dawson, Religion and the Modern State, pp. 61-71.

[108] "Dialectics and Prophecy," Criterion, vol. 14, 1934-1935, pp. 559-571; Religious Prospect, pp. 56-82 and 134-135; Religion and the Decline of Capitalism, pp. 23-33, 35-58, 88-99, 106, 111, 154-160 and 192-196. Canon Demant's idea of totalitarianism, of forced reintegration of a society disrupted by capitalism, is admittedly borrowed from K. Polanyi, Origins of Our Time (London, 1945).

[109] "Cultural Forces in the Human Order," in Prospect for Christendom, ed. by M. B. Reckitt, pp. 57-69.

desire to return to the womb," to that primitive stage at which culture and religion are one.[110] In this respect, moreover, democracy is no less hostile to culture than are openly totalitarian states. The duality of culture and religion, state and church, is, then, the only guarantee of distinction in cultural life and of justice in politics. If Lutheranism and Eastern Orthodoxy lead to totalitarianism because they destroy this duality in Erastianism, secularisms lead to the same result by eliminating religion as an active force in society and by reducing all life to a single level, the mundane. That is why the modern age is inherently self-destructive.

The New Wars of Religion

The argument of social theology is not limited to establishing a purely intellectual and institutional chain of causality from the Enlightenment to totalitarianism. It also takes psychological factors into account. Man, it is argued, is naturally predisposed to be religious. When he is denied the satisfactions of true religion, as he has been since the end of "the age of faith," he turns to secular religions. Totalitarian ideologies are primarily such substitute religions. That is their main evil, the challenge that makes them much more dangerous than the pale morality of liberalism. Thus T. S. Eliot notes, "The popular result of ignoring religion seems to be merely that the populace transfers their religious emotions to political theories. Few people are sufficiently civilized to afford atheism."[111] The only sort of faith that the secular era offered was the hope in progress, and when that faded, "a sort of metaphysical hatred against existence" took hold of people and turned them to anti-religions.[112] Secularism leaves a "horror vacuui" which

[110] *Notes towards a Definition of Culture* (London, 1948), pp. 27-34 and 68-69.
[111] "The Literature of Fascism," *loc.cit.*
[112] V. A. Demant, "Christianity and Western Civilization Now," *The Western Tradition. A Symposium* (Boston, 1951), p. 16.

people must escape at any price.[113] The substitute religions of Nazism and Communism fit the bill, for they give people at least some sense of purpose and solidarity.[114]

Totalitarianism, then, is not just a relapse into paganism but a new form of religion, "demonic para-theism," as Maritain calls it, whose chief aim and trait is a remorseless hatred of its one real rival, Christianity. Totalitarianism is first and foremost "anti-Christic."[115] Romano Guardini insists that the ex-Catholics who led the Nazi Party and "the savior of twelve years" exploited all the external manifestations of the true religion to destroy Christianity.[116] Dawson speaks of Communism as "the Godless Church Militant."[117] The "Satanic incarnation of our time," Brunner calls totalitarianism in words reminiscent of Maistre and Donoso Cortes.[118] In short, though Marxism is obviously atheistic, "the religious incurability of man" is such that it has become the "pseudo-theology of the communist church."[119] Indeed, Berdiaev claims that Bolshevism hates religion so intensely just because it too is a religion.[120]

The essence of the struggle is not political, not social at all. We are faced with a new war of religions—possibly the final battle. For, as Dawson writes of communism, "For the first time in the world's history the Kingdom of Anti-Christ has acquired political form and social substance and stands over

[113] H. Rommen, op.cit., pp. 71-73.
[114] V. A. Demant, Theology of Society, pp. 55-63.
[115] Scholasticism and Politics, pp. 15-18 and 244; Twilight of Civilization, pp. 18-26.
[116] Der Heilbringer, pp. 36-44.
[117] "Religion and the Totalitarian State," Criterion, vol. XIV, 1934-1935, pp. 7-13.
[118] Christianity and Civilization, vol. II, p. 121. Berdyaev too saw Satanism in communism especially, The End of Our Time, pp. 81-82 and 105.
[119] N. Micklem, The Theology of Politics, p. 13.
[120] Les Sources et le Sense du Communisme Russe, p. 213.

against the Christian Church as a *counter-church* with its own dogmas and its own moral standards. . . ."[121] Nazism, similarly, is "mystical neo-paganism," a "new public religion." Like communism, it is a fall to the lowest depth, left open by the "silence of the prophets" in an irreligious society.[122] It has even been suggested that the anti-semitism of the Nazis was really a form of "Christo-phobia," an attack on the person of Christ rather than just on contemporary Jewry.[123] Maritain suggests that the Communists reject democracy *because* they are anti-Christian.[124] Such views might be more convincing if there had never been any persecution of Jews by Christians, or if all Christians favored democracy as fervently as does Maritain. This, however, is scarcely the case. From the point of the historian—and of the Jew, it might be added—it is not a matter of staggering importance whether it is the hope of religious or racial uniformity that inspires violently anti-semitic policies.[125]

The main objection to the entire view of totalitarianism as a religious phenomenon is that it is simply too spiritual for reality. Even at the ideological level it is difficult to agree that anti-Christian fervor constitutes the core of totalitarianism. The church enjoyed rather better relations with Mussolini than with previous Italian regimes.[126] When, after his downfall, Mussolini came to regret his concessions to the church, it was for purely political never for ideological reasons.[127] Hit-

[121] *Religion and the Modern State*, p. 58; italics supplied; also pp. 57, 59, 111-113, and *Beyond Politics*, p. 113.

[122] *Beyond Politics*, pp. 81-82 and 104-108; *Religion and Culture*, p. 83.

[123] J. Maritain, *Redeeming the Time*, tr. by H. L. Binesse (London, 1943), pp. 125-126, 145-146, 153-154 and 157; A. Kolnai, *op.cit.*, pp. 494 and 511; N. Berdiaev, *The Fate of Man in the Modern World*, tr. by D. A. Lowrie (London, 1935), pp. 100-102.

[124] *Christianity and Democracy*, pp. 53-54.

[125] H. Butterfield, *Christianity in European History*, pp. 46-47.

[126] D. A. Binchy, *Church and State in Fascist Italy* (London, 1941).

[127] B. Mussolini, *The Fall of Mussolini*, tr. by F. Frenaye, ed. by M. Ascoli (New York, 1948). In this account of his own downfall writ-

ler's *Mein Kampf* is rather more concerned with racism, pan-Germanism, and militarism than with Christianity. Marx, who, to be sure, was a militant atheist, gave rather more thought to questions of economic change and class organization than to a religion which he expected to disappear in the due course of time. His attack on secular idealism was far more intense. In practice, moreover, the suppression of religious bodies in Germany was only an incidental part of a general drive against all centers of loyalty other than party and state. Indeed, scientific objectivity, artistic integrity, and political independence, all secular fields of activity, were crushed far more completely than religious autonomy. It was, at all times, possible in Nazi Germany at least to attend church services, while it was certainly not possible openly to profess sympathies for social democracy or Jews. In the USSR, although the social penalties of religion are very high, and the decision to open the churches was motivated by the purest expediency, the situation is much the same.[128] Because totalitarianism is a political phenomenon and operates upon political premises, its attitude to religion is determined entirely by political considerations. If the demands of political conformity require the harshest persecutions of the devout, there is no hesitation in undertaking it, but Anti-Christianity as an end in itself is not the sole, or even the primary, motive of such action.

---

ten during his last stand in Northern Italy, Mussolini came to regard the king and the church as the two main obstacles to his power. At no point does he make an ideological issue out of monarchy or religion.

It has been claimed that because Mussolini came to an agreement with the church, and because fascism was ideologically weak, the Italian fascist regime was only authoritarian, not totalitarian. Without political religion one cannot speak of totalitarianism, and the defining trait of such a religion is anti-Christianism. W. Gurian, "Totalitarian Religions," *Review of Politics*, vol. XI, 1952, pp. 3-14.

[128] M. Fainsod: *How Russia Is Ruled* (Cambridge, 1953), pp. 116, 483 and 497.

Social theology does not recognize this state of affairs, not because it wishes to dissemble, but because it does not see social life apart from its relation to religion. The idea of secular religions crowning the age of secularism is based on this; it reaches its height when it is claimed that all modern political thought, liberal, socialist, and totalitarian, is descended from a religious heresy, the "Gnosticism" of Joachim of Floris, and that in their general character *all* political theories since Hobbes are the same, since all are secular religions.[129] But this view is peculiar to Erich Voegelin, and represents an extreme version of the theory of social theology. It is, however, clear to all social theologians that the real conflict is a war between totalitarianism and Christianity, with no alternatives of a purely secular kind.

The Abolition of Man

There is a grand simplicity about looking at the modern age with one glance and rejecting it all. Secularism has been a failure, as an ethic because no secular power can really integrate society, as a pseudo-religion because it always deprives man of his true place in the divine order. The crowning indictment of the secular age is that by destroying man's inner concord it has led to ceaseless war. "War," Maurice Reckitt, a leader of the "Christendom" movement, writes, "is the truth about our civilization." It is "the catastrophic revelation of a secularized Europe."[130] War is the upshot of the unnatural social order that denies man's spiritual nature. That there never was a time of peace, even in the "natural" Middle Ages, does not seem to disturb Reckitt. After all, there is some doubt

[129] E. Voegelin, *The New Science of Politics*, pp. 107-189; *Die Politischen Religionen* (Stockholm, 1939), pp. 39-42, 49-63; on Hobbes' civil theology, see also N. Micklem, *op.cit.*, p. 41.

[130] M. B. Reckitt, "War: The Upshot of Peace," *Malvern*, 1941, p. 52; "The War behind the War," in J. H. Oldham et al., *The Church Looks Ahead* (London, 1941), pp. 44-51.

whether there ever was a "natural" order in the history of Western civilization. It is quite clear that social theology looks upon the Middle Ages as a model. It can be argued that life in the Middle Ages was far from conforming to the Christian ideal, being subject to non-religious motives in its secular life; also, to claim that it was an age of Christian behavior does Christianity no service, for the Middle Ages were neither so just nor so tranquil as to be a credit to their alleged guide and inspiration, the church.[131]

While it would be unfair to say that social theologians simply want a return to the Middle Ages, there is at least one aspect of mediaeval life, in addition to its religiosity, that strongly appeals to them, namely, the reverence for tradition. Christian traditionalism is not simply social conservatism; it is rather a matter of historical solidarity, a sense of shared responsibility both for the Christian message revealed in history and for the guilt of Adam that must be shouldered by all posterity. Each generation is bound to all past and future generations by "solidarity in sin and creation." No one can disconnect himself from either Adam's destiny or his guilt. In itself this idea of solidarity has no obvious connection to social institutions, but it has been characteristic of social theology from the first to regard it as a dogmatic basis for conservatism.[132] Few social theologians today are ready to go as far as Maistre,

[131] H. Butterfield, *History and Human Relations* (London, 1951), pp. 131-157. Two critical reviews of Dawson's and one of Maritain's historical works stress this point, as well as a liberal economist's critique of Canon Demant. A. Huxley, *The Olive Tree and Other Essays* (London, 1936), pp. 129-149. G. G. Coulton, "Mediaeval Religion," *The Cambridge Review*, vol. 56, 1934-1935, p. 48; "The Historical Background of Maritain's Humanism," *Journal of the History of Ideas*, vol. v, 1944, pp. 415-433; C. Wilson: "Canon Demant's Economic History," *The Cambridge Journal*, vol. vi, 1953, pp. 281-290.

[132] An especially illuminating discussion of solidarity in sin as a dogmatic defense of conservatism is that of Donoso Cortes, *op.cit.*, pp. 209-252, and Brunner, *The Theology of Crisis*, p. 83.

who, it is said, "made time God's prime minister."[133] However, many would agree with Brunner that since "the Church in her very essence is tradition, she also is the legitimate guardian of all natural and cultural tradition." Moreover, tradition is conceived as a support to man's weakened reason. Social theology therefore stands in opposition to rationalism and democracy, since one subjects every custom to the test of rationality, and the other holds today's decision to be as valid as that of yesterday.[134]

Christian traditionalism is, to be sure, selective; both Brunner and Dawson insist on the great impetus for change that Christianity has given Western culture. Indeed, it alone is said to have provided the dynamic element in European civilization.[135] Certainly it does not countenance old evils because of their age. On the other hand, it has attached a special value to specific institutions and social forms for the sake of tradition. Social theology, believing that there is a "natural" form of society, which alone corresponds to the divine intent for man, is not only concerned to preserve certain traditional values; it also insists on the inherent superiority of specific traditional institutions. Chief among these are social gradation, hierarchy, and a special feeling for the peasantry as the most stable group in society. To this extent at least Christian traditionalism is purely conservative. But the "need for roots," which is so strongly felt by social theologians, not only is a means to ensure a more natural social order; it is also necessary to preserve man as a spiritual entity. For the age of "extreme dissociation" is about to end in the "abolition of man" as part of humanity and his replacement by the masses.[136]

[133] H. Rommen, op.cit., p. 213.
[134] Brunner, Christianity and Civilization, vol. I, p. 122, and vol. II, pp. 29-42.
[135] Dawson, Religion and Culture, pp. 50-54.
[136] Demant, Religion and the Decline of Capitalism, p. 116. C. S. Lewis in The Abolition of Man (New York, 1947) insists that in

The less-than-human mass man is above all the victim of "religious homelessness (which) tears man out of his *metaphysical* structure of existence; he is no longer rooted in an eternal order."[137] For social theology, the masses are not the new Philistines that they are for romantics, nor are they a mere byproduct of technology, although its contribution to moral dissociation, and to irresponsibility, especially in war, is not ignored. However, it is not science or technology as such that is evil; on the contrary, they represent man's uniqueness in the order of creation, his God-given power over nature. It is the misuse of nature that is bound to occur in an "unnatural," irreligious age that makes the power of science and technology demonic or, to be exact, Satanic.[138] Man defies nature today as part of the rejection of God, hence the emergence of the non-human masses in the unwholesome environment of "unnatural" cities, the development of a destructive technology, and finally the de-humanization of man. Here is the great romantic fear, in religious form.

Although not all social theologians are ready to accept the ghastly picture of mankind in "flight from God" painted by Max Picard, his passionate lamentations represent only an extreme expression of a view generally held. In the "World of the Flight" there is neither love nor friendship, no enduring

---

democracies as in totalitarian states the "debunking" of tradition ends in destroying the specifically human element in man.

[137] Brunner, *Justice*, p. 164, italics supplied; *Man in Revolt*, tr. by O. Wyon (London, 1939), pp. 458-459.

[138] Brunner, *Christianity's Civilization*, vol. II, pp. 1-28; *Justice*, p. 172; Dawson, *The Judgment of Nations*, p. 6; *Religion and Culture*, pp. 214-215; *Understanding Europe*, pp. 225-240; Demant, *Religion and the Decline of Capitalism*, pp. 128-129, 159-161 and 191-194. P. Mairet, "The Nation behind the War," J. H. Oldham et al., *The Church Looks Ahead*, pp. 56-66; P. McLaughlin, "Nature and Rural Man," M. B. Reckitt, ed., *Prospect for Christendom*, pp. 100-113; R. Guardini, *Die Macht* (Wuerzburg, 1951), pp. 20-22, 25-28, 55. W. G. Peck, "The Essential Nature of the Problem," *Malvern*, 1941, pp. 19-35.

ideas, not even real faces—nothing lasts.[139] The symbol and true reality of this world is the radio—the instrument and master of discontinuity. It rules men who have lost their inner continuity, their personality, and thus all sense of responsibility. The concentration-camp guard of yesterday is the kindly clerk of today, without even feeling the incongruity of it all, for he is a different person at every moment. Hitler, the man without a face or personality, with just a screaming voice, was "in ourselves" long before he ever appeared on the scene. Having neither doctrine nor policy, he was absolutely nothing, in a world of universal emptiness. His dictatorship was only an extension of private discontinuity to the public sphere.[140] With Picard it is no longer just a matter of "mass-man"; man has already ceased to be.

Not all those who see man losing himself in a godless world go to Picard's lengths, but all feel the "need for roots" deeply. However, whether the remedies proposed involve a return to agricultural life, to a revival of the mediaeval "tour de France" for young workers, a return to political rule by the "old families" or "Christian federalism," very few theologians see in the present world the slightest basis for such developments.[141] Indeed, these desirable changes are all drawn from

[139] *The Flight from God*, tr. by J. M. Cameron (London, 1951), especially pp. 57-67.

[140] *Hitler in uns selbst* (Erlenbach-Zuerich, 1946). Even admirers of Picard have felt that this picture is an exaggeration and that he overemphasizes the single factor of discontinuity and the radio. His book apparently has met with great success, being translated into numerous languages. Max Pribilla, *Deutsche Schicksalsfragen* (Frankfurt am Main, 1950), pp. 253-283; S. Godman, "Max Picard: the Man and his Work," *The Dublin Review*, vols. 222-223, 1949, pp. 23-43.

[141] The idea of the "Tour de France" was suggested by Simone Weil, an author much admired by Christian writers. T. S. Eliot, for instance, has written an appreciative introduction to her book, *The Need for Roots*, tr. by A. Wills (New York, 1952), in which this idea is presented, pp. 52, 76 and 84. But in general her ideas are wildly individualistic. The return to the land is a constant theme with

the example of the Middle Ages. All these authors have taken great pains to show that the spirit which gave rise to them has been utterly destroyed. There is nothing in the world today that would give material support to a revival of religion, and without renewed religious faith there is no hope that the West will survive its present disasters. Some might find consolation in Dawson's words: "None knows where Europe is going and there is no law of history by which we can predict the future. Nor is the future in our own hands; for the world is ruled by powers that it does not know and the men who appear to be making history are in reality its creatures. But the portion of the Church is not like these. She has been the guest and the exile, the mistress and the martyr of nations and civilizations and has survived them all."[142]

For those who wish to improve the world by worldly means there is slender comfort in this. Christian fatalism is certain that the time for mere social reform is past, that not only are such efforts unavailing unless based on religious faith, but that nothing less than a complete spiritual reorientation will do. Europe, however, has been on the wrong path so long that even this is unlikely. The political misfortunes of today are not only signs of the spiritual depravity of the present; they may well mean the end of Christianity. For, as Canon Demant writes, "If Europe suffers cultural death it is very doubtful

---

every author mentioned here. Hierarchy, however, is not so universally stressed, Brunner and Eliot being its chief proponents, e.g., the former's *Justice*, pp. 40-46, 164-173, and the latter's *Notes toward a Definition of Culture*, pp. 35-49 and 83-89. "Christian federalism" is Brunner's term for pluralism, which is also cherished by other social theologians. Only Romano Guardini has suggested that anything positive could arise from the civilization of today. He envisions a new type of Stoicism emerging in which fortitude is the greatest virtue, but he insists that without Christian faith neither this nor anything else can survive in the modern world. *Das Ende der Neuzeit*, pp. 81-82.

[142] In H. G. Wood et al., *The Kingdom of God in History*, pp. 216-217.

whether Christendom will arise anywhere else."[143] On the evidence presented by social theology itself, Europe is no longer Christian and therefore doomed to cultural extinction. Social theology begins by making culture the creature of religion; it ends by making religion dependent on culture. There is, therefore, as little hope for those who would save Western society by spiritual means as for those who work only in the secular sphere.

There are, of course, Christians who protest against this, who warn against "a supernaturalism which escapes from a materialist post-Christian civilization in despair and without hope to re-Christianize it, and expects divine intervention or indulges in eschatological prophecies."[144] However, social theology has adopted just such an attitude. If totalitarianism and Christianity are our only choice, and if Europe is as de-Christianized as social theology insists it is, then there is no realistic reason for hopefulness. One can either put one's trust in a saving miracle, as Gabriel Marcel does,[145] or, if one is more conventional like Monsignor Knox, one can keep up the semblance of morale which is necessary for personal salvation. In neither case is there any belief in the self-regenerating powers of man as a social being, or in the possibilities of less drastic alternatives.

The road away from the Enlightenment has led to romantic despair and to Christian fatalism. Neither offers a really satisfactory account of the sequence of events that has brought Europe to its present condition, but neither can be blamed for its lack of social optimism. It is, after all, not only from the vantage point of the rejected that the present scene looks deplorable. The question is whether politics, the ability to act

---

[143] *Theology of Society*, p. 127.

[144] H. Rommen, *op.cit.*, p. 612.

[145] G. Marcel, "Preface" à *La Vingt-Cinquième Heure*, by C. V. Gheorghiu, p. x; *Men against Humanity*, pp. 159-171.

freely in history, is still able to offer a means of social improvement. For, even if the position of despair or fatalism is logically untenable, something more than mere criticism is needed. It is not just a matter of reviving the Enlightenment. The question is whether any adequate theoretical alternatives can be offered. At present nothing of the sort seems possible.

CHAPTER VI

The End of Radicalism

WHAT ANSWERS can be offered to these counsels of social despair? Romanticism refuses to analyze the social world with any degree of thoroughness, and Christian fatalism subjects modern history to an excess of simplification in order to satisfy its sense of outrage. But to have noted all these shortcomings is not a reply. In fact, no reply is forthcoming. The spirit of rational optimism which alone could furnish a reply does not flourish at present. The Enlightenment was not killed by its opponents; even its most natural followers found its leading conceptions inadequate in an age that has proved all their hopes false. There are, of course, traces of survival. Sartre, very characteristically, notes that the conformism of Americans is really due to their universal rationalism and optimism.[1] But even in America this spirit is no longer encountered among social philosophers. There are few serious people who really believe today that the advantages of democratic government are so self-evident that once it is established it must appeal to all. Probably President Wilson's Fourteen Points were the last great document to testify to that faith. By now it is only too well known that democracy is not inevitable, that it may be destroyed from within, and that even the most successful constitutional democracies are not the models of social perfection that the Enlightenment had dreamed about. This disenchantment—perhaps it is realism—even among the most consistent advocates of democratic government is the real measure of the decline of social optimism.

[1] *Situations III*, pp. 75-91.

What has happened is not only that the Enlightenment has no heirs but that radicalism in general has gone totally out of fashion. Radicalism is not the readiness to indulge in revolutionary violence; it is the belief that people can control and improve themselves and, collectively, their social environment. Without this minimum of utopian faith no radicalism is meaningful. At present, however, even those who regard themselves as adherents of the "spirit of 1789" seem to lack it. For instance, Stuart Hampshire, the Oxford philosopher, recently deploring the absence of radicalism today, defined it as the wish to expand the personal liberty of as many people everywhere as possible.[2] Quite rightly he notes that the mere defense of existing liberties is not enough, that this indeed is conservative. One cannot but agree with him that the necessary effort to ward off the dangers of fascism and communism has reduced libertarian efforts to just that. However, even he never explains why liberty is so valuable, what social ends it is to serve. Unlike the radicals of the 18th century, he does not promise that liberty will bring harmony, or that it will necessarily involve any moral elevation. It is, in fact, liberty for its own sake. It is good will, but not genuine radicalism.

If this were an isolated example, it would matter but little. However, it is just among the most obvious heirs of the Enlightenment, among liberals and democratic socialists, that the spirit of radicalism has most conspicuously disappeared. And it is this which prevents either one from offering anything like a complete answer to the theories of social despair. Ever since the French Revolution, liberalism has become increasingly uncertain of itself, so that at present there flourishes a conservative liberalism that is just as cheerless as Christian fatalism. Democratic socialism, on the other hand, if it exists at all as a systematic theory, has become purely defensive. Certainly

[2] Stuart Hampshire, "In Defence of Radicalism," *Encounter*, vol. v, 1955, pp. 36-41.

neither liberals nor socialists today believe in inevitable progress or in the ability of free, rational men to live without coercion in a perfectly harmonious society. The conservative school of liberalism has indeed turned against all rationalism as a destructive force. Its disdain for intellectuals and for rational political action is such as to amount to a rejection of political theory in general.

Socialism, even the democratic variety, has always occupied an equivocal position toward the Enlightenment. After all, the Webbs, no less than Marx, made the rejection of 18th-century utopianism the very basis of their thought. Moreover, the "scientist" pretensions of both are inherently opposed to the spirit of radicalism. In their view progress was impersonal, the inevitable course of supra-personal development, and human choice was limited to getting on or off the historical bandwagon. It was not man who made history, but history that propelled man. As has often been observed, such a philosophy owes far more to conservatism than to the Enlightenment. To be sure, there were socialists who tried to throw off the yoke of historicism and to create a socialist philosophy akin to that of the Enlightenment, but very few were able to abandon the tactical advantage of claiming that they were also in tune with the march of "history" or, rather, the inevitable course of economic and technological development. The cost of inevitabilism has been high. For when totalitarianism and war proved its "scientific" claims to be utterly false, socialists were left without a philosophy. There are, of course, other reasons for the virtual absence of socialist theory today. For years the need to be "anti-fascist," and now to resist communism, has consumed all its energies. These attitudes have become a substitute for theory. Moreover, the close alliance of socialist theory and the demands of the "movement" have always been an intellectual liability. But, above all, the evaporation of radicalism has affected socialism just as much as every other type of political theory.

As one looks back to the last century, the decline of radical hope seems like a steady process, especially in the case of liberalism, for the French Revolution dealt a blow to liberal radicalism from which it never recovered. The generations of liberals that followed that event were never able to regain the social self-confidence that had reigned during the 18th century, nor were they able to stand up to the challenge of the newly developed conservative philosophy. On the contrary, with the years liberalism absorbed more and more of its spirit. Two wars and totalitarianism have only completed the rout. Today orthodox liberalism owes more to Burke than to Locke. And, indeed, since the First World War Burke has been celebrated as a profound and prophetic figure.[3] Certainly his influence has been so enormous that any account of liberalism is as incomplete without him as one of conservatism would be.

The Conservative Challenge

Conservatism began as a philosophy of negation. It built itself around a denial of the spirit of the Enlightenment. To the Enlightenment's optimism it opposed a profoundly pessimistic outlook. Where the power of ideas had been extolled, habit, prejudice, and unreflecting action were now held up as the only hope for social order. Instead of trust in mankind's spontaneous sociability, the need for authority was now proclaimed. With a firm theological basis Maistre built these sentiments into a consistent system, but it was Burke, who was anything but a consistent thinker, who made them influential. Burke owes his present reputation to the very absence of a closely-knit body of ideas. There is something for everyone in his essays and speeches. Moreover, Maistre was necessarily of-

[3] "Introduction" to *Burke's Politics*, ed. by R. V. S. Hoffman and P. Levack (New York, 1949), pp. xi-xiii.

fensive to all but the most rigorous Catholics. In any case his gloom was too much for even his fellow Theocrats.[4] Certainly not even the most timid liberal can accommodate himself to a view in which sin and punishment are the two most important social realities. Burke, on the other hand, left more room for spontaneous social creativeness within the framework of tradition. Limited changes, progress, and freedom, especially in the economic sphere, were not abhorrent to him. He, unlike Maistre, belonged to the traditional school of natural law. To be sure, he too despised the philosophy of the 18th century and spoke of "Voltaire . . . Helvetius and the rest of that infamous gang," as the teachers of "the ethics of vanity."[5] Abstraction was his aversion no less than Maistre's, but he at least believed in the existence of secular values in morality and politics. That is what he meant when he spoke of the necessity for moral principles in politics. This, of course, weakens his case against "abstract" thinkers, for principles are no less abstract than "theories." One set of universally applicable precepts is no more and no less concrete than another. This simple scorn for "theory," combined with faith in "principles," has been a permanent intellectual liability to conservatism. But Burke, again unlike Maistre, was not prepared to condemn all non-theological thought. While he insisted that government could not be "made upon any foregone theory," he hastened to add that he did not "vilify theory and speculation . . . because that would be to vilify reason itself." It was only "fallacious, unfounded, or imperfect" theory that failed to take due account of man's "nature in general (and) as modified by his habits" that he condemned.[6] It is not altogether surprising that a

---

[4] H. Michel, *L'Idee de l'Etat* (Paris, 1947), p. 118.

[5] "Letter to a Member of the National Assembly," *Burke's Politics*, pp. 390 and 387. Maistre, *Soirées*, vol. I, p. 25.

[6] "Speech of May 7, 1782" in *Burke's Politics* (New York, 1949), pp. 228-229.

wholly sympathetic student of Burke's political philosophy was
forced to comment that: "There is, alas, more than a suspicion
of insincerity in Burke's reiterated denunciations of theorists.
Anyone who opposes him or who suggests any reform he dislikes can be disposed of by this means."[7] A parliament composed of solid citizens was only too pleased to hear him say
these things. His real objection to "theory" was that it seemed
to ignore the complexity of society. Society is not just a collection of fairly similar individuals. People are complicated
and diverse, as are their purposes and those of society.[8] Consequently any social action entails results that no one can
predict, and the best intentioned proposal may involve the
most disastrous results. "[That] which in the first instance is
prejudicial may be excellent in its remote operation, and its
excellence may arise even from the ill effects it produces in
the beginning. The reverse also happens; and very plausible
schemes, with very pleasing commencements, have often
shameful and lamentable conclusions. In states there are often
some obscure and almost latent causes, beings which appear
at first view of little moment, on which a very great part of
its prosperity or adversity may most essentially depend."[9]

Experience and more experience is required for political
affairs, Burke felt, and it always shows that purposeful change
of institutions is dangerous. Individuals are weak in their powers of judgment; even a whole generation is unwise; only "the
species" as a whole, working insensibly throughout the ages,
creates institutions and maxims that have permanent value.[10]
There can be no simple answer to the problems of legislation
or of education as Bentham and Helvetius thought. Social

[7] A. Cobban, *Edmund Burke* (London, 1929), p. 76.
[8] "Reflections on the Revolution in France," *Burke's Politics*, p.
305.
[9] *Ibid.*, pp. 304-305.
[10] "Speech of May 7, 1782," *Burke's Politics*, p. 227.

knowledge is always retrospective. This was the so-called "inductive" method in politics, as opposed to the "abstract" theories of the Enlightenment. Actually, the Enlightenment drew heavily on the history of antiquity to illustrate its principles. But if this practice was not consistent with the theory of progress, it was no better suited to the conservative theory of the uniqueness of each period and each nation. Logically Burke's reverence for tradition as such, whether American, Indian or British, might well have left him with no single standard of political judgment. Each situation would provide its own norms of action. History would then provide but little general guidance. However, Burke called upon it, as he did upon the law of nature, as much as any man. The fact is that there really was no genuine conflict between the Enlightenment and the first conservatives about the nature of historical knowledge and its uses; both misused it.

The real meaning of Burke's emphasis on history was the simple belief that age sanctifies institutions. For him there could, moreover, be no conflict between tradition and liberty. To continue in one's customary ways was the essence of freedom. To follow habit, not rational activity, was what men really wanted and what was "natural." When Burke, in a sentence that sounded like Locke, said that the state was bound to preserve the rights of man, he meant something very un-Lockeian. The rights to be upheld were prescriptive, prejudice, and custom. In this particular instance he was defending the rights of Catholics to profess their religion freely. They were, he noted, moved by those very motives that were of the highest value to society, "the implicit admiration and adherence to the establishments of their fathers."[11]

It is almost with a shock that one turns from these political and historical considerations to Burke's thoughts on econom-

[11] "Tract on the Popery Laws," Burke's Politics, pp. 157 and 159.

ics, for Burke was one of the first social theorists to base his economic and political ideas on entirely opposed principles. Adam Smith is alleged to have said that no one understood him as well as Burke.[12] Free trade, laissez-faire, the inalienable rights of private property—these were, in sum, his economic principles. As Cobban notes, "they are based on natural rights and unqualified individualism: which means that they are utterly alien from . . . his political ideas."[13] There is no trace of his ideas on communal solidarity, on the complexities of social life, and on the need for authority to be found in his, fortunately, scant writings on economic subjects. It is difficult to believe that the *Thoughts on Scarcity* were written by the same man who wrote the *Appeal from the New to the Old Whigs*. Burke was neither as consistent nor as logical as the philosophers of the Enlightenment but, then, it was just these qualities that conservatives have resented most in their opponents.

In view of its internal inconsistencies, its natural dependence on the historical antecedents to which each author looked, conservatism cannot be defined as a general philosophy.[14] Even Burke's reflections, taken alone, do not form a single theory. However, of the historic mission of conservatism there can be no doubt. In the words of Lord Hugh Cecil, "Conservatism

[12] Cobban, *op.cit.*, p. 193.   [13] *Ibid.*, p. 196.
[14] Thus philosophic conservatism also to be distinguished from "economic" conservatism, which has recently been defined as, "The desire to cling to one's economic privileges, if one is fortunate enough to have any. . . ." R. English, "Conservatism: the Forbidden Faith," *The American Scholar*, vol. 21, 1951-1952, p. 400. In fact, no list of essential traits ever exhausts the possibilities of conservative thought. F. J. C. Hearnshaw counted up a dozen such characteristics which included among others such virtues as piety and loyalty; *Conservatism in England* (London, 1933), pp. 22-23. A later scholar has cut down this formidable list to a mere six traits, which is no less curious, since "a buoyant view of life" has now been made an essential element of the conservative creed; R. Kirk, *The Conservative Mind* (Chicago, 1953), pp. 7-8.

arose to resist Jacobinism, and that is to this day its most essential and fundamental characteristic."[15] However, soon liberalism came to join conservatism in this preoccupation. Throughout the 19th century the fear of Jacobinism, no less than hostility to conservatism, disturbed liberal minds and contributed vastly to their uncertainty. Today a conservative school of liberalism has gone so far as to make anti-Jacobinism its primary aim, without, however, abandoning its liberal fear of authority and devotion to personal liberty. But this has not been the work of one day. It took many years of adversity to bring liberals to abandon the Enlightenment, and finally even to submit to the spirit of fatalism.

Liberalism without Self-Confidence

The French Revolution forced liberals no less than conservatives to review critically the assumptions of the Enlightenment. If one takes Benjamin Constant, de Tocqueville, John Stuart Mill, and Lord Acton as the most representative figures of the liberal movement one cannot fail to notice that their thought was a constant effort to define their attitude toward the Enlightenment and democracy on one hand and to conservatism on the other. That is why they always spoke of their time as "an age of transition" in which nothing could be settled.[16] In fact, it was for them a time for reconsideration. The faith in an all-conquering reason was gone, though the belief in education continued to be strong. Religion was no longer regarded with hostility; Constant and Tocqueville

[15] Lord Hugh Cecil, *Conservatism* (London, 1912), pp. 249 and 244. See also A. Cobban, *op.cit.*, p. 13, and F. M. Watkins, *The Political Tradition of the West* (Cambridge, Mass., 1948), p. 179.

[16] E.g., "Nous sommes une generation de passage," Constant wrote in a letter to Paris students in 1827. D. Bagge, *Les Idées Politiques sous la Restauration* (Paris, 1952), p. 26. Mill often made this point, e.g., *The Spirit of the Age* (Chicago, 1942), pp. 6 and 76.

thought it essential to a well-ordered society.[17] Lord Acton based his political principles on the moral values of Catholicism. Only Mill remained indifferent to and even suspicious of religion. This tolerance toward religion did not involve a decline in respect for the secular intellectuals. As during the Enlightenment, they were regarded as a "natural aristocracy." Tocqueville, indeed, already went so far as to doubt the political wisdom of "men of letters"; however, the great problem for him, as for all liberals, was that society at large had rejected their leadership.[18] In short, theirs was an intellectualism devoid of optimism. Tocqueville put his finger on the sorest spot of the battered liberal consciousness when he wrote, "If the men of the Revolution were more irreligious than we are, they were imbued with one admirable faith, which we lack: they believed in themselves."[19]

That public opinion should rule the state was accepted as it had been in the 18th century, but the rational and moral powers of the majority of men were no longer trusted. Indeed, intellectuals had to guard themselves against the ever-increasing power of unenlightened majorities. Freedom was still held to be the greatest good in society, but that a natural harmony would emerge did not now seem clear. Political power was regarded with all the misgivings of the 18th century, but liberals no longer expected it to disappear; indeed it seemed to

[17] Tocqueville remarked cannily that any class that feels its social power threatened will turn to religion as a support. This had happened in the case of the nobility, and was about to become evident among the bourgeoisie, especially after 1848. *The Recollections of Alexis de Tocqueville*, tr. by A. T. de Mattos, ed. by J. P. Mayer (London, 1948), p. 120; *The Old Régime and the Revolution*, tr. by J. Bonner (New York 1876), pp. 188-189.

[18] Tocqueville considered himself as one of the last heirs of an aristocratic tradition of public service. He did not think of himself as an "intellectual" only. Indeed he rather despised "men of letters" who played at politics. Lamartine typified for him this kind of person and he loathed the poet. *Recollections*, p. 75.

[19] *The Old Régime*, p. 190.

increase. This, as much as the new fear of the majority, was
part of the central conflict that followed the French Revolution, the war between liberalism and democracy, "the two
inseparable but opposed terms" as they have been called by
one eminent student of liberalism.[20] As for progress and political reform, neither seemed inevitable any longer. Liberals had
learned from conservatives that there was no obvious "art or
science of legislation." The Enlightenment's hopes on that
score were regarded as "sonorous phrases" and Mill came to
speak with some condescension of his father's and Bentham's
simplicities.[21] Burke's lesson that intangible factors, such as
national character and tradition, were at least as important as
the conscious desires of men had been well taken.[22] Of course,
no liberal was ready to follow Burke all the way. The binding
force of individual conscience was not disregarded. All agreed
with Acton that "no prescription is valid against the conscience of mankind."[23] But they doubted that the "majority"
had any conscience to call upon. The power to control social
life was limited by nature and by the inadequate moral capacities of most men. Mill was ready to admit that none of the
reforms of the 18th-century radicals had produced the desired
moral changes, and, in any case, he saw "the glory of the average man" in the ability to follow the guidance of his betters.[24]

[20] G. de Ruggiero, *The History of European Liberalism*, tr. by R.
G. Collingwood (London, 1927), pp. 82, 51, 370 and 378.
[21] E.g., Tocqueville, *The Old Régime*, pp. 170-181 and 251; B.
Constant, *Mélanges de Littérature et de Politique* (Bruxelles, 1829),
vol. I, pp. 132-133 and vol. II, pp. 89; Mill, *Autobiography*, pp. 133-
134 and 170-171; "Coleridge" in *Dissertations and Discussions* (Boston, 1864), vol. II, pp. 6-7.
[22] The greatest of Bentham's mistakes, Mill thus noted, was to disregard national character. For "(a) philosophy of laws and institutions, not founded on a philosophy of national character, is an absurdity." "Bentham," *Discussions and Dissertations*, vol. I, p. 391.
[23] G. Himmelfarb, *Lord Acton* (London, 1952), p. 136.
[24] *Autobiography*, pp. 201-202; *On Liberty* (Everyman's Library,
London, 1910), p. 24.

These reflections are, of course, incompatible with the theory of progress. Mill sometimes hoped that society might reach a serene "stationary state" in which social life would be more harmonious, but he was often harassed by doubts.[25] Cultural decay was, he feared, inevitable. The history of civilization involved the slow accretion of habits until the capacity for innovation was quite stifled.[26] Tocqueville, too, warned that societies are ever in danger of internal decay, and that modern Europe might well go the way of ancient Rome. He was not, however, inclined to regard this as an inevitable fate.[27] In fact, Tocqueville rejected all forms of historical determinism, but this meant only that he did not believe in general schemes. Historical events seemed to him partly inevitable and partly accidental, a notion that does not leave much to conscious human direction.[28]

It was, however, not only a sense of the weight of the past that came to dampen liberal zeal. The moral and intellectual deficiencies of the majority of men now appeared an equally serious obstacle to reform. The will to power, too, now seemed a permanent curse, so that the first task of liberalism tended to be reduced to simply trying to ward off the encroaching activities of the state. Positively, its political efforts were directed toward promoting the influence of "the educated classes," as Mill called them. Such social progress as might reasonably be expected was to come from this enlightened minority, acting in the interest of the majority, but also in opposition to its prevailing opinions. As long as the majority did

[25] *Principles of Political Economy* (New York, 1909), pp. 452-455.
[26] "M. de Tocqueville on Democracy in America," *Dissertations and Discussions*, vol. ii, pp. 141-142, "Civilization," *ibid.*, vol. i, pp. 197-198 and 243-231; *J. S. Mill's Philosophy of Scientific Method*, ed. by E. Nagel (New York, 1950), pp. 344-346.
[27] *Democracy in America*, tr. by H. Reeve, ed. by P. Bradley (New York, 1951), vol. ii, pp. 47, 228-229 and 249-263.
[28] *Recollections*, p. 68.

not obstruct these efforts, it had done all it could do to improve society.

If, like the romantics, liberal intellectuals began to feel that they were outcasts in a society dominated by the middle classes or by "the people," or by both, they did not choose to retire from the world of politics. Mill made a powerful argument in favor of the educational values of representative government, and for the intellectual's place in it. He supported Hare's scheme for proportional representation mainly because he saw in it a means of gaining parliamentary seats for intellectuals.[29] Lord Acton too insisted that this was the one way of combining popular government with the leadership of the intellectuals.[30] If they feared "the tyranny of the majority," as liberals fear all tyranny, they were still prepared to offer their services to that ungrateful "majority." For they never abandoned the 18th-century's democratic demand that the benefit of "society as a whole" or the "greatest good of the greatest number" must be the sole aim of government. They had only lost the old intellectualist hope that philosophers would dominate public opinion in order to achieve this end. Moreover, the French Revolution had given them second thoughts about the nature of power.

In general, it was clearly recognized that political power was both necessary and dangerous. Constant thus explicitly rejected Godwin's notion that the state is simply evil. In its proper sphere, he argued, it should be strong. On the other hand, the Revolution had convinced him that all political power, even that of the well-intentioned men of 1789, was incompatible with liberty and justice.[31] Lord Acton's dictum on the subject

[29] *Representative Government*, pp. 195-207, 211-218 and 256-275; *Autobiography*, pp. 219-220.

[30] "Sir Erskine May's Democracy in Europe," *Essays on Freedom and Power*, ed. by G. Himmelfarb (Boston, 1948), pp. 160-165.

[31] *Mélanges*, vol. I, pp. 185-187. *Cours de Politique Constitutionelle,*

will not bear repetition. Nothing filled Mill with greater anxiety than the prospect of a bureaucracy that would absorb all the existing talents of society, and turn them from free development to administrative pedantry.[32] But although liberalism sees a constant threat to individual liberty in the power of the state, it is not concerned with the possibility of a conflict between the individual and society. This is the preoccupation of romanticism. The two can appear together at times, and Mill was as much a romantic as a liberal, but the differences between romantic and liberal thinking remain clear enough. Liberalism is a political philosophy, romanticism a *Weltanschauung*, a state of mind which can adapt itself to the most divergent types of political thought. The basic problem of liberalism is the creation of an enlightened public opinion to secure the civil rights of individuals and to encourage the spontaneous forces of order in society itself. It has nothing to say about defying convention, except to extend it legal protection. The liberal sees the rights of individuals as based on justice or utility. The romantic makes a virtue of self-expression as an end in itself, and sees individuality as necessarily involving an opposition to prevailing social standards. The liberal fears majorities, because they may be too powerful to be just, and too ignorant to be wise. The romantic is revolted by their docility, their indifference to genius, their undistinguished emotional life. The liberal sees only the dangers of power abused. That the state may not interfere with society is a concept of an entirely different order than the idea that a man's first duty is to develop an original personality. Majority rule and minority rights are the two central themes of liberal thought; the unique individual and his enemies, the masses, need never enter its considerations. The romantic does

---

ed. by E. Laboulaye (Paris, 1875), vol. i, pp. 7-17, 275-281, vol. ii, pp. 537-560.
    [32] *On Liberty*, pp. 167-168.

not offer society anything but his defiance. Liberalism, on the
other hand, attempts to regulate the relations of the individual
to society and the state, and of these two to each other, by law.

The idea of constitutional government was thus both the
resolution of the inner conflict of liberal thinking and its greatest contribution to social theory. A constitution, the liberals
argued, was to express both the traditions and the moral will
of society. Essentially this is a position halfway between Burke
and Paine, for progress and order were inseparable, as Mill
claimed.[33] Thus Constant conceded that constitutions are
made by the ages, and should be slowly moulded, but men
may, from time to time, make deliberate alterations in their
structure.[34] To the prestige of prescription the weight of moral
principle was to be added in the writing of constitutions. Constant wanted it to be a conservative force in society, as well
as a statement of principle and a guarantee of individual freedom. It was to grant the rights that the Enlightenment had
championed and, also, to preserve the existing social structure
and the privileges that conservatives cherished.

In their relation to socialism the 19th-century liberals were
rather indefinite. Certainly anti-socialism was not one of their
major concerns. Constant, to be sure, swore by Adam Smith,
but he devoted only a few paragraphs to the subject.[35] Tocqueville feared socialism as impractical, but he had little fondness
for the existing order.[36] Mill separated economic from political
liberalism, insisting that the former was justified only by its
practical advantages at a given time, not by any intrinsic virtues. While he remained relatively orthodox in his economic
thinking, he had a sentimental sympathy for socialism, as did

[33] *Representative Government*, pp. 185-192; "Vindication of the
French Revolution of February 1848," *Dissertations and Discussions*,
vol. III, p. 15.
[34] *Cours de Politique Constitutionelle*, vol. I, pp. 265-271.
[35] *Ibid.*, vol. I, pp. 357-370.
[36] *Recollections*, pp. 82-85.

Lord Acton.[37] All of them feared the class legislation that democratically elected, and thus they supposed, proletarian parliaments would contemplate. But, actually, for all their somber fears, they gave rather little thought to the exact steps by which "democratic tyranny" was to be brought into being. Certainly socialism was not a sufficiently important movement to merit much of their attention. When they thought of tyranny, they usually thought in terms of older historical forms, and this is a theoretical liability that they have bequeathed to their 20th-century admirers. Thus, although both Mill and Tocqueville have been called prophets of the present age, the future that both dreaded bears no resemblance to totalitarianism. Tocqueville foresaw a novel form of despotism, quite unlike any of the past, and, one might add, any that has yet appeared. It would be mild in character, for "the principle of equality which facilitates despotism, tempers its rigor." The power of the democratic state will be "absolute, minute, regular, provident and mild."[38] The happy disappearance of the military spirit was observed by him as well as by Mill. Peaceful inanity was the real danger. Everyone would be the same though isolated, each living alone under the benevolent omnipotence of the state. This too was the fear of the first critics of socialism. Not its potential violence, but its stultifying, softening effect was dreaded.

Even if at first liberals could afford to treat socialism light-

[37] *On Liberty*, pp. 150-151. Under the influence of Harriet Taylor, Mill became increasingly sympathetic to socialist aspirations, but his ultimate ideal did not go beyond voluntary profit-sharing between entrepreneurs and workers. Even in his last and most favorable essay on socialism he showed no liking for public ownership. For an indication of these changes in Mill's general outlook, one need only compare the first and the final editions of his *Principles of Political Economy* (London, 1848), vol. II, pp. 313-333 and 504-549, and (New York, 1866), pp. 341-381 and 558-603. See also M. St. John Packe, *The Life of John Stuart Mill* (New York, 1954), pp. 297-298, 313-314, 488-491.

[38] *Democracy in America*, vol. II, pp. 317-318.

ly, it did present them with a serious problem. In fact, it forced them to choose between two of the main beliefs that they had inherited from the Enlightenment, and which had come to seem contradictory. Were they to seek a more rational form of society at any price, or was the danger to freedom, inherent in radical political action, too great? Were they to trust the power of reason expressed in political action, after all, or were they to limit themselves to a purely defensive battle on behalf of the acquired freedoms in economic and intellectual life? The liberals who chose the first path, of whom T. H. Green was surely the outstanding example, are now regarded as the precursors of democratic socialism.[39] The second alternative, which Herbert Spencer chose, is the one that conservative liberalism follows today. Not that anyone is still impressed by Spencer's pseudo-scientific pretensions. It is his view that the state is the source of all evil that has prevailed. In socialism he saw the rise of a "New Toryism," a return to absolutism. Spencer was no conservative in his views on authority; indeed he was not a terribly consistent thinker.[40] His hostility to all state interference in economic life was based both on the conservative idea that society is an organic growth which must not be disturbed and on the old radical notion that whatever is given to the state is taken away from the individual.[41] The state, in his system, is reduced to the position of a bacillus, whose origins and continued existence within the social organism are entirely inexplicable. This incongruity has continued to plague contemporary efforts to combine liberalism and conservatism. Certainly the organic ideal bears little resemblance to the theory of social harmony which had first

[39] A. Ulam, *The Philosophical Foundations of English Socialism* (Cambridge, Mass., 1951).

[40] E. Barker, *Political Thought in England* (London, n.d.), pp. 84-131.

[41] D. G. Ritchie, *Principles of State Interference* (London, 1891), pp. 3-50.

animated classical liberalism. To Spencer capitalism insured the social predominance of the fittest, that is, the economically successful.[42] In short, it is an ideal of harmony devoid of all ethical content. What is, however, most significant about Spencer's theory is the social fatalism it implies. Freedom, he argued, cannot survive in any form without absolute economic liberty, or, to put it negatively, as he did, without absolute inactivity on the part of the state. With Spencer, freedom had already become less a matter of doing what one feels ought to be done, and more a matter of not being told what to do by political authorities. It was absence of restraint, not moral and intellectual self-fulfillment. If the phrases of 18th-century radicalism still appear in his works, it is without their original spirit. By the end of the last century there had appeared a liberalism that denied the Enlightenment altogether.

The Fatalism of Conservative Liberalism

Nothing that has occurred since the First World War could conceivably encourage the orthodox liberal. In fact, liberalism has become increasingly conservative and fatalistic. If during the last century it still offered an alternative to romantic escapism or religious orthodoxy, it has now succumbed to the spirit of despair as well. It is only another expression of social fatalism, not an answer to it. To those who lack the aesthetic and subjective urges of the romantic, or find it difficult to accept formal Christianity, conservative liberalism offers the opportunity to despair in a secular and social fashion. But those who seek the remnants of the Enlightenment must look elsewhere.

Who are the conservative liberals? First of all, there are the groups organized about the annual publication, *Ordo*, and in the Mont Pelerin Society. The late Walther Eucken and Pro-

[42] H. Spencer, *The Man versus the State* (Boston, 1950), pp. 127-128.

fessors Roepke, Ruestow, Hayek, and Bertrand de Jouvenel are among their most distinguished members. In England Professor Michael Polanyi is in many respects close to this group, as is John Jewkes, who has translated some of Eucken's writings into English. Among historians Alfred Cobban and J. L. Talmon share their outlook. In economic theory, though not in other respects, Ludwig von Mises is also at one with them. These authors share a real community of opinion.[43] In their analysis of modern history, especially, all agree. It is evident to all that European society has been deteriorating steadily since the French Revolution. Totalitarianism is but the latest and most calamitous expression of this decline, and one that the intellectual climate of the modern age made all but inevitable. To them, too, it appears that Western civilization is on the point of collapse. In short, though they shun theology and dislike romanticism, they are very far from refuting them with a contemporary equivalent of the philosophy of the Enlightenment. Instead, they provide only another form of fatalism, for theirs is the liberalism of defeat.

The feeling that all social life today is unsatisfactory does not in itself constitute a form of fatalism. Neither does the increasingly conservative temper of liberalism. The belief that liberty has been destroyed by democracy and economic planning, or a Burkean appreciation for the inarticulate bases of society are not in themselves fatalistic. The political fatalism of conservative liberalism emerges only in its interpretation of the entire course of modern history, not in these specific ideas, important as they are to the theory in general. It is in a view of history as a rigid sequence of causes and effects that conservative liberalism displays its fatalism. First of all, it adheres

[43] For a general description of the group see E.-W. Duerr, *Wesen und Ziele des Ordoliberalismus* (Winterthur, 1954), and C. J. Friedrich, "The Political Thought of Neo-Liberalism," *American Political Science Review*, vol. XLIX, 1955, pp. 509-525.

to a theory of intellectual determinism. This is nothing less than turning Enlightenment intellectualism against itself. Where it was once held that social progress must inevitably accompany the advancement of scientific knowledge, it is now argued that social decline has unavoidably followed the false "rationalism" that has dominated modern thought. Moreover, the first political expression of this rationalism, the French Revolution, is seen as something akin to a second fall of man, a calamity that has forever warped European life. Every contemporary disaster, totalitarianism, the threatened destruction of civilization, is deduced, step by inexorable step, as a necessary consequence from this one event. Modern history is represented as nothing but an account of its baneful results. Thus Professor Roepke, in a representative passage, writes, "The world would not be in its present hopeless state . . . if the errors of rationalism—more fatal than all misguided passions —had not caused the promising beginnings of the eighteenth century to end in a gigantic catastrophe of which we can still feel the effects: the French Revolution."[44]

To these considerations a simple economic determinism has been added. "Rationalism," it is claimed, has led to the destruction of the free market and to the introduction of economic planning by political authorities. Without economic freedom, however, conservative liberals insist, no other kind of liberty, intellectual or civic, can possibly survive. Here, too, is a display of disenchanted liberalism. The positive aspect of Enlightenment anarchism, the belief in natural harmony, has been discarded, but the hostility to state action remains. "Planning" especially is an unnatural interference with the organic structure of society. The Burkean belief that there are permanent limits upon man's ability to alter society has replaced the hopes of the Enlightenment. "Human nature" or

[44] *The Social Crisis of Our Times*, tr. by A. and P. Schiffer Jacobsohn (London, 1950), p. 41.

the interdependence of economic factors provides insuperable barriers to the best-intentioned reforms. There is more here than *Ordo's* statement of policy which declares that only free competition can solve the social problems of our time and that "planning" must be shunned as the enslavement of man by bureaucracy.[45] It is really felt that every political catastrophe of the age, war no less than totalitarianism, is the direct and *necessary* effect of "planning" and that without the free market these political and social manifestations can not and will not be avoided. This indeed is an apparently Marxist type of determinism—not quite, however, for its fatalism is reinforced by non-materialist consideration. Not only do economics determine the state of society; economic life itself is controlled by the climate of opinion, which in turn is ruled by the intellectuals, who throughout the modern age have occupied a social position that all but forces them to attack and destroy the free market, and to institute rationalist schemes of economic planning.

All this amounts in the end to a rejection of purposeful social thought and action. For, ultimately, society is too complex and human knowledge forever insufficient to allow men to alter their social environment with any degree of success. It is not, however, this political quietism that renders conservatism so fatalistic. It is, rather, its either/or approach to social ideas and deeds. Every philosophic position must lead to a corresponding action; every dangerous thought end in some lengthy chain of political errors. In the realm of economics *any* incompatible state interference with the price mechanism, or *any* attempt to regulate employment must at all times and in every place lead by an iron chain of causes and effect to the establishment of totalitarian rule.[46] In short, in a time of

[45] *Ordo*, vol. 1, 1948, pp. vii-xi.
[46] Even commentators wholly sympathetic to this school of thought have noted the strain of fatalism in this form of argument. E.g., J.

hopelessness the Enlightenment's old belief that logic dominates social life has been transformed into a theory of pure fatality. Yet this is as true an expression of liberal thinking, and certainly as thorough and well-considered, as any at the present time.

Rationalism and the Intellectuals

In their attitude toward the intellectuals, conservative liberals seem to have abandoned the liberal tradition most conspicuously in favor of conservatism. The 19th-century liberals never doubted that society depended on intellectuals for its welfare. They feared only that the rest of mankind was tragically incapable of recognizing this fact. Conservative liberals today, however, feel that the professional intellectual and his works are directly responsible for every social misfortune. This is quite in keeping with the theory of intellectual determinism. At its simplest this is the assumption that historical events mirror logical sequences of ideas, that metaphysical premises lead necessarily to predictable forms of behavior. Thus, rationalism sooner or later must and did lead to totalitarianism. It is the logical and necessary cause of all our present difficulties. Not that this attempt to deduce forms of action from metaphysical predispositions is peculiar to conservative liberalism alone. Theorists of the most diverse sort have tried to establish such relationships. Hans Kelsen and Bertrand Russell have argued that a belief in absolutes leads to authoritarianism. However, moralists and theologians insist with equal certainty that it is the lack of such a faith that brings about the destruction of liberty.[47] The sad fact is that the relation be-

---

W. N. Watkins, "Walther Eucken, Philosopher Economist," *International Journal of Ethics*, vol. 63, 1953, pp. 131-136.

[47] H. Kelsen, "Absolutism and Relativism in Philosophy and Politics," *American Political Science Review*, vol. 42, 1948, pp. 906-914. B. Russell, *Philosophy and Politics* (London, 1947).

tween rationalism and authoritarianism, and empiricism and liberalism, or any other metaphysical theory and political thought and action, is very tenuous. For example, one can defend democracy, or any political system, simply because it "works," or because one likes it, or, because it is *a priori* the best, and the only rational form of government.[48] Nor is there much evidence that specific metaphysical beliefs lead to definite psychological or moral conditions, or to political states of mind. One must first translate a belief in absolutes into intolerance or uprightness, empiricism into generosity or dissoluteness, rationalism into pride, and pragmatism into humility, to prove such connections. This is, in fact, what all these theorists, especially the conservative liberals, do.

The difficulty here is not only that systematic philosophy is given an exaggerated importance as an agent of social change, but also that the inner validity of a theory is never separated from its presumed social effects—a practice that is common to Christian fatalists as well. To conservative liberals, rationalism is always both a metaphysical concept and a psychological and moral condition. Of these two the second is by far the more important. Moreover, following Burke's errors, no adequate separation of these two quite distinct aspects of the problem is made. Rationalism as an epistemological theory cannot be invalidated because it may have morally undesirable consequences. Such a criticism is logically irrelevant, even if it were based on factual evidence and not on some rather speculative psychological thinking. It is one thing to say that no rational *a priori* political principles can be established, because no generalizations at all can be made about an indefinite and unknown number of separate and unique events and persons, but it is quite another matter to claim that this sort of thinking

[48] The entire argument presented here is based largely on F. Oppenheimer, "Relativism, Absolutism, and Democracy," *American Political Science Review*, vol. 44, 1950, pp. 951-960.

inclines men toward radicalism, hence to totalitarianism and to social destructiveness.

The difficulties caused by this confusion of ideas are well illustrated by Professor Hayek's attack on rationalism. Thus he argues that, "(Human) Reason, with a capital R, does not exist in the singular, as given or available to any particular person as the rationalist approach seems to assume."[49] Cartesian thought, which is the first great example of such rationalism, is, therefore, an obstruction to the study of society, because it tries to reduce social realities to an illusory level of simplicity and regularity. Society cannot be understood as a single whole. It is impossible to make comprehensive generalizations about society or history, since each event and every given set of circumstances are unique, and since they depend on such incalculable entities as the will and ideas of individual persons.[50] From this critique of Cartesian methodology, however, Professor Hayek turns to a quite different sort of attack. Descartes, it seems, was the first "engineering mind," intent upon making society over in accordance with a preconceived plan. Through Rousseau and the French Revolution, his influence extends to contemporary "planners" and thus to totalitarianism.[51] Again, historicism, or the effort to see social life in terms

[49] *Individualism and Economic Order* (Chicago, 1948), p. 15.

[50] *Ibid.*, e.g., pp. 8, 125-127; *The Counter-Revolution of Science* (Glencoe, Ill., 1952), pp. 39-53 and 65. E. Nagel in his review of Hayek's *The Counter-Revolution of Science*, *Journal of Philosophy*, vol. XLIX, 1952, pp. 560-565, points out that the sharp difference drawn between the methods of the natural and social science here is based on a false concept of the former.

[51] *Individualism*, p. 10. Actually the celebrated passage to which Professor Hayek refers, and which he quotes only in part, is a defence of royal absolutism against petulant reformers. Descartes used the analogy of the architect to justify royal rule—that is, the status quo. The origin of the argument is, in fact, Platonic. If it proves anything about Descartes at all, it shows that he dislikes innovation in political matters.

See also W. Roepke, *Mass und Mitte* (Erlenbach-Zuerich, 1950),

of "wholes," constitutes a "methodological collectivism" which must ultimately realize itself in political collectivism.[52] This vice too is common to "rationalists," for the "rationalist" is not only a person who holds certain opinions; he becomes a specific human type. He is the man who respects nothing that he cannot explain, and this initial error conditions his approach to every realm of thought and action. Here one element of the fatalism of conservative liberalism emerges. If rationalism were but an opinion, it would presumably be responsive to argument, but since it is an all-pervasive state of mind, it is beyond alteration. Moreover, since political developments depend on such states of mind, they become inevitable. Philosophy, intellectual determinism argues, creates a certain kind of person and, thus, a society. As Professor Roepke observes, today rationalist, that is "unnatural," non-habitual attitudes dominate all spheres of life. All modern existence lacks "measure, proportion and naturalness." Men have become blind to the limits imposed by the inescapable external circumstances which surround society. The spirit of "eternal Saint-Simonism" is everywhere. It can be seen in "the cult of the colossal," which is an "absolutist optimism" emanating from the "overtrust in the intellect," and from the "intoxication of the critical spirit."[53] The tragedy is that reason itself can survive only if men submit to the forces of convention and tradition. As Professor Hayek notes, "the most dangerous stage in the growth of civilization may well be that in which man has come to regard all these beliefs as super-

---

pp. 28-29 and 50-51, in which these arguments are in substance repeated, and even exaggerated. Professor Roepke holds that the idea that men and society can be "made" at will is at the bottom of communism, and reveals its rationalistic 18th-century origins. Such an accusation of voluntarism, if directed at Marx, would surely have surprised the prophet of determinism.

[52] *The Counter-Revolution of Science*, pp. 44-63.

[53] *The Social Crises of Our Time*, p. 48; *Civitas Humana*, tr. by C. S. Fox (London, 1948), pp. 43-82.

stition and refuses to submit to anything he does not rationally understand."[54]

This critique of rationalism is not only anti-intellectualist in that it objects to conscious efforts to influence the course of social life and to social theory in general. It is also an attack on the manufacturers of ideas, the intellectuals—and not surprisingly so. For, conservative or not, as liberals they still see history as made by the men of ideas, and it is they who are responsible if history has gone wrong. In some respects the most extreme and consistent version of the conservative liberal view of the social role of intellectuals was offered by Professor Schumpeter, who, in other ways, was not representative of this school of thought. The intellectuals, he argued, stand outside society as mere observers of the capitalist order. As such they have a vested interest in criticism. This sustained critical effort, along with the decline of entrepreneurial initiative in a technological society, he rated as the two chief factors in the decline of that system. Both, moreover, are the inevitable creations of the very society that they destroy, for capitalism, resting on freedom, cannot find the strength to suppress intellectual liberty. It also increases educational opportunities to such an extent that a considerable number of unemployed or unsatisfactorily employed intellectuals are produced. Consequently, capitalism creates a reservoir of leadership upon which all discontented groups can, and do, draw. Moreover, with their ability to control public opinion the intellectuals create a temper hostile to capitalism, and so encourage the rise of such groups.[55]

To this theory Bertrand de Jouvenel has added some vivid touches. The secular intellectuals of the modern age, he

[54] The Counter-Revolution of Science, p. 92. See also Individualism, etc., p. 32.
[55] Capitalism, Socialism, and Democracy (New York, 1950), pp. 145-155.

claims, are opposed to every authority except their own, which is based on persuasion. First they destroyed the clergy, which rested its authority on revelation. Then they turned upon the power of the sword, the monarchy. Since the French Revolution they have fought the moneyed classes, the power of wealth. Conflict between the businessman and the intellectual is, moreover, inevitable. The latter is a Pharisee intent upon forcing the public to do what he thinks it ought to do. The former, on the other hand, is a good Samaritan, who gives the public what it wants. Their standards of behavior are, thus, totally incompatible. Jouvenel, no more than Professor Hayek, doubts that the intellectuals, through their iron hold on public opinion, must ultimately control the course of social life. Indeed, lately the historians have come to join the engineers in Professor Hayek's rogues' gallery; it is solely due to their deliberate misinterpretations that capitalism is misunderstood today, and that anti-capitalist movements flourish everywhere. They and all the other "second-hand" dealers in ideas, especially journalists and intellectuals who leave their "fields" for political activity, rule public opinion with absolute power.[56] If Constant saw institutions as nothing but the embodiment of ideas, he had at least not yet discovered that the peddlers of ideas were themselves the helpless products of their environment. To the contemporary conservative liberal the social power of intellectuals is dangerous not only because it cannot be limited but also because it is inevitably bad. The intellectuals are doomed to ruin society. They threaten society because their character and opinions are entirely determined by their historical fate, their psychological weakness, and their odd social position.

[56] B. de Jouvenel, "The Treatment of Capitalism by Continental Intellectuals," *Capitalism and the Historians*, ed. by F. A. Hayek (Chicago, 1954), pp. 116-121. F. A. Hayek, "History and Politics," *ibid.*, pp. 3-29, and "Socialism and the Intellectuals," *University of Chicago Law Review*, vol. 16, 1949, pp. 417-433.

Democracy and Totalitarianism

The rejection of the intellectuals has not led conservative liberals to a sudden appreciation of the untutored intelligence of the common man. The old fear of "democratic tyranny" flourishes today, especially in the theory of "totalitarian democracy." Democracy too is regarded as an offspring of rationalism and of the French Revolution. As such it is both a form of absolutism, the liberals' ancient enemy, and of "unnatural politics," the conservatives' greatest horror. Moreover, the history of modern Europe is a march toward this disastrous condition. As a recent student of "totalitarian democracy" concludes, "Totalitarian democracy, far from being a phenomenon of recent growth, and outside the Western tradition, has its roots in the common stock of eighteenth-century ideas. It branched out as a separate and identifiable trend in the course of the French Revolution and has had unbroken continuity ever since."[57]

Here again, the origins of an entire social structure are to be found in the realm of political philosophy. According to Professor Talmon, Rousseau's "general will" lies at the root of our troubles, for this notion is a "Cartesian truth," a social imperative constructed by pure reason, to which no one may legitimately object.[58] It is totalitarian because it tries to create a "natural order" by imposing a single system of values upon diverse and discordant people. It is democratic because its realization is made to depend on the active participation of all members of the community.[59] Historically, democracy is the incarnation of Rousseau's ideas, expressed in Jacobinism and in the tireless attempt to force a single pattern of action upon a society whose essence is variety in political and social life. That is why democracy is inherently totalitarian. Sum-

---

[57] J. L. Talmon, *The Rise of Totalitarian Democracy* (Boston, 1952), p. 249.
[58] *Ibid.*, pp. 1-3 and 25-29.   [59] *Ibid.*, pp. 43-49.

ming up this entire line of thought, Professor Cobban writes, "Dictatorship is both the logical and the historical consequence of the theory of the General Will. . . . Democracy, in the form imposed on it by the theory of popular sovereignty, requires as its logical corollary the existence of the General Will. The attempt to put the abstract idea of the General Will into practice produces dictatorship."[60]

Democracy, according to conservative liberals, depends on a unanimity of social views, and this can usually be achieved only by means of coercion. In a liberal society, on the other hand, no general ethical or political objectives could or should be shared by all. That is why it seems incompatible with the democratic urge to enforce conformity. However, as true followers of Burke, "empiricists" conservative liberals are by no means the moral anarchists that such deprecations of moral absolutism might logically indicate. The present social crisis, Professor Hayek writes, is largely due to our refusal to think in terms of fixed social principles.[61] It is not really the abstract *a priori* character of rationalist morality that upsets conservative liberals. After all, "sound principles" are no less abstract. What really worries them is the belief that rationalist democrats will try to force agreement upon society.[62] Moreover, democracy, no less than any other state form, is an instrument of coercion, and the political life of democracies a matter of pure violence. In their hostility to political power, at least, conservative liberals remain the true sons of the Enlightenment.

What is disturbing in this analysis is that no attention at all is given to the actual course of events. The inner urge to fatalism has obliterated all those distinctions among actual

[60] *The Crisis of Civilization* (London, 1941), p. 67.

[61] *Individualism*, pp. 1-2.

[62] E.g., Professor Roepke claims that "everyone knows that democracy is possible only where a state of virtual unanimity exists on all major social questions." *The Social Crisis*, pp. 88-89.

forms of government, and the real sequence of events ceases to matter. It is of no importance here that totalitarianism has not, in fact, triumphed in countries that were at all notable for their democratic government. What is "democratic," in actual totalitarian rule? What justifies Professor Polanyi's amazing remark that "the more cruel a dictatorship, the more democratic can—and will in general—be its institutions"?[63] All that matters to the liberal conservative is the logic inherent in history, a rationalism they would deprecate in others. It is democracy *in general*, not as it exists in various countries, that is made to appear as a precursor of totalitarianism. Again, its institutions are discussed as abstractions. It is ideological discussion *in general* and political parties *in general* that simply must, as inherent aspects of democratic government, lead to totalitarianism, or at least to social disintegration. Not forms of ideology, not types of parties, but the general idea as such is reprehensible, and causes democracy to mix disorder with tyranny. Thus Walther Eucken, for example, identifies ideology as a byproduct of the competition between various power blocks within society, and so a hindrance to any sound policy. The basic evil, however, is the too rapid change of leadership groups in modern society. Using Pareto's classification of élites, he insists that a too continuous "circulation of élites" leads to disorganization within society, until the state alone is capable of maintaining order. Moreover, control of the state's increased power becomes the goal of these competing groups, which want to use it for their own advantage.[64] Totalitarianism is nothing but the final triumph of one of these groups. From "the anarchy of pressure groups" it is but a step to totalitarianism.[65]

[63] *The Contempt of Freedom* (London, 1940), p. 97.
[64] *Grundsaetze der Wirtschaftspolitik* (Bern-Tuebingen, 1952), pp. 16-17, 139, 147, 177-183 and 233-234.
[65] E.g., W. Roepke, *Mass und Mitte*, pp. 65-75.

Equality of opportunity in social and political life is simply too unsettling. Political parties, according to Bertrand de Jouvenel, are the means by which this unrest turns into tyranny. Though, in fact, power remains in the hands of a small group, a great many people can expect to become ministers eventually, and consequently, no one wants to limit the powers of these offices. Parliamentary government in a democracy degenerates into a party struggle instead of providing guidance by "an elite of independent citizens." The citizenry is, moreover, lulled into a false sense of security by the myths of popular sovereignty; in any case, it is pleased by any diminution of the influence of its social superiors.[66] From this democratic system of party competition to totalitarianism it is but a short step: "Let one of these machines put more method into its organization and more cunning into its propaganda, let it boil down its doctrine still further into propositions which are at once simpler and falser, let it surpass its adversaries in insult, treachery and brutality, let it once seize the coveted prey and, having seized it, never let it go—and there you have totalitarianism."[67]

There is no effort made here to analyze the differences between totalitarian and democratic parties, either before or after a totalitarian regime has been established. Dissimilarities in internal structure, leadership, social composition, and general aims and procedures are completely ignored. Only the compelling force of events matters, as it does in all fatalist theories.

However fatalistic the conservative liberal account of rationalism, of intellectual deterioration, and of democratic life may seem, they are mild, in comparison with its view on economic life. "Plan and perish" might well be its motto. The argument here is simplicity itself. Any economic planning by

[66] *On Power*, tr. by J. F. Huntington (New York, 1949), pp. 9-11 and 236-279.
[67] *Ibid.*, p. 275.

the state must and has led to political tyranny and implies the end of civilization. Moreover, our rationalist heritage has made us all fall into this fatal practice. It is this, above all, which demonstrates the real hopelessness of the present situation. In keeping with the usual method, the question of what types of planning are dangerous and of whose freedom suffers under a fully or partially planned economy can thus be disregarded. Nor do the political conditions under which any specific type of planning is undertaken matter. The purposes, the way in which plans are conceived, and their scope are similarly dismissed.[68] The only thing that matters is the inherently totalitarian dynamic of all political interference in the operations of the free market.

In all cases it is a matter of an absolute either/or, an unyielding chain of cause and effect. Professor Roepke speaks for all when he insists that any state intervention in economic life that is incompatible with the operation of the free market must result in "an unending dynamic chain of cause and effect, and everything begins to go downhill." The state must fight an unending battle with the reactions of the market until "it has reached the *ultima ratio* of all incompatible interventions, and of all forms of collectivism, i.e., capital punishment. . . . The motto of incompatible interventionism is always: *aut Caesar aut nihil.*" In proof of this he, amazingly, points to foreign exchange control.[69]

But the fatalism of iron causality is not the limit of conservative liberal determinism. The works of Professors Eucken, Hayek, Jewkes, Mises, and Roepke are all largely devoted to proving that all forms of liberty—political and cultural—are the products of the free market and are entirely dependent

[68] See C. J. Friedrich, *Constitutional Government and Democracy* (Boston, 1950), pp. 487-510, for a criticism of the political premises on which these attacks are based, and for an account of the great variety of forms that "planning" actually can take.

[69] *The Social Crisis of Our Time,* p. 161.

upon its existence. Thus Professor Mises speaks for all when he writes, "The essential teaching of liberalism is that social cooperation and the division of labor can be achieved only in a system of private ownership of the means of production, i.e., within a market society, or capitalism. All other principles of liberalism—democracy, personal freedom of the individual, freedom of speech and of the press, religious tolerance, peace among the nations—are consequences of this basic postulate. They can be realized only within a society based on private property."[70]

Not surprisingly, this has been called an economic determinism comparable to Marxism.[71] This is of course an exaggeration, since the roots of false economics are spiritual. Its ultimate cause is rationalism. However, the negative form of this argument, which is used to explain all contemporary difficulties, amounts to a complete fatalism. "Planning" has been made intellectually unavoidable, and from there on economic necessities must bring about the decline of civilization. What the actual consequences of full or partial planning have been is of no consequence here. Neither is the difference in democratic or totalitarian planning. Speculative necessity alone matters. Planning will always be repressive, for it is doomed to failure as a logical impossibility. The assumption of planners that they are omniscient is dangerous pride, since economic

[70] *Omnipotent Government* (New Haven, Conn., 1944), p. 48.

No planned economy has ever operated without destroying all freedom, according to Professor Jewkes, because when economic freedom goes, so do all others; for "(Property) is the means by which the individual creates independence for himself against the powers of the State and the powers of organized opinion in the community." J. Jewkes, *Ordeal by Planning* (London, 1948), pp. 189-195. Also W. Roepke, *Mass und Mitte*, pp. 29-30, and *The Social Crisis of Our Time*, p. 108; F. A. Hayek, *The Road to Serfdom* (Chicago, 1944), is almost entirely devoted to this argument, as is W. Eucken, *Grundsaetze der Wirtschaftspolitik*.

[71] H. Finer, *Road to Reaction* (Boston, 1945), pp. 38 and 133.

life is made up of innumerable decisions taken separately by
an indefinite number of individuals. No one can know the
ultimate consequences of any of his deeds. We can calculate
accurately only within the narrow framework of our personal
experiences and environment.[72] To attempt to guide the economic activities of any sizable group is therefore sheer folly.
The planners discover this eventually, when they see their
plans go awry and note the discontent that they have created.
To halt any rebellion, they embark on a policy of repression,
thus increasing their unpopularity, and a vicious cycle of revolt
and terror is established.[73] Lastly, there is, in Professor Hayek's
opinion, a necessary cause for extreme discontent in any
"planned" economy, which depends on human nature, rather
than on the general success or failure of the planners. Individuals can no longer ascribe their personal failures to "natural" forces within society, but only to a specifically human
agency,[74] and this, it seems, is intolerable. While this prefer-
ence for the "natural" to the "artificial" and man-made is an
assumption deeply rooted in conservative social theory, there
is actually little evidence to show that people really like the
inexplicable. The conservative liberal analysis of the rationalist
temper itself contradicts such an idea. The very development
of technology and the demand for "social engineering" express a desire to overcome "nature." To be able to blame
someone known and obvious for one's troubles seems more
satisfactory to many people than to submit meekly to the mystical forces of a "cycle."

If "planning" is intellectually and psychologically impossible, and hence repressive, it is also inherently the "rule of

[72] Hayek, *The Counter-Revolution of Science*, pp. 98-102, *Individualism*, etc., pp. 77-91 and 120-127; L. von Mises, *Omnipotent
Government*, pp. 54-55; Roepke, *Civitas Humana*, p. 20; *The Social
Crises*, pp. 88-90 and 159-163.
[73] E.g., Jewkes, *op.cit.*, pp. 208-209.
[74] *The Road to Serfdom*, pp. 106-107.

the worst." The "planners," in deciding on production and prices, must necessarily make decisions of a moral nature. No agreement on such matters, however, exists among the most intelligent, well-educated, and imaginative persons, and the standards of the lowest common denominator will prevail. No fine or varied goods will be produced; the tastes developed by education and leisure will be disregarded until they disappear.[75] Since agreement on values is essential in carrying out these schemes, moreover, only "the worst" will succeed in such a political system. Power will necessarily fall into their hands, since "the best" are unable or unwilling to meet the conditions of such a regime.[76] In short, the tyrannous flaw in democracy, its supposed dependence on unanimity, also affects all "planning."

That liberals should be profoundly disturbed by the growth of bureaucratic activity which comes with planning is perfectly natural. On the other hand, it cannot be shown that totalitarianism in Italy or Germany had its origins in "planning" or that this was even a vital characteristic of these regimes. Even in Russia the terror clearly began as a means of eliminating political opposition rather than as an adjunct to the planned economy. The polemic against planning cannot, therefore, be regarded as a serious analysis of current history. It is rather a matter of warning, of predicting. It is the certainty of social disaster that has inspired all these prognostications. As such they are hardly likely to move romantics or Christian fatalists to reconsider their views.

The relationship of conservative liberals to romanticism and social theology is not simple. Among romantics only Jaspers

[75] *Ibid.*, pp. 59-61 and 110-114; Jewkes, *op.cit.*, pp. 225-226; B. de Jouvenel, *The Ethics of Redistribution* (Cambridge, 1951), pp. 40-41.

[76] Hayek, *The Road to Serfdom*, p. 138; B. de Jouvenel, *Problems of Socialist England*, tr. by J. F. Huntington (London, 1949), pp. 146-152.

has declared himself in favor of conservative liberal thinking, at least as far as economic planning is concerned.[77] However, romantic "illumination" of the external world remains as far as ever from the society-centered thinking of liberalism. Conservative liberals are quite aware of this. Romantic ideas of individuality and their latter-day corollary, the fear of the masses, play no part in their thinking. Professor Polanyi thus makes an explicit distinction between the romantic "private" and the liberal "public" freedoms. The anarchism of private life that the former generates is to him and to Professor Hayek one of the most disagreeable and un-libertarian aspects of contemporary life. In keeping with this hostility to romanticism, Hayek also dismisses the word "masses" as mere jargon.[78] Again, von Mises ridicules the very idea that the "herd" could ever play a significant role in history. It is the intellectuals, and they alone, who matter and who are responsible for such events as the triumph of Nazism.[79] Only Professor Roepke is a romantic by admission.[80] With his exception, however, conservative liberals remain true to the civic ideal of the Enlightenment and abhor the cult of individuality.

In their conception of history also the conservative liberals are at odds with the romantics. To the latter, causality in history is an intolerable limitation on the freedom, or rather, the unpredictability, of human action. But the fatalism of conservative liberals rests precisely in their too rigid adherence to a single chain of causality. Though they detest all "scientism," history is for them still nothing but an inevitable and very limited series of causes and effects. Certain ideas will

[77] *Origin and Goal of History*, pp. 281-283.

[78] *The Logic of Liberty* (Chicago, 1950); Hayek, *Individualism*, pp. 25-29.

[79] *Omnipotent Government*, pp. 118-120; *Planned Chaos* (New York, 1947), p. 90; and *Human Action* (New Haven, 1949), pp. 859-860.

[80] *Mass und Mitte*, pp. 33-34.

cause predictable actions, and economic actions are bound to be followed by foreseeable results in the intellectual and social realm. Indeed, if romanticism makes history incomprehensible by denying it all rational continuity, the conservative liberal confuses history with fate by envisaging causality as the operation of a small number of all-embracing principles.

Though conservative liberalism remains unreconciled to romanticism, it does not offer the uncommitted observer an alternative to social despair. It does not even hold out to the unhappy consciousness the consolation that Hegel offered. For to it, self-realization in social activity is as impossible in the modern state as it is to the romantic. The conservative liberal feels quite as excluded from the rationalist world as does the romantic. History seems to have gone against both.

As might be expected, the revulsion against rationalism has brought conservative liberals closer to Christianity. In any case, the old liberal hostility to religion has abated. Thus Elie Halévy, for instance, could still describe the liberalism of his youth as "anti-clerical, democratic and republican."[81] A conservative liberal of the "new school" would regard such views as obsolete. Thus Professor Michael Polanyi writes, of the post-war coalitions of Liberal and Catholic parties in Europe, "(On) the day that the modern sceptic placed his trust in the Catholic Church to rescue his liberties against the Frankenstein monster of his own creation, a vast cycle of human thought had come full swing. The sphere of doubt has been circumnavigated. The critical enterprise which gave rise to the Renaissance and the Reformation, and started the rise of our science, philosophy, and art, had matured to its conclusion and had reached its final limits. We have thus begun to live in a new intellectual period, which I would call the post-critical age of Western civilization. Liberalism today is becom-

[81] *L'Ere des Tyrannies* (Paris, 1938), p. 216.

ing conscious of its own fiduciary foundations and is founding an alliance with other beliefs kindred to its own."[82]

Professor Roepke especially feels that a merging of liberal and conservative-religious thinking is desirable as a means of combatting totalitarian ideology.[83] Again, Professor Hayek affirms that the values that liberalism serves are essentially those of traditional Western Christianity.[84] These admissions, as well as the conservative liberal critique of rationalism, should be highly gratifying to Christian theorists. Moreover, the intellectual determinism of this school is in some ways very close to the historical analysis of Christian fatalists. In any case, the admission of defeat inherent in conservative liberalism ought to comfort the latter. However, their dislike of liberalism is far too deep for that. Canon Demant speaks for all when he says that from the Christian point of view there is nothing to choose between Hayek and Finer.[85] He is quite right. Conservative liberalism, for all its rejection of rationalism, remains a purely secular theory. Its approach to society owes nothing to theology. Its central conceptions about history, the role of the intellectuals and of economics, are not Christian categories. History remains for them a purely man-made process, even if it is not a matter of premeditated action. If, unlike the Enlightenment, conservative liberals do not regard religious dogma as false, they still ignore it. They do not think of themselves as liberators from religion—indeed their social quietism precludes such a thought—but they have come no nearer to a religious view of history. What matters most here, however, is that conservative liberalism offers no genuine substitute for Christian fatalism. It has only added its own fatalism to it, and to the romantics' despair. Armed with the intellectual heritage of

[82] *The Logic of Liberty*, p. 109.
[83] *Mass und Mitte*, pp. 59-60 and 152; *Civitas Humana*, p. xvii.
[84] *Individualism*, pp. 1-2. Only Professor Mises remains unfriendly to the clergy and to religion.
[85] *Religion and the Decline of Capitalism*, p. 106.

liberalism, conservative liberalism has joined the ancient enemies of the Enlightenment.

The Silence of Socialism

To a democratic socialist it would seem ridiculous to treat
conservative liberalism as an offspring, however distant and unwilling, of the Enlightenment. Only social democracy, he
might well argue, can be regarded as the true representative
of the radical, liberal spirit. From a theoretical point of view
this proposition, however, is highly dubious. First of all, nothing like a socialist philosophy can be said to exist at present.
Moreover, historically the two dominant forms of socialist
theory, Marxism and Fabianism, began by explicitly and resolutely rejecting the philosophy of the Enlightenment. To
Marx it was only the ideology of the rising bourgeoisie that
was rejected; to Fabians the ideas of Bentham, especially, were
obnoxious as an unscientific justification of laissez-faire. To
be sure, there were earlier socialist philosophies which had
their origins in the Enlightenment, but they were all but
routed by the intellectual success of Marxism and English
Fabianism. In recent years there has been a general revulsion
against materialism and scientism among socialists, and with
it a belated return to the principles of the Enlightenment.
However, socialism has not been able to recover the lost spirit
of utopian idealism and it is neither radical nor hopeful today.
Neither in terms of its history nor in terms of its present disposition, therefore, can socialism be regarded as an heir, a
defendant, or contemporary supporter of the Enlightenment.
As such, its present position in general, and its inability to
provide an alternative to social despair in particular, do not
demand an extensive treatment. All that need really be stated
is that socialism no longer has anything to say.

From the first, democratic socialist theory, whether Marxian
or Fabian in origin, has suffered from one great liability—its

pseudo-scientific attachment to historical determinism. It has been just this movement away from the humane idealism of the Enlightenment that ultimately deprived it, in evil days, of both its radical impetus and of its philosophical backbone. Historical inevitabilism is a double-edged sword. In times of success it undoubtedly makes those who think that they are riding "the wave of the future" feel doubly strong. But when they are forced to recognize that history has not gone according to "scientific" plan, it leaves them totally at sea, incapable alike of explaining the present or of planning for the future. Moreover, since the "inevitable" involves nothing less than the collapse of the entire social edifice, as it does in Marxist theory, it amounts to a confirmation, rather than a refutation, of all other fatalist theories. In fact, directly or indirectly, Marx is surely the originator of most current culture-fatalism, even when its adherents dislike him intensely, for no one has given greater impetus to this form of social thinking than he.

In spite of these considerations, it has been the misfortune of democratic socialists to cling to the belief that socialism was an economic and technological inevitability, even when they had already abandoned Marx's theories of class war, imminent pauperization, and revolutionary violence. Some, indeed, notably Jean Jaurès and Léon Blum, felt that socialism was both the fulfillment of a law of history and an independent, rational moral ideal. But this entirely inconsistent outlook did nothing to explain either the failure of socialism to reach power or the dying moral fervor of democratic socialists. In England the Webbs provided an equally illiberal basis for socialism. Far from being the untheoretical and, therefore, un-Marxian John Bulls that they have frequently been pictured, they accepted the social Darwinism and general historical materialism so popular in their day. It was poor theory, to be sure, but it was no less a theory than Marxism. For the early Fabians, as for Marx, freedom meant only adjustment to historical necessity. Individuals can do no more than follow the tide of the inevitable. Like Marx, they scorned all utopian hopes and all ideals.[86] Sidney Webb indeed disposed of the Enlightenment with one phrase: "humanity intoxicated." To him only institutions, not individuals, had any meaning, and history was the movement of large, impersonal forces, all evolving in scientifically predictable ways. He was convinced by the "scientific" gospel according to Spencer.[87] It really is worth noting that both Marxism and Fabianism are far closer to the conservative doctrine of organic necessity in society than to the radical notion that men make their own history freely.[88] Dialectical materialism and the Webbs' "insensible sweep of history" allow the individual no more genuine choice than the theories of Burke or Maistre.

In other respects as well, Marx and the early Fabians spurned the Enlightenment. Not only individualism was anathema to them. Natural harmony as the product of human reason seemed equally absurd.[89] For Marx it remained a distant goal to be reached only after violent social convulsions. To some Fabians the development of class-consciousness, though not of revolution, seemed an inevitable part of capitalist development.[90] Anarchy too was indefinitely postponed by Marx, while the Webbs did not believe in it at all, but looked toward state-directed socialism. Hence their eventual enthusiasm for the USSR. The intellectualism of the Enlightenment fared no better than the rest of its outlook in Marxist hands. To be sure, some traces of it remained, but the reduction of all

[86] L. Woolf, "The Political Thought of the Webbs" in *The Webbs and Their Work*, ed. by M. Cole (London, 1949), pp. 251-264.

[87] S. Webb, "Historic" in *Fabian Essays in Socialism*, ed. by G. B. Shaw (London, 1889), p. 32.

[88] In Marx's case this was part of the Hegelian heritage, I. Berlin, *Karl Marx*, pp. 51 and 142.

[89] S. Webb, *op.cit.*, p. 57.

[90] H. Bland, "The Outlook," in *Fabian Essays*, p. 219.

philosophy to mere "ideology"—that is, the expression of the needs of a class at a given point in its historical development —is perhaps the worst blow that has ever been dealt philosophy. Nevertheless, for Marx the intellectuals were at least free to choose their class affiliation. They alone could decide whether to remain bourgeois or to join the working class, while all other men were forced into their social positions and opinions by their place in the productive process.[91] The "sociology of knowledge," too, which is an offspring of the Marxian theory of ideology, assumes that intellectuals can somehow rise to scientific independence and so free their discoveries from the social determination of class-interest and environment. It is this possibility that makes feasible the emergence of an élite of planners which, according to Karl Mannheim, the chief expounder of the sociology of knowledge, must ultimately direct society.[92] But this élite, like the glorified civil-service types whom the Webbs hoped to breed, is a long way from the ideal of the Enlightenment, though it undeniably derives from it.

The writers who have remained faithful to historical determinism can clearly offer no answer to the far less fatalistic writers of the Christian and liberal schools, or to romantic escapists. They denounce them vehemently, of course, but they too regard the end of Western society as it has existed so far as a foregone conclusion. The difference is that they accept this as a happy event. Mrs. Webb was, apparently, at the end of her life converted to Marxism, and saw ahead an inevitable struggle between the United States and Soviet Russia in which the latter would happily triumph, because West-

[91] M. M. Bober, *Karl Marx's Interpretation of History* (Cambridge, Mass., 1927), pp. 105-107.
[92] *Ideology and Utopia*, tr. by L. Wirth and E. Shils (Harvest Books, New York, 1955), pp. 153-164, and *Man and Society in an Age of Reconstruction*, tr. by E. Shils (London, 1940).

ern society had decayed beyond saving under bourgeois and Christian domination.[93] Again, Harold Laski saw the crisis of the age in the coming demise of the "acquisitive society," and with it the end of all existing forms of social and cultural life. To him T. S. Eliot, Christopher Dawson, and Huxley were no more than "reactionaries" or, rather, people who failed to see and to accept the inevitable in history.[94] More recently, Simone de Beauvoir and Sartre have tried to lay down the burdens of romanticism by submitting to the demands of communism, and this, characteristically, without a trace of utopian fervor. The urge to destroy the "oppressors," not to assist the oppressed, and a sudden wish to march with the inevitable are the obvious motives here. The communists, they argue, at present enjoy the confidence of most workers; therefore the intellectual who wants to be one with the proletariat must follow its lead and be a communist. The end of such action is violent revolution, and to speculate about the outcome of this cataclysm, to dream of some happier future state, is regarded as childish and somehow "un-Marxian."[95] The inevitability and desirability of revolution have become the sole end. In her analysis of the writers who foresee the collapse of Western civilization, Mme. de Beauvoir calmly announces that the cultural death which they fear is only the collapse of bourgeois society. In short, to all purposes and intents she agrees with them about the course of events that must occur, but she finds the prospect desirable, even though she refuses to think about what the outcome of this revolution is to be. As one of her collaborators on Les Temps Modernes

[93] B. Drake, "The Webbs and Soviet Communism" in The Webbs and their Work, pp. 221-232.

[94] H. Laski, Faith, Reason and Civilization (New York, 1944), pp. 73-129.

[95] J.-P. Sartre, "Réponse a Claude Lefort," Les Temps Modernes, vol. 8, 1953, pp. 1571-1629; S. de Beauvoir, "La Pensée de Droite Aujourd'hui," ibid., vol. x, 1955, pp. 1537-1575 and 2219-2261.

puts it, there is no room for a "left humanism";[96] anything beyond the necessity of violence, any adherence to specific social values, is a false utopianism. The result is not a socialist theory at all but an utter devotion to fatality as such. But this is not altogether surprising, for such immersion in "reality" is quite common among ex-romantics.

Inevitabilism, then, has rendered one section of socialist thought as unradical as it is hopeless. As such, it really is only a confirmation of fatalism. Its adherents hate the present so much that they long for the end of the modern age in a dramatic collapse. The Christian fatalist and the romantic are at least not so totally estranged and envenomed. They deplore the state of the modern world, but they still regret its inevitable decline. Moreover, the refusal to contemplate a better future is particularly appalling among people who are so ready to bring about the end of all existing institutions. That romantics and conservatives should not indulge in hopes of social amelioration is understandable, but that revolutionaries should decline to do so is remarkable. Yet it is only the most logical end of pure historical determinism—unradical, unutopian, and inhuman.

There have, fortunately, been a number of honest Marxists to whom it has become obvious that the theory of economic determinism and especially the notion of an inevitable class war ending in a classless society have been proved wrong. Neither Soviet communism nor German Nazism had been in any way predicted by Marx, nor can either be readily explained in Marxian terms.[97] Their attempts to bring socialist theory up to date have not, however, brought about a revival

[96] C. Lanzmann, "L'homme de Gauche," Les Temps Modernes, vol. x, 1955, pp. 1626-1658.

[97] For the shortcomings of Marxian explanations of Nazism, see R. Bendix, "Social Stratification and Political Power" in R. Bendix and S. M. Lipset, eds., Class, Status and Power (Glencoe, Ill., 1953), pp. 596-609.

of radicalism. Like the votaries of pure determinism today they are even less utopian than Marx. This is not surprising, since it was the success of totalitarianism which made these revisions of Marxism necessary. One response to the loss of Marxist expectations is romanticism such as Emil Lederer's. Here the theory of dialectical materialism is retained, and only its utopian end dismissed. Capitalism has, indeed, perished according to plan but it has been succeeded, not by the classless society of free men, but by the totalitarian mass-state. A rather similar adaption of Marxist theory is James Burnham's conception of the managerial state. Here economic necessity still rules history and the foretold extinction of capitalism is taken as accomplished. However, finance capital has been ousted, not by the proletariat but by bureaucrats and executives. In view of the economic power of this group, moreover, it is inevitable that they should assume political control as well. Such is the "iron law of history"—or at least the Marxian "law" that political power is the mere tool of economic classes. To Burnham it seems that this has been the sequence of events in Russia and Germany, and he is certain that it must also be the path of the United States.[98]

In addition to these relatively limited adjustments of Marxism, there have been at least two socialists who were too perceptive to allow socialist theory to remain stationary in view of recent events. Rudolf Hilferding thus came to reject economic determinism entirely. Since the First World War, he argued, political power alone not economic necessity, had become the real source of social change. To him, the Soviet rulers constituted a political class which controlled the economic life of Russia by means of political power. The system itself he chose to call "state capitalism," since the means of pro-

[98] *The Managerial Revolution* (New York, 1941); H. H. Gerth and C. W. Mills, "A Marx for Managers," *International Journal of Ethics*, vol. LII, 1941-1942, pp. 200-215.

duction were employed in the interest of the political group controlling the state.[99] According to Franz Neumann, another socialist, this was the aim of the Nazis as well. Unlike Burnham he was not ready to regard this managerial state as an inevitability, nor did he raise political power to the theoretical position formerly occupied by economic power. History for him was not just a meaningless struggle for power but also a purposeful development of ideas. This, in fact, is as far as socialism today can go, apparently.[100] The new recognition of the autonomy of politics in history need not end in Machiavellism, but it does not seem to lead to a new radicalism. Though it implies that men are free to determine their fate, it has simply not stirred socialists to new hope. But, since pure power was revealed to socialists for the first time in its most abhorrent, totalitarian form, this is only natural.

Perhaps the most serious objection to all theories of historical inevitability is that they make it impossible to hold individuals responsible for political actions or, indeed, to exercise any moral judgment at all. Everyone is simply the agent of some larger uncontrollable and impersonal force, and as such he can hardly be praised or blamed as an individual.[101] Such a position is as offensive to common sense as it is to morality. To absolve Hitler and his cohorts as mere pawns of higher historical forces is neither sensible nor morally acceptable. In a day when political evil has been demonstrated so starkly over and over again, very few people really care for theories which blur good and bad into a single indefinable

[99] R. Hilferding, "State Capitalism or Totalitarian State Economy," *Modern Review*, vol. 1, 1947, pp. 266-271; "The Modern Totalitarian State," *ibid.*, pp. 597-605. See also A. Rosenberg, *Democracy and Socialism*, tr. by G. Rosen (New York, 1938), pp. 339 and 343, for the notion of "state capitalism" in the USSR.

[100] "Approaches to the Study of Political Power," *Political Science Quarterly*, vol. 65, 1950, pp. 161-180.

[101] For this issue, see I. Berlin, *Historical Inevitability* (London, 1954).

shade of historical necessity. However, even before the totalitarian age, the moral weakness—and, incidentally, the lack of radical idealism—was evident to many socialists. French *possibilistes* before Jaurès denounced Marxism as a theory opposed to the Enlightenment, as fatalistic, and as destructive of socialist incentive.[102] The latter, too, at various times warned that socialism was also a moral position, a continuation of "the spirit of 1789," but he also regarded it as an historical inevitability, as an economic and technological necessity. In the end he simply declared that there was no separating moral and material elements in history and that neither was the cause of the other.[103] This is certainly not orthodox Marxism, which clearly insists on material factors as the ultimate cause of other cultural manifestations. However, it does nothing to give socialism a moral purpose apart from its economic mission, either. This indecision also marked Jaurès' disciple's, Léon Blum's, view. Still a believer in inevitable progress in the year 1944, Blum could, nevertheless, see in totalitarianism a pure regression to barbarism. Assured that technological and economic changes had already brought about the fall of the bourgeoisie and made them incapable of ever holding power again, he was, however, forced to bemoan the inability of socialists to seize and exercise power. In order to urge them on to greater efforts, he appealed to their moral sense, to their devotion to the "rights of man," and to their general feeling for justice.[104] But why did "history" not put them in power, as it had put the bourgeoisie out? Here there can be no compromise. It is an absolute decision: inevitability or moral responsibility. Either socialists must do without the joys (and the sorrows) of historical certainty or they must cease to regard

[102] H. R. Weinstein, *Jean Jaurès* (New York, 1936), p. 27.
[103] L. Levy, ed., *Anthologie de Jean Jaurès* (London, 1947), pp. 183-190.
[104] *For All Mankind*, tr. by W. Pickles (New York, 1946).

themselves as the heirs of the Enlightenment and as the bearers of a moral message.

It was of course difficult in the years before the First World War to renounce the theory of historical inevitability. When the spirit of optimism flourished, the theory of evolutionary progress easily became the staple of every popular political creed. It was just this widespread confidence which led the German socialist Eduard Bernstein to substitute unilinear evolution for Marx's idea of dialectical progress. Improvement would thus be gentle, not revolutionary, and it would be steady and democratic rather than a matter of universal pauperization, revolution, and proletarian dictatorship. To be sure, progress for him was still a certainty, but it was a concept he employed chiefly to combat the unrealistic and extremist theory of the orthodox Marxists. It is, moreover, worth noting that Jaurès took the Marxist side. Thus, though he suffered from the infirmities of his age, Bernstein was more free than most of his contemporaries to return to the Enlightenment. Aligning himself with those neo-Kantians who regarded socialism as an extension of their ethics, he clearly called for a return to morality. Liberalism, as expressed in the philosophy of the Enlightenment, he recognized, had a universal validity which it was the duty of socialists to propagate.[105] With Jaurès and Blum he shared another view common to all liberals. All three were unenthusiastic about centralized political power. Municipal socialism, rather than the state as the sole employer, was much to be preferred.[106] It was, in short, a return to the gospel of reasoned persuasion, of social self-sufficiency and harmony, and of justice as the highest social good, though

[105] E. Bernstein, *Evolutionary Socialism*, tr. by E. C. Harvey (New York, 1912), pp. 148-154 and 200-224; P. Gay, *The Dilemma of Democratic Socialism* (New York, 1952), pp. 136-146, 141-151 and 296-301.

[106] *Anthologie de Jean Jaurès*, pp. 145-150; Blum, *op.cit.*, pp. 61-62 and 136-138.

these three continental revisionists were by no means equally clear or consistent in their attachment to the Enlightenment.

In England today the moral shortcomings of materialist determinism have become perfectly obvious to most socialist theorists. Thus Professor G. D. H. Cole explicitly mentions the Marxian theory that morality is only a rationalization of class interest as one of the main causes for the cruelties of Soviet totalitarianism. His own socialism is explicitly based on a moral credo which includes all the social and private values of humanity, tolerance, liberty, and justice which liberals have traditionally cherished.[107] Nothing, moreover, could be more striking than the attitude of Mr. Richard Crossman, the editor of the *New Fabian Essays*. Except for the title, there is scarcely any resemblance to the celebrated earlier volume. Philosophically one is in a new world. Materialism is denounced as morally unpalatable. Instead of inevitability the editor demands that man dominate history, and this he insists can be accomplished only by the individual conscience and will. The great aim of socialists is now to moralize human institutions, and in this he openly declares that socialists are only assuming the task of 19th-century liberalism.

This reconciliation to liberalism implies more than Mr. Crossman is, perhaps, ready to recognize. For his theory resembles 19th-century liberalism most in its loss of confidence. It is the same defensive attitude of good-will at bay that was characteristic of Tocqueville, Mill, and Acton. Progress is neither inevitable nor indeed likely, to Mr. Crossman. In any case, material advances mean little, since prosperity does not make men good. At best one may speak of occasional periods of progress. But dangers exist on every side today. There is

[107] G. D. H. Cole, *Essays in Social Theory* (London, 1950), pp. 83-84, 7-10 and 245-251; see also E. F. M. Durbin, *The Politics of Democratic Socialism* (London, 1940); V. Gollancz, *Our Threatened Values* (London, 1946).

Soviet Russia, the most capitalist country of all. There is the perpetual danger of the managerial society. It is against these that socialism must direct its efforts. There is also a need for a new theory. Indeed Mr. Crossman blames the inner stagnation of the Labour Party on its lack of any firm philosophy.[108] But his attempt to provide one could hardly be less adequate. Like the 19th-century liberals he is quite definite about what he hates—and he despises the same things they deplored. But when it comes to an affirmation he is as silent as they were, and for the same reason. The spirit of radicalism has deserted socialists. Their return to the Enlightenment was too late. Face to face with historical disaster they have not been able to find a doctrine that could support them in their difficulties. They have not been able to adapt liberalism; they have only come to share its disillusion.

Success is probably an important cause of the theoretical decline of socialism. Sidney Webb's prediction that "the slow and gradual turning of the popular mind" was toward socialism has been realized.[109] Everyone is a bit socialist today, especially in England. Consequently there is no room for a specifically "socialist" philosophy. That, too, was the fate of liberalism. Success has meant that socialism has lost much talent. As long as it was the champion of the dispossessed, it could count on the artistic and polemic support of many romantic minds anxious to join the battle against the philistines. Once these artists discovered that a socialist state would do no more for them than any other, their ardor cooled markedly, and the revival of purely aesthetic romanticism began.[110] Then, the too close relationship of socialist theory to

[108] "Toward a Philosophy of Socialism," *New Fabian Essays*, ed. by R. H. S. Crossman (London, 1952), pp. 1-32.

[109] *Op.cit.*, p. 34.

[110] One of their group is even perfectly ready to say so, C. Conolly, *Ideas and Places* (New York, 1953), pp. 158-160.

the "movement" is a particular liability, because theory tends to become mere official propaganda and election material. Lastly, the concentration on pure anti-fascism and then anti-communism has left the socialists intellectually exhausted and has forced both the parties and the theorists into permanently defensive states of mind.[111]

However, after mentioning all these external, historical causes for the absence of anything resembling a socialist philosophy, the main point still remains—utopianism is dead, and without it no radical philosophy can exist. In this socialists not only share the spirit of the times; they are also historically, as Marxists and Fabians, responsible for the discrediting of all utopian thought. However, today when all the "scientist" illusions have gone, socialists are more completely at a loss than other groups deprived of hope for the future. For, though their aspiration to change society continues, they are incapable of showing that change will bring anything morally or socially worthwhile. As a result, socialists cannot challenge the theories of Christian fatalism and of romanticism, nor do they seem to have seriously tried. Against the attacks of conservative-liberals they have long been able to defend themselves, but then that is an argument carried on on common ground. To those who simply deny the civic creed they can give no answer. On the contrary, the fact that socialism no longer exists as an intellectual faith has been the greatest single cause for the prevalence of the unhappy consciousness, for its passing deprived many of the last possible "cause" and thus indirectly forced them into complete social alienation. As for Christian fatalists, the decline of socialism only confirms in their eyes the inherent weakness of all secular movements and their inevitable defeat by the powers of pure evil. In fact, however,

[111] For an excellent account of the sagging morale of French socialism see M. Duverger, "S.F.I.O.: Mort ou Transfiguration," *Les Temps Modernes*, vol. x, 1955, pp. 1863-1885.

their present aversion to materialism may very well lead socialists, if only in a fumbling way, to a return to Christianity or at least to a new feeling for the moral advantages of religious belief. In this socialists would again be retracing the steps of 19th-century liberals. In any case it can be said with some certainty that socialism has nothing to offer to romantics, to Christians, or to those who seek some alternative to them.

Socialists and liberals are by no means unaware of their own sad state. Nothing could be more revealing than Professor Hayek's impassioned warning to his fellow-liberals that they cannot hope to survive without some utopian impulses. For a liberal to become nothing but a defender of the existing or past state of affairs is fatal. Some program that will arouse the emotions and the imagination of intellectuals at least is absolutely essential for liberalism, he insists.[112] Socialists might well echo his sentiments. This seems a far cry from the time, less than thirty years ago, when Julien Benda was denouncing intellectuals for indulging in political passions, instead of serving humanity as a whole by tending civilization, as he supposed the clergy did in ancient times.[113] The fact is that a curious situation exists in which everyone talks about or around politics, but no one really cares—at least, no one is sufficiently concerned philosophically to be capable of renewing the tradition of political theory. Yet everyone is perfectly aware that it is in the realm of political life that our present condition and future life are largely determined. Politics impinge upon every moment of our existence, and yet we are incapable of synthesizing our experience into a theoretical picture. It is not only the civic consciousness of the Enlightenment but the entire tradition of political theory that is at a standstill.

[112] "Socialism and the Intellectuals," loc.cit.
[113] The Betrayal of the Intellectuals, tr. by R. Aldington (Boston, 1955).

Conclusion

The Impasse of Political Thought

WHY POLITICS? After all, romanticism and social theology themselves are not primarily political philosophies. Why not simply turn to some entirely different realm, if these enemies of the Enlightenment are unacceptable and if the Enlightenment itself has withered? The fact is that intellectually there is no escaping politics. Romanticism is surely not political in its initial inspiration, yet ultimately it too is forced to concern itself with questions of politics, even if it is only to exploit or to bewail. Indeed, the disgust with omnipresent political activity is the greatest incentive to romanticism. Again, Christian fatalism is espoused by persons not really at home in any conceivable historical situation. In both cases politics has induced an estrangement from the entire social world and with it a mixture of hatred for, and anxiety about, the future of European culture as a whole. That is why the question is one of politics, even though it is quite obvious that among romantics a non-political mentality, and among Christians an only partially social concern, can and does prevail. One might well speak of their being imprisoned by politics. But both these attitudes exist today as political conditions. The romantic suffers from political claustrophobia. The social theologian has allowed political and cultural involvement to encompass his faith. Since they exist and arose, at least to a degree, in a political environment, they must be dealt with by some more comprehensive, if not necessarily more enthusiastic, political philosophy. Yet no such theoretical renovation seems at all possible. The answer to the quasi-politics of despair would be a new justification of some form of politics as culturally valuable and intellectually necessary. Yet such a thing is beyond us, even after all the countless failings of Christian fatalism and romantic despair—the two most extreme expressions of much general opinion—have been demonstrated. Paradoxically the fact remains that many people could never be satisfied by despair or by gloomy contemplation of the apocalypse. To a great extent the success of these attitudes is due to the absence of a satisfactory secular social philosophy.

Skepticism, however rational, tends to be an attitude of expectation; at worst it leads to the unhappy consciousness. But what other state of mind is possible when one is philosophically marking time? At present we know too little to feel justified in cultural despair. The examination of romanticism and Christian fatalism does show that. On the other hand, we know too much to fall into even the slightest utopianism, and without that grain of baseless optimism no genuine political theory can be constructed. However, it is not only the experience of liberalism and socialism and the very events of recent years that defy the spirit of civic hopefulness. The lessons of psychology, the masses of empirical data accumulated about the workings of political institutions, and the self-consciousness that theories such as the sociology of knowledge have bred in all of us, prevent the renewal of radical hopes. Everyone is excessively aware of the emptiness of even the most qualified generalization. Everyone is introspectively worried about his bias. Too many who once indulged in excesses of radicalism have returned with their fingers burnt.

Traditionally political theory has turned around and around two poles, the notions of power and of justice. Purely empirical studies of various power structures and of various conceptions of justice can and do exist in quantity, of course, but these do not add up to a theoretical picture. To speak of justice has become intellectually hazardous. The inhibitions bred by our historical experience and by analytical honesty are overpowering. Moreover, the very notion of political justice implies a moral imperative—and as such an end beyond what is known to exist. Unless we admit that the very notion is senseless, it demands at least an ounce of utopianism even to consider justice, and this utopianism, as we have amply seen, is absent today. All that our lack of confidence permits is to say that it is better to believe in it than not—and that is hardly a theory of politics in the grand tradition. Relativism, Marxism, the era of "debunking" have left no one in an intellectual condition to write about justice. The entire mood of the times is against it. Yet, the distressing course of recent history has made cheap cynicism out of fashion. On one hand there is a good deal of eagerness to deal with politics in moral terms; on the other, the insights of psychology and anthropology and of political observation have silenced the urge. It is again a matter of knowing too much to be daring.

To limit oneself purely to power, the other main subject of political theory, as the sole question of concern is neither realistic nor morally particularly attractive. Psychologically it is not possible to isolate power as the single motivation in political conduct. In short, a pure concentration on power is anything but realistic. Moreover, totalitarian ideology and practice have so crassly revealed the tendencies of theories of pure power that they make all but the most obtuse uneasy. In any case, on the purely political plane it has become more difficult to be as certain about the nature of power, as Hobbes, for example, could be. The sources of power in non-totalitarian societies are not easily discerned. The theories of inevitability and of historical "forces" have influenced most thinkers enough to make the location of social power next to impossible. Here, too, it is a case of knowledge having bred uncertainty.

The grand tradition of political theory that began with Plato is, then, in abeyance. A reasoned skepticism is consequently the sanest attitude for the present. For even skepticism is politically sounder and empirically more justifiable than cultural despair and fatalism. For neither logic nor history is in accord with these, and this even when no happier philosophies flourish.

Bibliography

Books and Monographs

Acton, Lord J. E. E. D. A. *Essays on Freedom and Power,* ed. by G. Himmelfarb. Boston, 1948.

——. *Letters to Mary Gladstone.* London, 1905.

Adams, H. *The Education of Henry Adams.* New York, 1931.

Alain, *Elements d'une Doctrine Radicale.* Paris, 1933.

Allen, E. L. *Existentialism from Within.* London, 1953.

Allen, J. W. *The History of Political Thought in the Sixteenth Century.* London, 1941.

Almond, G. *The Appeals of Communism.* Princeton, N.J. 1954.

The Amsterdam Assembly Series, *Man's Disorder and God's Design.* New York, 1952.

Anschutz, R. P. *The Philosophy of J. S. Mill.* Oxford, 1953.

Arendt, H. *The Origins of Totalitarianism.* New York, 1951.

Arnold, M. *Culture and Anarchy.* Cambridge, 1946.

Aron, R. *L'Homme contre les Tyrans.* New York, 1944.

——. "Remarques sur les Rapports entre Existentialisme et Marxisme," *L'Homme, le Monde, l'Histoire, Cahiers du Collège Philosophique.* Grenoble et Paris, 1948.

Auden, W. H. *Collected Poetry.* New York, 1945.

——. *The Enchafèd Flood.* New York. 1950.

Babbitt, I. *Rousseau and Romanticism.* Boston, 1919.

Bagge, D. *Les Idées Politiques sous la Restauration.* Paris, 1952.

Baillie, J. *What Is Christian Civilization?* London, 1945.

Balthasar, H. U. von. *Apokalypse der Deutschen Seele,* 3 vols. Salzburg-Leipzig, 1939.

Banville, T. de. *Poésies Complètes*, vol. III. Paris, 1883.

Barker, E. *Political Thought in England*. London, n.d.

Barth, K. *Church and State*, tr. by G. R. Howe. London, 1939.

———. "No," *Natural Theology*, tr. by P. Frankel, ed. by J. Baillie. London, 1946.

———. *The Only Way*, tr. by M. N. Neufeld and R. G. Smith. New York, 1947.

Barthélemy, J. *L'Introduction du Regime Parlementaire en France sous Louis XVIII et Charles X*. Paris, 1904.

Barzun, J. *Berlioz and the Romantic Century*, 2 vols. Boston, 1950.

———. *Romanticism and the Modern Ego*. Boston, 1944.

Baudelaire, C. *L'Art Romantique*. Paris, 1868.

———. *Intimate Journals*, tr. by C. Isherwood. Hollywood, Cal., 1947.

Beauvoir, S. de. *The Ethics of Ambiguity*, tr. by B. Frechtman. New York, 1948.

———. *L'Existentialisme et la Sagesse des Nations*. Paris, 1948.

———. *Must We Burn De Sade?* tr. by A. Michelson. London, 1953.

Becker, C. *The Heavenly City of the Eighteenth Century Philosophers*. New Haven, Conn., 1952.

Belloc, H. *The Crisis of Civilization*. New York, 1937.

Benda, J. *The Betrayal of the Intellectuals*, tr. by R. Aldington. London, 1955.

Bendix, R., and Lipset, M. S. *Class, Status and Power*. Glencoe, Ill., 1953.

Benn, G. *Ausdruckswelt*. Wiesbaden, 1949.

———. *Doppelleben*. Wiesbaden, 1950.

Berdiaev, N. *The End of Our Time*, tr. by D. Atwater. London, 1933.

———. *The Fate of Man in the Modern World*, tr. by D. A. Lowrie. London, 1935.

———. *Les Sources et le Sens du Communisme Russe*, tr. by A. Nerville. Paris, 1951.

———. *Towards a New Epoch*, tr. by O. F. Clarke. London, 1949.

Berlin, I. *The Hedgehog and the Fox*. New York, 1953.

———. *Historical Inevitability*. London, 1954.

———. *Karl Marx*. London, 1948.

Bernstein, E. *Evolutionary Socialism*, tr. by E. C. Harvey. New York, 1912.

Bevan, E. *Christians in a World at War*. London, 1940.

Binchy, D. *Church and State in Fascist Italy*. London, 1941.

Blankenagel, J. C. *The Dramas of Heinrich von Kleist*. Chapel Hill, N.C., 1931.

Bloch, M. *The Historian's Craft*, tr. by P. Putnam. New York, 1953.

Blum, L. *For All Mankind*, tr. by W. Pickles. New York, 1946.

Boas, G. *French Philosophies of the Romantic Period*. Baltimore, 1925.

Bobbio, N. *The Philosophy of Decadentism*, tr. by D. Moore. Oxford, 1948.

Bober, M. M. *Karl Marx's Interpretation of History*. Cambridge, Mass., 1927.

Bollnow, O. F. *Existenzphilosophie*. Stuttgart, 1949.

Bossuet, J. B. *Oeuvres*, 4 vols. Paris, 1841.

Brailsford, H. N. *Godwin, Shelley and their Circle*. London, 1951.

Brentano, C. *Werke*, ed. by M. Preitz, 3 vols. Leipzig, 1914.

Brinton, C. *The Political Ideas of the English Romantics*. Oxford, 1926.

Brunner, H. E. *Christianity and Civilization*, 2 vols. London, 1949.

———. *Communism, Capitalism and Christianity*, tr. by N. P. Goldhawk. London, 1949.

Brunner, H. E. *Justice and the Social Order*, tr. by M. Hottinger. London, 1945.

——. *Die Kirche zwischen Ost und West*. Stuttgart, 1949.

——. *Man in Revolt*, tr. by O. Wyon. London, 1939.

——. "Nature and Grace," *Natural Theology*, tr. by P. Frankel, ed. by J. Baillie. London, 1946.

——. *The Theology of Crisis*. New York, 1929.

Burke, E. *Burke's Politics*, ed. by R. J. S. Hoffman and P. Levack. New York, 1949.

Burckhardt, J. *Briefe*, ed. by F. Kaphahn. Leipzig, 1935.

——. *Force and Freedom*, ed. by J. H. Nichols. New York, 1943.

Burnham, J. *The Managerial Revolution*. New York, 1941.

Buthman, C. *The Rise of Integral Nationalism in France*. New York, 1938.

Butler, E. M. *The Tyranny of Greece over Germany*. Cambridge, 1935.

Butterfield, H. *Christianity in European History*. London, 1953.

——. *History and Human Relations*. London, 1951.

Byron, Lord G. G. *Poetical Works*. Oxford, 1945.

Caillois, R. "Le Monde Vécu et l'Histoire," *L'Homme, le Monde, l'Histoire, Cahiers du Collège Philosophique*. Grenoble et Paris, 1948.

Camus, A. *Actuelles I, 1944-1948*. Paris, 1950.

——. *Actuelles II, 1948-1953*. Paris, 1953.

——. *Le Mythe de Sisyphe*. Paris, 1942.

——. *The Rebel*, tr. by A. Bower. London, 1953.

Carlyle, R. W. and A. J. *A History of Mediaeval Political Theory in the West*, 6 vols. New York, 1950.

Carlyle, T. *Heroes and Heroworship*. New York, n.d.

Cassirer, E. *Kant's Leben und Lehre*. Berlin, 1918.

——. *The Myth of the State*. New Haven, Conn., 1946.

———. *The Philosophy of the Enlightenment*, tr. by F. C. A. Koelln and J. P. Pettegrove. Princeton, N.J., 1951.

———. *The Question of Jean-Jacques Rousseau*, tr. by P. Gay. New York, 1954.

———. *Rousseau, Kant, Goethe*, tr. by J. Gutman, P. O. Kristeller and J. H. Randall, Jr. Princeton, N.J., 1945.

Cecil, Lord H. *Conservatism*. London, 1912.

Chateaubriand, F. A. de. *Le Génie du Christianisme. Oeuvres*, vol. II. Paris, 1874.

Cobban, A. *The Crisis of Civilization*. London, 1941.

———. *Dictatorship*. London, 1939.

———. *Edmund Burke and the Revolt against the Eighteenth Century*. London, 1929.

Cochrane, C. N. *Christianity and Classical Culture*. London and New York, 1944.

Cole, G. D. H. *Essays in Social Theory*. London, 1950.

Cole, M., ed. *The Webbs and Their Work*. London, 1949.

Coleridge, S. T. *Philosophical Lectures*, ed. by K. Coburn. New York, 1949.

———. *Selected Poetry and Prose*, ed. by D. A. Stauffer. New York, 1951.

———. *Works*, ed. by W. G. T. Shedd. 7 vols. New York, 1853-1854.

Comfort, A. *Art and Social Responsibility*. London, 1946.

———. *Authority and Delinquency in the Modern State*. London, 1950.

———. *The Novel and Our Time*. London, 1948.

———. *The Pattern of the Future*. London, 1949.

Constant, B. *Cours de Politique Constitutionelle*, ed. by E. Laboulaye, 2 vols. Paris, 1872.

———. *Mélanges de Littérature et de Politique*, 2 vols. Bruxelles, 1829.

Condorcet, M.-J.-A.-N.C. de. *Esquisee d'un Tableau Histo-*

rique des Progrès de l'Esprit Humain, ed. by O. H. Prior. Paris, 1933.

Croce, B. *Europe in the Nineteenth Century,* tr. by H. Furst. New York, 1933.

——. *European Literature in the Nineteenth Century,* tr. by D. Ainslie. New York, 1924.

——. *History as the Story of Liberty,* tr. by S. Sprigge. New York, 1941.

——. *What Is Living and What Is Dead in the Philosophy of Hegel,* tr. by D. Ainslie. London, 1915.

Crossman, R. H. S., ed. *The God That Failed.* London, 1950.

——. ed. *New Fabian Essays.* London, 1952.

Daiches, D. *The Novel in the Modern World.* Chicago, 1939.

D'Arcy, M. C. *A Monument to Saint Augustine.* London, 1930.

Dawson, C. *Beyond Politics.* New York, 1939.

——. et al. *Essays in Order.* New York, 1931.

——. *The Judgment of Nations.* New York, 1942.

——. *Progress and Religion.* London and New York, 1933.

——. *Religion and Culture.* London, 1948.

——. *Religion and the Modern State.* London, 1935.

——. *Understanding Europe.* London, 1952.

Demant, V. A. *Religion and the Decline of Capitalism.* London, 1952.

——. *The Religious Prospect.* London, 1939.

——. *Theology of Society.* London, 1947.

Dilthey, W. *Das Erlebnis und die Dichtung.* Leipzig, 1929.

Donoso Cortes, J. *An Essay on Catholicism, Authority and Order,* tr. by M. V. Goddard. New York, 1925.

Duerr, E. W. *Wesen und Ziele des Ordoliberalismus.* Winterthur, 1954.

Duhamel, G. *America the Menace,* tr. by C. M. Thompson. Boston, 1931.

Durbin, E. F. M. *The Politics of Democratic Socialism*. London, 1940.

Eckermann, J. P. *Gespraeche mit Goethe*, ed. by O. Roquette. Stuttgart, n.d.

Eliot, T. S. *After Strange Gods*. New York, 1934.

———. *Notes towards a Definition of Culture*. London, 1948.

———. *Selected Essays*. New York, 1950.

Ellis, M. B. *Julie ou la Nouvelle Heloise*. Toronto, 1949.

d'Entrèves, A. P. *The Medieval Contribution to Political Thought*. Oxford, 1939.

Eucken, W. *Grundsaetze der Wirtschaftspolitik*. Bern Tuebingen, 1952.

Evans, D. O. *Social Romanticism in France*. Oxford, 1951.

Faguet, E. *Politiques et Moralistes du 19ièm Siècle*, 3 vols. Paris, 1891.

Fainsod, M. *How Russia Is Ruled*. Cambridge, Mass., 1953.

Fairly, B. *A Study of Goethe*. Oxford, 1947.

Ferguson, W. K. *The Renaissance in Historical Thought*. Boston, 1948.

Ferrero, G. *The Principles of Power*, tr. by T. R. Jaeckel. New York, 1942.

Fichte, J. G. *Popular Works*, tr. by W. Smith, 2 vols. London, 1889.

———. *The Science of Knowledge*, tr. by A. E. Kroeger. Philadelphia, 1868.

Figgis, J. N. *The Political Aspects of St. Augustine's "City of God."* London, 1921.

Finer, H. *The Road to Reaction*. Boston, 1945.

Forster, E. M. *Two Cheers for Democracy*. New York, 1951.

Frank, E. *Philosophic Understanding and Religious Truth*. New York, 1945.

Friedrich, C. J. *Constitutional Government and Politics*. Boston, 1950.

———. *The Inevitable Peace*. Cambridge, Mass., 1948.

Friedrich, C. J., ed. *Totalitarianism*. Cambridge, Mass., 1954.

Gautier, T. *Histoire du Romantisme*. Paris, 1874.

Gay, P. *The Dilemma of Democratic Socialism*. New York, 1952.

Gide, A. *The Journals*, tr. by J. O'Brien, 4 vols. New York, 1948.

Gillies, A. *Herder*. Oxford, 1945.

Ginsberg, M. *The Idea of Progress*. Boston, 1953.

Godwin, W. *Political Justice*, ed. by F. E. L. Priestley, 3 vols. Toronto, 1946.

———. *Political Justice* (1st ed.). London, 1793, 2 vols.

———. *Thoughts on Man*. London, 1831.

Gollancz, V. *Our Threatened Values*. London, 1946.

Gooch, G. P. *Germany and the French Revolution*. London, 1920.

Guardini, R. *Das Ende der Neuzeit*. Basel, 1950.

———. *Der Heilbringer*. Zuerich, 1946.

———. *Die Macht*. Wuerzburg, 1951.

Guilday, P., ed. *The Catholic Philosophy of History*. New York, 1936.

Gundolf, F. *Goethe*. Berlin, 1922.

Gurian, W. *Die Politischen und Sozialen Ideen des Franzoesischen Katholizismus*. 1789-1914. M. Gladbach, 1929.

Halevy, E. *L'Ere des Tyrannies*. Paris, 1938.

———. *The Growth of Philosophic Radicalism*, tr. by M. Morris. London, 1934.

Hamilton, A., et al. *The Federalist* (Modern Library). New York, n.d.

Hayek, F. A. *The Counter-Revolution of Science*. Glencoe, Ill., 1952.

———. *Individualism and the Economic Order*. Chicago, 1948.

———. *The Road to Serfdom*. Chicago, 1944.

———. ed. *Capitalism and the Historians*. Chicago, 1954.

Hayes, C. J. H. *The Historical Evolution of Modern Nationalism.* New York, 1950.

Haym, R. *Hegel und seine Zeit.* Berlin, 1857.

Hazlitt, W. *The Spirit of the Age.* London, 1910.

Hearnshaw, F. J. C. *Conservatism in England.* London, 1933.

Hegel, G. W. F. *The Introduction to Hegel's Philosophy of Fine Arts,* tr. and ed. by B. Bosanquet. London, 1905.

——. *Lectures on the History of Philosophy,* tr. by E. S. Haldane and F. H. Simson, 3 vols. London, 1896.

——. *The Phenomenology of the Mind,* tr. by J. B. Baillie. London, 1931.

——. *The Philosophy of History,* tr. by J. Sibree. New York, 1900.

——. *Philosophy of Right,* tr. and ed. by T. M. Knox. Oxford, 1942.

Heidegger, M. *Existence and Being,* ed. by W. Brock. London, 1949.

——. *Holzwege.* Frankfurt am Main, 1952.

——. *Sein und Zeit.* Tuebingen, 1953.

——. *Die Selbstbehauptung der Deutschen Universitaet.* Breslau, 1934.

——. *Ueber den Humanismus.* Frankfurt am Main, 1949.

Heiden, K. *Der Fuehrer.* Boston, 1944.

Heine, H. *The Romantic School,* tr. by S. L. Fleischman. New York, 1882.

——. *Werke,* ed. by E. Elster, 7 vols. Leipzig, n.d.

Heineman, F. H. *Existentialism and the Modern Predicament.* London, 1953.

Heller, E. *The Disinherited Mind.* Cambridge, 1952.

Helvetius, C. A. *A Treatise on Man,* tr. by W. Hooper, 2 vols. London, 1810.

Herder, J. G. *God: Some Conversations,* tr. and ed. by F. H. Burckhardt. New York, 1949.

——. *Werke,* ed. by B. Suphan, 33 vols. Berlin, 1877-1913.

Highet, G. *The Classical Tradition.* New York, 1949.

Himmelfarb, G. *Lord Acton.* London, 1952.

Hocking, W. E. *The Lasting Elements of Individualism.* New Haven, Conn., 1937.

Hoelderlin, F. *Werke,* ed. by A. Brieger, 1 vol. Salzburg, 1952.

Holl, K. *Gesammelte Aufsaetze zur Kirchengeschichte,* vol. I. Tuebingen, 1921.

Huch, R. *Ausbreitung und Verfall der Romantik.* Leipzig, 1902.

———. *Die Bluethezeit der Romantik,* Leipzig, 1899.

Hughes, H. S. *Oswald Spengler.* New York and London, 1952.

Hugo, V. *Hernani,* Paris, 1943.

Humboldt, W. von. *The Sphere and Duties of Government,* tr. by J. Coultard. London, 1854.

Huxley, A. *Ends and Means.* London, 1946.

———. *The Olive Tree and Other Essays.* London, 1936.

———. *Themes and Variations.* New York, 1943.

James, W. *Pragmatism.* New York, 1909.

Jaspers, K. *Existentialism and Humanism,* tr. by E. B. Ashton. New York, 1952.

———. *Man in the Modern Age,* tr. by E. and C. Paul. London, 1951.

———. *The Origin and Goal of History,* tr. by M. Bullock. London, 1953.

———. *The Perennial Scope of Philosophy,* tr. by R. Manheim. New York, 1949.

———. *Philosophie,* 3 vols. Berlin, 1932.

———. *The Question of German Guilt,* tr. by E. B. Ashton. New York, 1947.

———. *Rechenschaft und Ausblick.* Muenchen, 1951.

———. *Tragedy Is not Enough,* tr. by H. A. T. Reiche, H. T. Moore, and K. W. Deutsch. Boston, 1952.

———. *Von der Wahrheit.* Muenchen, 1947.

——. *The Way to Wisdom*, tr. by R. Manheim. New Haven, Conn., 1951.

Jewkes, J. *Ordeal by Planning*. London, 1948.

Joel, K. *Nietzsche und die Romantik*. Jena, 1923.

Jouvenel, B. de. *The Ethics of Redistribution*. Cambridge, Eng., 1951.

——. *On Power*, tr. by J. F. Huntington. New York, 1949.

——. *Problems of Socialist England*, tr. by J. F. Huntington. London, 1949.

Juenger, F. G. *The Failure of Technology*, tr. by F. D. Wiek. Hinsdale, Ill., 1949.

——. *Maschine und Eigentum*. Frankfurt am Main, 1949.

Kahn, L. *Social Ideas in German Literature, 1770-1830*. New York, 1938.

Kant, I. *Critique of Practical Reason and Other Writings in Moral Philosophy*, tr. and ed. by L. W. Beck. Chicago, 1949.

——. *The Philosophy of Kant*, ed. by C. J. Friedrich. New York, 1949.

——. *Werke*, ed. by E. Cassirer, 11 vols. Berlin, 1912-1922.

Kaufmann, W. A. *Nietzsche*. Princeton, N.J., 1950.

——. "Philosophie, Dichtung und Humanitaet," *Offener Horizont, Festschrift fuer Karl Jaspers*. Muenchen, 1953.

Kierkegaard, S. *Concluding Unscientific Postscript*, tr. by D. F. Swenson and W. Lowrie. Princeton, N.J., 1944.

——. *Either/Or*, tr. by W. Lowrie, 2 vols. Princeton, N.J., 1949.

——. *Fear and Trembling* and *The Sickness unto Death*, tr. by W. Lowrie. New York, 1954.

——. *The Journals*, tr. and ed. by A. Dru. London, 1938.

——. *The Point of View*, tr. by W. Lowrie. London, 1939.

——. *The Present Age*, tr. by A. Dru. London, 1940.

Kirk, R. *The Conservative Mind*. Chicago, 1953.

Kluckhohn, P. *Das Ideengut der Deutschen Romantik.* Halle, 1942.

———. *Persoenlichkeit und Gemeinschaft.* Halle Saale, 1925.

Knox, R. *God and the Atom.* London, 1945.

Koestler, A. *The Invisible Writing.* London, 1954.

———. *The Yogi and the Commissar.* New York, 1946.

Kolnai, A. *The War against the West.* New York, 1938.

Kroner, R. "Introduction" to Hegel's *Early Theological Writings,* ed. by T. M. Knox. Chicago, 1948.

Kurz, B. *The Pursuit of Death.* New York, 1933.

Lamartine, A. de. *History of the French Revolution of 1848,* tr. anon. London, 1905.

Laski, H. *Authority in the Modern State.* New Haven, 1919.

———. *Faith, Reason and Civilization.* New York, 1944.

———. *The Rise of European Liberalism.* London, 1947.

Layton, Lord W. T., et al. *The Western Tradition.* Boston, 1951.

Lea, F. A. *Shelley and the Romantic Revolution.* London, 1945.

LeBon, G. *The Crowd,* tr. anon. London, 1896.

Lederer, E. *State of the Masses.* New York, 1940.

Leon, X. *Fichte et son Temps,* 3 vols. Paris, 1924.

Leroy, M. *Histoire des Idées Sociales en France (de Montesquieu à Robespierre).* Paris, 1946.

Levy, L., ed. *Anthologie de Jean Jaurès.* London, 1947.

Lewis, C. S. *The Abolition of Man.* New York, 1947.

Litt, T. *Kant und Herder.* Heidelberg, 1949.

Lovejoy, A. O. *Essays in the History of Ideas.* Baltimore, 1948.

Loewith, K. *Jacob Burckhardt.* Luzern, 1936.

———. *Heidegger: Denker in Duerftiger Zeit.* Frankfurt am Main, 1953.

———. *Meaning in History.* Chicago, 1949.

Lowrie, W. *Our Concern with the Theology of Crisis.* Boston, 1932.

——. *Sören Kierkegaard*. Princeton, 1951.

Maistre, J. de. *Oeuvres*, 14 vols. Lyon, 1884-1886.

Malraux, A. *The Conquerors*, tr. by W. S. Whale. New York, 1929.

——. *The Voices of Science*, tr. by S. Gilbert. New York, 1953.

——. "Man and Artistic Culture," tr. by S. Gilbert, *Reflections on Our Age*, ed. by D. Hardman. New York, 1949.

——. *The Walnut Trees of Altenburg*, tr. by A. W. Fielding. London, 1941.

Malvern, 1941: *The Life of the Church and the Order of Society*. London, 1941.

Mannheim, K., *Ideology and Utopia*, tr. by L. Wirth and E. Shils. Harvest Books, New York, 1955.

——. *Man and Society in an Age of Reconstruction*, tr. by E. Shils. London, 1940.

Marcel, G. *The Philosophy of Existence*, tr. by M. Harari. London, 1948.

——. *Men against Humanity*, tr. by G. S. Fraser. London, 1952.

Marcuse, H. *Reason and Revolution*. New York, 1941.

Maritain, J. *Christianity and Democracy*. New York, 1945.

——. *Redeeming the Time*, tr. by H. L. Binesse. London, 1943.

——. *Scholasticism and Politics*, tr. by M. J. Adler. New York, 1940.

——. *The Twilight of Civilization*, tr. by L. Landry. New York, 1944.

Massis, H. *Allemagne d'Hier et d'Apres-Demain*. Paris. 1949.

——. *Chefs*. Paris, 1939.

——. *Découverte de la Russie*. Montreal, 1944.

——. *The Defence of the West*, tr. by F. S. Flint. New York, 1928.

——. *Jugements*. Paris, 1923.

Massis, H. *Maurras et Notre Temps*, 2 vols. Paris, 1951.

Mayer, J. P. *Prophet of the Mass Age*, tr. by M. M. Bozman and C. Hahn. London, 1939.

McCloskey, R. G. *American Conservatism*. Cambridge, Mass., 1951.

Meinecke, F. *Die Entstehung des Historismus*. Muenchen, 1946.

———. *Vom Geschichtlichen Sinn und vom Sinn der Geschichte*. Leipzig, 1939.

———. *Weltbuergertum und Nationalstaat*. Muenchen, 1919.

Merleau-Ponty, M. *Humanisme et Terreur*. Paris, 1947.

Merton, R. K. ed., *Reader in Bureaucracy*. Glencoe, Ill., 1952.

Michel, H. *L'Idee de L'Etat*. Paris, 1896.

Micklem, N. *The Theology of Politics*. London, 1941.

Miliukov, P. *Outlines of Russian Culture*, 3 vols., tr. by V. Ughet and E. Davis, ed. by M. Karpovich. Philadelphia, 1942.

Mill, J. S. *Autobiography*. London, 1924.

———. *Dissertations and Discussions*, 3 vols. Boston, 1864.

———. *J. S. Mill's Philosophy of Scientific Method*, ed. by E. Nagel. New York, 1950.

———. *The Spirit of the Age*. Chicago, 1942.

———. *Utilitarianism, On Liberty, Representative Government*. London, 1910.

Mises, L. von. *Bureaucracy*. New Haven, Conn., 1944.

———. *Human Action*. New Haven, Conn., 1949.

———. *Omnipotent Government*. New Haven, Conn., 1944.

———. *Planned Chaos*. New York, 1947.

Monro, D. H. *Godwin's Moral Philosophy*. Oxford, 1953.

Moody, J. N., et al. *Church and Society*. New York, 1953.

Mussolini, B. *The Fall of Mussolini*, tr. by F. Frenaye, ed. by M. Ascoli. New York, 1948.

Namier, L. *In the Nazi Era*. London, 1952.

Neumann, F. *Behemoth*. New York, 1944.

Nicolson, H. *Benjamin Constant.* New York, 1949.

Niebuhr, R. *The Children of Light and the Children of Darkness.* New York, 1944.

Nietzsche, F. *The Philosophy of Nietzsche.* (Modern Library), New York, n.d.

———. *Works,* ed. by O. Levy, 18 vols. New York, 1914.

Novalis. *Werke,* ed. by H. Friedman, 4 vols. Leipzig, n.d.

Oakeshott, M. *The Social and Political Doctrines of Contemporary Europe.* Cambridge and New York, 1947.

Oldham, J. H., et al. *The Church Looks Ahead.* London, 1941.

Orwell, G. *The Lion and the Unicorn.* London, 1941.

Ortega y Gasset, J. *Betrachtungen ueber die Technik,* tr. by F. Schalk. Stuttgart, 1949.

———. *Concord and Liberty,* tr. by H. Weyl. New York, 1946.

———. *The Dehumanization of Art,* tr. by H. Weyl. Princeton, N.J., 1948.

———. *Mission of the University,* tr. by H. Nostrand. Princeton, N.J., 1949.

———. *The Revolt of the Masses,* tr. anon. New York, 1950.

———. *Toward a Philosophy of History,* tr. by H. Weyl.

Packe, M. St. J. *The Life of John Stuart Mill,* New York, 1954.

Pareto, V. *Systèmes Socialistes,* ed. by G. H. Bosquet. Paris, 1926.

Pascal, R. *The German Sturm und Drang.* Manchester, 1953.

Peterson, E. *Der Monotheismus als Politisches Problem.* Leipzig, 1935.

Picard, M. *The Flight from God,* tr. by J. M. Cameron. London, 1951.

———. *Hitler in uns selbst.* Erlenbach-Zuerich, 1946.

Picard, R. *Le Romantisme Social.* New York, 1944.

Picker, H. *Hitler's Tischgespraeche.* Bonn, 1951.

Pieper, J. *The End of Time,* tr. by M. Bullock. London, 1954.

Plamenatz, J. *The English Utilitarians.* Oxford, 1949.

Plamenatz, J. *German Marxism and Russian Communism.* London, 1954.

Polanyi, K. *The Origins of Our Time.* London, 1945.

Polanyi, M. *The Contempt of Freedom.* London, 1940.

———. *The Logic of Liberty.* Chicago, 1951.

———. *Science, Faith and Society.* London, 1946.

Popitz, H. *Der Entfremdete Mensch.* Basel, 1953.

Popper, K. R. *The Open Society and Its Enemies.* Princeton, N.J., 1950.

Pribilla, M. *Deutsche Schicksalsfragen.* Frankfurt am Main, 1950.

Read, H. *Education through Art.* London, 1943.

———. *Poetry and Anarchism.* London, 1938.

———. *The Politics of the Unpolitical.* London, 1943.

———. *The True Voice of Feeling.* London, 1953.

———. ed. *Surrealism.* London, 1936.

Reckitt, M., ed. *Prospect for Christendom.* London, 1945.

Ritchie, D. G. *Principles of State Interference.* London, 1891.

Roepke, W. "Barriers to Immigration," *Twentieth Century Economic Thought,* ed. by G. Hoover. New York, 1950.

———. *Civitas Humana,* tr. by C. S. Fox. London, 1948.

———. *The German Question,* tr. by E. W. Dickes. London, 1946.

———. *Internationale Ordnung.* Erlenbach-Zuerich, 1945.

———. *Mass und Mitte.* Erlenbach-Zuerich, 1950.

———. *The Social Crisis of Our Times,* tr. by A. and P. Schiffer Jacobsohn. London, 1950.

Romier, L. *Who Will Be Master?* tr. by M. Josephson. New York, 1928.

Rommen, H. *The State in Catholic Thought.* St. Louis and London, 1950.

Rousseau, J-J. *Citizen of Geneva: A Selection from the Letters of Jean-Jacques Rousseau,* tr. and ed. by C. W. Hendel. New York and London, 1937.

————. *Confessions*, tr. anon. (Modern Library), New York, n.d.

————. *Oeuvres*. Paris, 1826.

————. *The Political Writings of Rousseau*, ed. by C. E. Vaughan, 2 vols., Cambridge, 1915.

————. *The Social Contract and Discourses*, tr. by G. D. H. Cole. New York and London, 1950.

Roustan, M. *The Pioneers of the French Revolution*, tr. by F. Whyte. Boston, 1926.

Rowse, A. L. *The End of an Epoch*. London, 1947.

Ruestow, A. *Zwischen Kapitalismus und Kommunismus*. Godesberg, 1949.

Ruggiero, G. de. *The History of European Liberalism*, tr. by R. G. Collingwood. London, 1927.

Russell, Lord B. *Mysticism and Logic*, London, 1953.

————. *Philosophy and Politics*. London, 1947.

Sainte-Beuve, C-A. *Portraits Littéraires*, 2 vols. Paris, n.d.

Sartre, J.-P. *Anti-Semite and Jew*, tr. by G. J. Becker. New York, 1948.

————. *Baudelaire*, tr. by M. Turnell. New York, 1950.

————. *L'Etre et le Néant*. Paris, 1949.

————. *L'Existentialisme est un Humanisme*. Paris, 1946.

————. *The Flies and In Camera*, tr. by S. Gilbert. London, 1946.

————. *Situations III*. Paris, 1949.

————. *What is Literature?* tr. by B. Frechtman. New York, 1949.

Scott, J. A. *Republican Ideas and the Liberal Tradition in France 1870-1940*. New York, 1951.

Schiller, F. *On the Aesthetic Education of Man*, tr. and ed. by R. Snell. London, 1954.

Schlegel, F. "Ideen," *Athenaeum*, III (1800).

The Philosophy of History, tr. by J. B. Robertson. London, 1846.

Schleiermacher, F. D. E. *Soliloquies*, tr. and ed. by H. L. Friess. Chicago, 1926.

——. *Ueber die Religion*, ed. by M. Rade. Berlin, n.d.

Schmitt, K. *Die Politische Romantik*. Muenchen und Leipzig, 1925.

Schopenhauer, A. *Essays*, tr. by T. B. Saunders. New York, n.d.

Schumpeter, J. A. *Capitalism, Socialism and Democracy*. New York, 1950.

Seillière, E. *Romanticism*, tr. by C. Sprietsma. New York, 1929.

——. *Jean-Jacques Rousseau*. Paris, 1921.

Shaw, G. B. *Saint Joan*. London, 1946.

——. ed. *Fabian Essays*. London, 1889.

Shelley, P. B. *Essays and Letters*, ed. by E. Rhys. London, 1887.

——. *Poetical Works*. Oxford, 1945.

Shinn, R. L. *Christianity and the Problem of History*. New York, 1953.

Siebeck, H. *Goethe als Denker*. Stuttgart, 1922.

Silz, W. *Early German Romanticism*. Cambridge, Mass., 1929.

Simmel, G. *Kant und Goethe*. Leipzig, 1916.

——. *The Sociology of George Simmel*, tr. and ed. by K. H. Wolf. Glencoe, Ill., 1950.

Simon, Y. *Philosophy of Democratic Government*. Chicago, 1951.

Smith, A. *The Wealth of Nations*, ed. by E. Cannan. New York, 1937.

Smith, L. P. *Words and Idioms*. Boston and New York, 1925.

Smith, P. *The Life and Letters of Martin Luther*. Boston, 1911.

Spencer, H. *The Man versus the State*. Boston, 1950.

Spender, S. *The Creative Element*. London, 1954.

——. *World within World.* New York, 1951.

Spengler, O. *The Decline of the West,* tr. by C. F. Atkinson, 2 vols. New York, 1939.

——. *Preussentum und Sozialismus.* Muenchen, 1922.

Strich, F. *Deutsche Klassik und Romantik.* Bern, 1949.

——. *Goethe and World Literature,* tr. by C. A. M. Sym. London, 1949.

Talmon, J. L. *The Rise of Totalitarian Democracy.* Boston, 1952.

Thiel, R. *Luther.* Wien, 1952.

Thomson, D. *The Democratic Tradition in France and England.* Cambridge, 1940.

Tillich, P. *The Courage to Be.* New Haven, Conn., 1952.

Tocqueville, A. de. *Democracy in America,* tr. by H. Reeve, ed. by P. Bradley, 2 vols. New York, 1951.

——. *The Old Regime and the Revolution,* tr. by J. Bonner. New York, 1876.

——. *The Recollections of Alexis de Tocqueville,* tr. by A. T. de Mattos, ed. by J. P. Mayer. London, 1948.

Troeltsch, E. *Deutscher Geist und Westeuropa.* Tuebingen, 1925.

Ulam, A. *The Philosophical Foundations of English Socialism.* Cambridge, Mass., 1951.

Unamuno, M. *Essays and Soliloquies,* tr. by J. E. C. Flitch. New York, 1925.

——. *The Tragic Sense of Life,* tr. by J. E. C. Flitch. New York, 1954.

Unger, R. *Hamann und die Aufklaerung,* 2 vols. Saale, 1925.

——. *Herder, Novalis und Kleist.* Frankfurt am Main, 1922.

Vaughan, C. E. *The Romantic Revolt.* Edinburgh and London, 1923.

Vernadsky, G. *A History of Russia.* New Haven, Conn., 1951.

Viëtor, K. *Goethe the Poet,* tr. by M. Hadas. Cambridge, Mass., 1949.

Viëtor, K. *Goethe the Thinker*, tr. by B. Q. Morgan. Cambridge, Mass., 1950.

Vigny, A. de. *Journal d'un Poète*, ed. by P. Flottes. Paris, 1949.

——. *Stello*. Paris, 1852.

——. *Théatre Complèt*. Paris, 1864.

Villasenor, J. S. *Ortega y Gasset Existentialist*, tr. by J. Small, Chicago, 1949.

Voegelin, E. *The New Science of Politics*. Chicago, 1952.

——. *Die Politischen Religionen*. Stockholm, 1939.

Wahl, J. *Etudes Kirkegaardiennes*. Paris, 1949.

——. *Le Malheur de la Conscience dans la Philosophie de Hegel*. Paris, 1929.

Walzel, O. *German Romanticism*, tr. by A. E. Lussky. New York, 1932.

——. *Das Prometheussymbol von Shaftsbury zu Goethe*. Muenchen, 1932.

Watkins, F. M. *The Political Tradition of the West*. Cambridge, Mass., 1948.

Weil, S. *The Need for Roots*, tr. by A. Wills. New York, 1952.

Weinstein, H. R. *Jean Jaurès*. New York, 1936.

Welleck, R. *A History of Modern Criticism 1750-1950*, 2 vols. New Haven, 1955.

Wells, H. G. *Mind at the End of Its Tether*. London, 1945.

White, R. J., ed. *The Political Tracts of Wordsworth, Coleridge and Shelley*. Cambridge, 1953.

Whitehouse, H. R. *The Life of Lamartine*, 2 vols. Boston, 1918.

Wood, H. G., et al. *The Kingdom of God and History*. Chicago and New York, 1938.

Zévèas, A. *Le Socialisme en France*. Paris, 1934.

Anderson, E. N. "German Romanticism as an Ideology of Cultural Crisis," *Journal of the History of Ideas*, II (1941), 301-317.

Arendt, H. "What Is Existenz Philosophy," *Partisan Review*, XIII (1946), 34-56.

Ayer, A. J. "Sartre," *Horizon*, XII (1945), 12-26 and 101-110.

Barth, K. "No Christian Marshall Plan," *The Christian Century*, LXV (1948), 130-133.

Beauvoir, S. de. "La Pensee de Droite Aujourd'hui," *Les Temps Modernes*, X (1955), 1537-1575 and 2219-2261.

Berlin, I. "Political Ideas in the Twentieth Century," *Foreign Affairs*, XXVIII (1950), 351-385.

Briefs, G. "The Economic Philosophy of Romanticism," *Journal of the History of Ideas*, II (1941), 279-300.

———. "Intellectual Tragedy," *The Commonweal*, XXXIII (1940-1941), 25.

Coulton, G. G. "The Historical Background of Maritain's Humanism," *Journal of the History of Ideas*, V (1944), 415-433.

Dawson, C. "The End of an Age," *Criterion*, IX (1929-1930), 386-401.

———. "Religion and the Totalitarian State," *Criterion*, XIV (1934-1935), 7-13.

Demant, V. A. "Dialectics and Prophecy," *Criterion*, XIV (1934-1935), 559-571.

Duverger, M. "S.F.I.O.: Mort ou Transfiguration," *Les Temps Modernes*, X (1955), 1863-1855.

Eliot, T. S. "The Action Française," *Criterion*, VII (1928), 195-203.

———. "The Literature of Fascism," *Criterion*, VIII (1928-1929), 280-290.

Eliot, T. S. "A Reply to Mr. Ward," *Criterion*, VII (1928), 84-88.

English, R. "Conservatism: the Forbidden Faith," *The American Scholar*, XXI (1951-1952), 393-412.

Friedrich, C. J. "The Political Thought of Neo-Liberalism," *American Political Science Review*, XLIX (1955), 509-525.

———. "Review of F. A. Hayek's *The Road to Serfdom*," *American Political Science Review*, XXXIX (1945), 575-579.

Gerth, H. H. "The Nazi Party," *American Journal of Sociology*, XLV (1940), 517-541.

Gerth, H. H., and Mills, C. W. "A Marx for Managers," *International Journal of Ethics*, LII (1941-1942), 200-215.

Godman, S. "Max Picard: the Man and his Work," *The Dublin Review*, CCXXII-CCXXIII (1949), 23-43.

Grene, M. "Authenticity: An Existentialist Virtue," *International Journal of Ethics*, LXII (1946), 266-274.

Gurian, W. "Totalitarian Religions," *Review of Politics*, XIV (1952), 3-14.

Hampshire, S. "In Defence of Radicalism," *Encounter*, V (1955), 36-41.

Hayek, F. A., "Socialism and the Intellectuals," *University of Chicago Law Review*, XVI (1949), 417-433.

Hilferding, R. "The Modern Totalitarian State," *The Modern Review*, I (1947), 597-605.

———. "State Capitalism or Totalitarian State Economy," *The Modern Review*, I (1947), 266-271.

Huszar, G. de. "Nietzsche's Theory of Decadence and the Transvaluation of all Values," *Journal of the History of Ideas*, VI (1945), 259-272.

Jaspers, K. "The Fight against Totalitarianism," *Confluence*, III (1954), 251-266.

———. "The Importance of Nietzsche, Marx and Kierkegaard in the History of Philosophy," tr. by S. Godman, *Hibbert Journal*, XLIX (1950-1951), 226-234.

Kecskemeti, P. "Existentialism, a New Trend in Philosophy," *Modern Review*, I (1947), 34-51.

————. "How Totalitarians Gain Absolute Power," *Commentary*, XIV (1952), 537-546.

Kelsen, H. "Absolutism and Relativism in Philosophy and Politics," *American Political Science Review*, XLII (1948), 906-914.

Kohn, H. "Romanticism and the Rise of German Nationalism," *Review of Politics*, XII (1950), 443-472.

Lanzmann, C. "L'Homme de Gauche," *Les Temps Modernes*, X (1955), 1626-1658.

Loewith, K. "Les Implications Politiques de la Philosophie de l'Existence chez Heidegger," tr. by J. Rovan, *Les Temps Modernes*, II (2) (1946), 343-360.

Marcuse, H. "Remarks on Jean-Paul Sartre's *L'Etre et le Néant*," *Philosophy and Phenomenological Research*, VIII (1947-1948), 309-336.

Mcrae, D. G. "The Politics of Lord Acton," *The Political Quarterly*, XXIV (1953), 285-292.

Nagel, E. "Review of F. A. Hayek's *The Counter-Revolution of Science*," *Journal of Philosophy*, XLIX (1952), 560-565.

Nathanson, M. "Jean-Paul Sartre's Philosophy of Freedom," *Social Research*, XIX (1952), 364-380.

Neumann, F. "Approaches to the Study of Political Power," *Political Science Quarterly*, LXV (1950), 161-180.

Niebuhr, R. "We are Men not Gods," *The Christian Century*, LXV (1948), 1138-1140.

Oakeshott, M. "Contemporary British Politics," *The Cambridge Journal*, I (1947-1948), 474-490.

————. "Rationalism in Politics," *The Cambridge Journal*, I (1947), 81-98 and 145-157.

————. "The Tower of Babel," *The Cambridge Journal*, II (1948), 67-83.

O'Boyle, L. "The Class Concept in History," *Journal of Modern History*, XXIV (1952), 391-397.

Oppenheimer, F. "Relativism, Absolutism and Democracy," *American Political Science Review*, XLIV (1950), 951-960.

Ordo, 1 (1948), VII-XI.

Pollock, J. K. "An Areal Study of the German Electorate, 1930-1933," *American Political Science Review*, XXXVIII (1944), 89-95.

Sartre, J-P. "Réponse à Claude Lefort," *Les Temps Modernes*, VIII (1953), 1571-1629.

Schumpeter, J. A. "Science and Technology," *American Economic Review*, XXXIX (1949), 345-359.

Silone, I. "Ferrero and the Decline of Civilization," *Partisan Review*, IX (1942), 379-383.

Tillich, P. "Existential Philosophy," *Journal of the History of Ideas*, V (1944), 44-70.

Viner, J. "Bentham and J. S. Mill," *American Economic Review*, XXXIX (1949), 360-382.

Waehlens, A. de. "La Philosophie de Heidegger et le Nazisme," *Les Temps Modernes*, II (5) (1947), 115-127.

Watkins, J. W. N. "Walter Eucken: Philosopher Economist," *International Journal of Ethics*, LXIII (1953), 131-136.

Weil, E. "Le Cas Heidegger," *Les Temps Modernes*, II (5) (1947), 128-138.

Wilson, A. "The Novels of William Godwin," *World Review*, II (June, 1951), 37-40.

Wilson, C. "Canon Demant's Economic History," *The Cambridge Journal*, VI (1953), 281-290.

Wollheim, R. "The Political Philosophy of Existentialism," *The Cambridge Journal*, VII (1953), 3-19.

Wolin, S. S. "Hume and Conservatism," *American Political Science Review*, XLIII (1954), 999-1016.

Index